P9-AOU-121

EVERSON REVISITED

Religious Forces in the Modern Political World
General Editor Allen D. Hertzke, The Carl Albert Center,
University of Oklahoma at Norman

Religious Forces in the Modern Political World features books on religious forces in politics, both in the United States and abroad. The authors examine the complex interplay between religious faith and politics in the modern world, emphasizing its impact on contemporary political developments. This new series spans a diverse range of methodological interpretations, philosophical approaches, and substantive concerns. Titles include:

EVERSON REVISITED

Religion, Education, and Law at the Crossroads

Edited by Jo Renée Formicola
and Hubert Morken

ROWMAN & LITTLEFIELD PUBLISHERS, INC.
Lanham • Boulder • New York • Oxford

ROWMAN & LITTLEFIELD PUBLISHERS, INC.

Published in the United States of America
by Rowman & Littlefield Publishers, Inc.
4720 Boston Way, Lanham, Maryland 20706

12 Hid's Copse Road
Cummor Hill, Oxford OX29JJ, England

Copyright © 1997 by Rowman & Littlefield Publishers, Inc.

Portions of the first section of Chapter 1, "The Everson Case in the Context of New
Jersey Politics" by Daryl R. Fair, originally appeared in "Remote from the
Schoolhouse," New Jersey History 99 (Spring/Summer 1981): 49–65. Reprinted by
permission of the New Jersey Historical Society.

Quotation in Chapter 6 from "The Road Not Taken" from *The Poetry of Robert
Frost* edited by Edward Connery Lathem, copyright 1944 by Robert Frost.
Copyright 1916, © 1969 by Henry Holt and Co. Reprinted by permission of Henry
Holt & Co., Inc.

All rights reserved. No part of this publication may be reproduced, stored in a
retrieval system, or transmitted in any form or by any means, electronic, mechani-
cal, photocopying, recording, or otherwise, without the prior
permission of the publisher.

British Library Cataloguing in Publication Information Available

Library of Congress Cataloging-in-Publication Data

Everson revisited : religion, education and law at the
  crossroads / edited by Jo Renée Formicola and Hubert Morken.
      p.   cm. — (Religious forces in the modern political world)
    Includes bibliographical references and index.
    ISBN 0–8476–8650–7 (cloth : alk. paper). — ISBN 0-8476-8651-5
  (pbk. : alk. paper)
    1. Religious education—United States.   2. Religion and state—
  United States.   3. United States—Religion—1960– . I. Formicola,
  Jo Renée, 1941– .   II. Morken, Hubert.   III. Series.
  BL42.5.U5E94   1997
  379.2'8'097309045—dc21   97–12642
                                                                   CIP

ISBN 0–8476–8650–7 (cloth : alk. paper)
ISBN 0–8476–8651–5 (pbk. : alk. paper)

Printed in the United States of America

⊖™   The paper used in this publication meets the minimum requirements of
American National Standard for Information Sciences—Permanence of Paper for
Printed Library Materials, ANSI Z39.48–1984.

Contents

Acknowledgments

John Littel at Regent gave unstinting support at every stage of the project. We wish to thank Timothy Tardibono, whose indefatigable labors included producing the index; and Candice Zouhary, who assisted in research. Cheryl Hoffman, Lawrence Paulson, and Kim Cooper were most helpful. Our editors, Allen Hertzke, Stephen Wrinn, Robin Adler, and Julie Kirsch, smoothed the way for early publication. We are especially grateful to the chapter authors, who brought diverse perspectives and professional acumen to their analysis of religion, education, and law in this the fiftieth year after *Everson.*

Jo Formicola wishes to dedicate this book to Allan and Mary B., "for always believing in me, and helping me to believe in myself."

Hubert Morken dedicates this book to the Stony Brook School, "where my four children went to high school, and to its vision of 'Character before Career.'"

Preface

February 10, 1997, marked the fiftieth anniversary of *Everson v. Board of Education*. The case took place in New Jersey, when Arch Everson brought suit against Ewing Township for using tax money to transport Catholic students to a parochial high school in Trenton. What seemed to involve only a small town and a negligible expense escalated into more serious constitutional questions: What was meant by the establishment clause of the First Amendment, and was child benefit theory a valid legal reason to use tax dollars for busing Catholic students to a religious school? Because of the ruling's sweeping interpretation of the nonestablishment provision of the First Amendment, espousing a "wall" of separation that was unyielding yet so flexible as to allow state-funded busing of Catholic students, *Everson* generated controversy right from the beginning. As a result, it became the basis for virtually every argument made for and against religious accommodation and separation in the last half century.

In this book, we concentrate on the aspect of *Everson* that is still most relevant: the relationship between religion, education, and the law. As editors, we believe that public education is at a point of strategic change, indeed at a crossroads, and that church-, synagogue-, and mosque-related schools have the potential to play a role as alternative educational choices for a growing cadre of disaffected American parents and students. A confluence of events leads us to this conclusion.

First, there is a general level of malaise and dissatisfaction with current American public education. This is evidenced in the increasing support for school choice, vouchers, and tuition tax credits. Very recently, Minnesota, Wisconsin, and Vermont began to explore new alternatives to their educational systems. The mayor of Jersey City, Bret Schundler, has called for vouchers to save his city's floundering school system. Mayor Rudolf Giuliani of New York asked John Cardinal O'Connor of the Archdiocese of New York to assist the city when overcrowding was about to compromise the effectiveness of the Big Apple's schools in 1996, and thus a new voluntary program involving New York City and religious schools will be implemented in the fall of 1997 to help those who are educationally "troubled."

Second, there is a growing move toward home schooling, reflecting parents' increased desire to play a larger role in both the secular and the value-centered parts of their children's education. With a generation of highly educated mothers and fathers among the "baby boomers" and the "thirteenth generation," this trend is likely to continue.

Third, the fear of violence and concern about a lack of moral training are leading many parents, particularly in the inner city, to flee public educational systems and opt for church-related schools. Often the choice is a Catholic school, as its mission has traditionally been to educate the middle and lower classes, particularly immigrants and those who have historically been rejected by the elites of American society. Catholic schools have changed to meet this new challenge, and now their charge is to educate those of diverse religions and backgrounds, preparing them for a place in the political, social and economic infrastructure, just as the schools provided for Catholics in the past century.

All these lead to a fourth change: the increasing number of different kinds of religious and other private schools emerging in the United States. Chief among them now are the Evangelical schools in the South and in the heartland, Christian schools whose purpose it is to inculcate traditional family values and spiritual standards along with secular subjects. Islamic schools are burgeoning as well, and Jewish academies are springing up, particularly on the East and West Coasts.

Fifth, there is a renewed sense of ecumenism on church-related education. Today, Catholics and Evangelicals are working together to advance their similar educational agendas. During the 1996 election, for example, more than 250,000 Catholics joined the religious right through the Christian Coalition in order to send a message about their dissatisfaction with much of the liberal thinking of the Democratic Party and one of its main supporters, the National Education Association.

Sixth, the introduction and debate about the Religious Equality Amendment during the last session of Congress reflect a grassroots fear about the place of religion in society, a concern that should be questioned and rejected only if the protections of the First Amendment remain fully effective. However factually based or exaggerated these apprehensions may be, many Americans think that religious liberty is eroding and will soon disappear entirely from schools unless there is a renewed commitment to maintain a benevolent neutrality toward religious access in schools and other institutions of society.

Finally, the Supreme Court itself has taken unprecedented action this term in deciding to rehear *Aguilar v. Felton*, the case that insisted that public teachers offering remedial education for children in religious schools teach at neutral sites, such as mobile vans parked across the street from such schools. The Supreme Court's willingness to reconsider its stance clearly portends a dramatic shift in judicial thinking about religion and education in America, a possibility that could give rise to a completely different understanding of *Everson* in the future.

For these reasons, we decided to look more closely at *Everson* and to engage a number of nationally known scholars in the area of church-state relations in discussion about the future relationships of religion, education, and the law as the millennium approaches. We asked these experts to reconsider the influence and relevance of *Everson* from their diverse and even conflicting vantage points, and we were surprised both by their concerns and by their reflections. These authors provide historical, religious, philosophical, and legal analyses of the holding in the case and assess whether *Everson* will continue to create problems within American society, or whether it will solve them. Taken together, their views have produced Everson *Revisited: Religion, Education, and Law at the Crossroads.*

This book begins, logically, with the history of the case. Daryl Fair, a professor at the College of New Jersey in Trenton, with ready access to the files of the New Jersey state legislature and the Ewing Township Board of Education, investigates and explains the legislative background, political struggles, and judicial steps that led to the emergence of parochial school busing as the most important Supreme Court case of the 1947 term.

The first historical chapter is followed by that of Daniel Dreisbach, who, after tracing the literature and subsequent interpretations of *Everson*, examines *Everson*'s use of history, showing how the case has survived as a paradigm of separationist (and even accommodationist) thought during the last fifty years.

The two following chapters by Hubert Morken and Jo Formicola look at *Everson* through Evangelical and Catholic lenses, articulating the unintended effects of *Everson* on their respective church agendas and jurisprudence.

Angela Carmella examines the effort by *Everson* to deal properly with two dimensions of religion, its transcendent quality, and the more concrete and daily activities of God-fearing people. She shows how *Everson* spawned two schools of legal thought about both religion and religious education, thus bringing the current conflicts and concerns to the fore.

Stephen Monsma strongly objects to *Everson* and to its restraint on what he considers the necessary and inevitable ties between religious organizations and civil government. He argues instead for a constitutional theory of "neutrality" that would permit tuition tax credits and other forms of assistance to church schools.

Addressing a specific issue, Derek Davis challenges the moment of silence in public schools that is being legislated in some states. He presents ethical arguments that lead him to suggest that even if such silence legislation is constitutional, it is imprudent, if not immoral, to pass it.

In an imaginatively framed essay, Robert Booth Fowler lays out the postmodern rationale for school aid, claiming that the irreligious can make a case for assistance to religious schools as a way to promote diversity in culture and liberty in a liberal context.

Mary Segers shows how *Everson* has created a continuing quandary, leading some in the 104th Congress to advance the Religious Equality Amendment, which seeks to guarantee equal treatment of religious persons and organizations. She questions the advisability of this remedy.

Finally, we present the recollections of William Bentley Ball, a distinguished attorney and author whose legal career has been defined in part by his professional attempts to understand and to interpret *Everson*. Having argued ten cases before the Supreme Court on matters of religion and education since 1947, he brings a lifelong involvement with the case and shows how *Everson* will continue to speak to issues of religion, education, and the law. We asked Mr. Ball to present his professional experiences and views in the form of a personal memoir.

As editors, we have come to the conclusion that despite the difficulties and controversies related to schools, some of them created by *Everson,* we are optimistic about the prospects for educational reform in America. As scholars and educators ourselves, we constantly seek new ways to create better teaching and learning environments. Thus, together we salute the other authors of this book, who out of respect for religion, education, and law have accepted the challenge to seek solutions to unresolved conflicts.

We also believe that *Everson* has endured, not only because of its infamous ambiguity, but also because of its unappreciated flexibility. This is potentially its greatest strength, namely, that it speaks both to accommodation via child benefit theory and to separation. Although *Everson* too sweepingly defines the establishment clause in attempting to solve the dilemma of giving aid to religious education without establishing religion, the Court left room for future adjustments on matters of church and state. We expect that positive changes will be made in the law and in judicial interpretation, encouraging communities to redesign their educational systems, to make the most of local resources, to provide real cooperation by government, to promote religious liberty, and to meet the needs and desires of parents, educators, and students.

We also are convinced that a reorientation of the relationships between public education and religion and between private education and the state is needed for the new millennium. A one-sided application of *Everson* that makes little or no room for religion and government to work side by side for the common good in public and private schools is antiquated at best and idolatrous at worst. We think a proper respect for the independence and interdependence of church and state, religion and education, will necessarily grow, bringing together a coalition of legislators, jurists, educators, and parents. The coming millennium's first century holds great promise and excitement for those who will labor to energize America's schools. We hope this book will lead to an understanding of how the very *Everson* that shaped the entire structure and ethos of American education for the past fifty years can have a decisive and different impact in the future, preparing the way for a diversity of dynamic community schools.

1

The *Everson* Case in the Context of New Jersey Politics

Daryl R. Fair

The *Everson v. Board of Education* case emerged out of a four-year struggle in the New Jersey legislature over state funding of transportation for
parochial school students.[1] From 1937 to 1941 the legislature grappled
with the issue. When the legislators finally agreed on a bill, the parties who
had fought against parochial school busing in the legislature turned to the
courts, where they used state constitutional grounds in their opposition,
because there was little U.S. constitutional law on establishment of religion. Everson's attorney added a Fourteenth Amendment claim as an afterthought; only when the case reached the U.S. Supreme Court did the federal constitutional issues get substantial attention. There were, of course,
earlier cases questioning state government action that aided religion,[2] but
these were never squarely based on the contention that such aid violated
the United States Constitution's establishment of religion clause, made
applicable to the states by the Fourteenth Amendment. By addressing this
claim, *Everson* became the first of the modern establishment of religion
cases.

Both the litigants and the courts seemed to proceed in a gingerly fashion
with the *Everson* case. Interest groups that were involved in the litigation, and
even in the legislative contest, seemed reluctant to be in the public eye. The
courts, including the U.S. Supreme Court, appeared reticent about certain
aspects of the case. The awkwardness of litigants and jurists may have been
due in part to the new legal ground they were breaking, but it was also
undoubtedly related to the sensitive subject matter of religion. The case, after
all, raised not only constitutional questions about church-state relations but
also politically volatile issues of interfaith relations. This chapter explains the
history of the case, including the prior legislative process and the stages of litigation in the courts.

1

The Origins of Parochial School Aid in New Jersey

The issue of whether and how much public funding should be used to support parochial schools had simmered for over a century before the *Everson* decision. In New York, Bishop Hughes spoke out in 1840 against the Protestant and anti-Catholic bias of the public schools, seeking equal public funding for Catholic schools. The New York legislature responded in 1844 by passing a law prohibiting public expenditures to support schools teaching religious sectarian doctrines or using books prejudicial to the doctrines of any Christian sect. A similar provision was written into the 1894 state constitution, and other states had similar prohibitions against public funding of sectarian institutions.

Catholics, naturally enough, felt that these provisions were discriminatory. While Catholics paid school taxes, they often did not use the public schools funded by those revenues, preferring instead to educate their children in parochial schools. As the number of Catholics in the industrialized states grew, and as Catholics attained positions of political power, challenges to these provisions mounted.[3]

Initial efforts focused on securing public funds for textbooks and transportation. New York was the scene of one early campaign. Despite the 1894 constitutional provision banning public expenditures to support religious schools, known popularly as the "Blaine amendment," the state legislature passed a bus transportation program for parochial school students in 1936. Governor Herbert H. Lehman vetoed the bill, but it eventually became law in amended form. The New York Court of Appeals then declared the legislation unconstitutional because it conflicted with the Blaine amendment. Subsequently, New York amended its state constitution to permit the use of public funds to provide bus transportation for parochial school students, and in 1939 Governor Lehman signed another parochial school bus bill.[4]

Meanwhile, in New Jersey, efforts to secure public transportation for parochial school students were also under way. After the passage of the comprehensive school code of 1903, New Jersey permitted local school boards to provide for transportation of children to the public schools. The relevant section of law provided that "whenever in any district there shall be children living remote from the schoolhouse, the board of education of such district may make rules and contracts for the transportation of such children to and from school."[5]

On May 26, 1937, Thomas G. Walker, the speaker of the general assembly, introduced a bill permitting boards of education to furnish transportation for pupils who attended schools other than public schools.[6] The assembly passed Walker's bill the day after it was introduced. The senate, however, squeezed by the calendar, adjourned for a month on the same day it received the bill from the assembly and failed to pass the legislation. The proponents of parochial school busing had missed a golden opportunity in 1937. The assembly approved the bus bill easily, and the senate probably would have done so as well, had Walker introduced the bill earlier.

The composition of the senate remained basically the same in 1938, when the senate passed a new version of the bill, but the makeup of the assembly changed drastically after 1937. As a result, the assembly blocked the path of parochial school bus subsidies, and no bus bill was reported out of committee in the assembly in 1938, 1939, or 1940.

In 1941, supporters of the parochial school bus bill made a major new effort to pass the legislation, pursuing a different strategy. This time the bill, S. 152, was introduced first in the senate by Majority Leader Alfred Driscoll of Camden County. Grant Scott, the senate president, referred it to the strongly supportive Miscellaneous Business Committee, chaired by Arthur F. Foran of Hunterdon County. Cumberland County Republican George H. Stanger was also a member of that committee. Scott, Foran, and Stanger were among seven GOP senators who had earned the nickname "Hague Republicans" by voting in 1939 to confirm Frank Hague Jr., a Democrat, as a lay judge of the Court of Errors and Appeals (New Jersey's highest court), and they tended to support religious accommodation.[7] The other two members of the committee were Democrat John E. Toolan of Middlesex County and Republican Charles E. Loizeaux of Union County, who at the time was reportedly interested in running for governor in 1943 and was therefore disinclined to alienate a large bloc of voters.[8]

The Miscellaneous Business Committee reported the bill two weeks after receiving it. The Republican caucus brought it to the floor the same day, and it passed the senate by a vote of 18-1. The sole dissenting vote was cast by Senator Howard Eastwood of Burlington County, a member of the Junior Order of United American Mechanics (JOUAM), an organization that was to play a major role in opposition to public funding of parochial schools in New Jersey.

The Junior Order of United American Mechanics emerged in the 1840s as a secret nativist fraternal organization. By the 1890s it was the leading group of this type in the country. Originally anti-Catholic in emphasis, the JOUAM eventually became more antiradical and anti-immigrant. After World War I the order gradually lost its nativist emphasis, and by the time parochial school busing was being considered and litigated in New Jersey, it was a fraternal benefit life insurance society. However, its history made it anathema to Roman Catholics in the 1930s and 1940s, and its stance as a promoter of the free public schools sometimes brought it into conflict with the Catholic Church over public benefits for parochial school students.[9]

The parochial school bus bill then went to the assembly, where Speaker

Roscoe McClave referred it to the Education Committee. Since the assembly had been the graveyard of this bill for the past three years, supporters of S. 152 began almost immediately to petition the Education Committee to report the bill to the floor. Opponents, not to be outdone, lobbied committee members to stand firm and keep the bill safely within their jurisdiction. The Catholic Daughters of America, for example, sought the release of the bill from committee, while the executive committee of the New Jersey Education Association opposed it.[10]

Newspaper reports indicated that one member of the Education Committee (Joseph W. Cowgill [D-Camden County]) favored the bill, three opposed it (Olive C. Sanford [R-Essex County], chair of the committee; Mattie S. Doremus [R-Passaic County]; and Clarence W. Beers [R-Warren County]), and one was uncommitted (A. Matlack Stackhouse [R-Burlington County]).[11] Mrs. Sanford, it appears, wanted hearings on the bill but thought the supporters of the bill should request them.[12] The bill's supporters did not see the need for hearings and instead sought to demonstrate statewide support for the bill by delivering to Mrs. Sanford 15,409 petitions containing 489,518 signatures. Frederick J. Gassert, corporation counsel for the Newark Archdiocese, president of the Catholic Lawyers' Guild of New Jersey, and mayor of the Hudson County municipality of Harrison, delivered these petitions on April 21.[13] Shortly after the petitions were delivered, Mrs. Sanford, for reasons that are not apparent, announced that hearings on S. 152 would be held on May 2.[14]

Before and during the hearing, individuals on both sides of the issue attempted to disguise their affiliation with groups and organizations. Groups opposing the bill included the Federated Boards of Education of New Jersey, the New Jersey State Board of Education, the New Jersey Education Association, the New Jersey Taxpayers Association, the state Chamber of Commerce, the American Association of University Women, the New Jersey League of Women Voters, the Junior Order of United American Mechanics, the Patriotic Order of Sons of America, and the Seventh-Day Adventists.[15] Among these groups were some of the most influential lobbying organizations in the state: the Chamber of Commerce, the New Jersey Education Association, and the New Jersey Taxpayers Association.[16]

Supporters of the bill included the Catholic Daughters of America, the Hudson County and New Jersey Young Republicans, the New Jersey Council of the Knights of Columbus, the Newark City Commission, the *Newark Evening News*, the *Jersey Journal*, and the *New Jersey Voter*.[17] In an interesting bit of reporting, the *Newark Evening News* identified individuals who testified against S. 152 at the May 2 hearing by the groups they represented (e.g., "Albert McCay of Palmyra, representing the Jr. O.U.A.M. and the P.O.S. of A. and affiliates") but identified supporters of the bill only by characteristics such as title or residence.[18] The people so identified were, according to *Newark Sunday Call* columnist Carteret, "an almost solid list of Hague folk."[19] They were also in some cases identifiable with groups quietly supporting S. 152. John A. Matthews, advisory master of the Court of Chancery of New Jersey, for example, was a prominent Roman Catholic layman who was close to Monsignor Ralph J. Glover, director of the Associated Catholic Charities of the Archdiocese of Newark and a supporter of the parochial school bus bill.[20]

The school bus bill now had considerable support from New Jersey Democrats, "regular" Republicans, Roman Catholic organizations, and some labor leaders as well. Newark City Commissioner Vincent J. Murphy, who was also secretary-treasurer of the state Federation of Labor, made a strong statement in favor of the bill the night before the hearings in Trenton.[21] Pressure on the Education Committee to release the bill began to grow. Prior to the hearings, Assembly Speaker McClave received entreaties, including one from U.S. Representative J. Parnell Thomas, urging that S. 152 be released from committee.[22] Pressure also came from the senate before the hearings. A bill on the rights of married women in the workforce, sponsored by Mattie Doremus, passed the assembly, but when it reached the Senate Labor Committee, Senator Foran, the chair, announced that he would not report it until Doremus agreed to support release of the parochial school bus bill from the assembly Education Committee.[23] On May 10 the annual convention of the New Jersey Knights of Columbus unanimously petitioned the assembly to release S. 152 from committee.[24] As the school bus bill became more and more difficult to contain, the committee began to consider amending and reporting the bill.

On May 20 the *Newark Evening News* reported that the Education Committee had agreed to amendments but would not make them public until the following week. These amendments reportedly limited transportation of parochial school students to bus routes then in service and limited the number of buses to the number then in service.[25] The *Evening News* reported about a week later that Mrs. Sanford wanted to bring these suggested amendments before the Republican caucus and to consult with proponents of the bus bill about the pending changes before reporting the bill out of committee.[26]

On June 2 the Education Committee met with proponents and opponents of the bill to discuss possible amendments. One amendment would have placed under the jurisdiction of the state board of education and commissioner of education all public and parochial schools with students taking advantage of transportation facilities provided by the bill. Proponents of the legislation quite naturally opposed this amendment but indicated that they would accept any of the other proposed amendments. These would have limited transportation service to parochial school students living along highways traveled by public school buses, limited the number of buses to the number then in use, and limited transportation to existing bus routes. Supporters of the bill preferred the latter amendment, with the understanding that extensions of those routes would be permitted with the approval of local school boards. Mrs. Sanford indicated that the Republican caucus would discuss the matter further and then adopt amendments.[27] Monsignor Glover and Mayor Gassert represented the supporters of the bill at this meeting.[28]

The following day, the GOP caucus discussed the bill and the proposed amendments, deciding to support passage of the bill with the amendment preferred by its proponents.[29] The Education Committee then reported the bill without recommendation, and the assembly amended it as agreed and passed it by a vote of 40-15.[30] The bill, which was of primary interest to the Democrats,[31] passed with support from a coalition of nineteen Republicans and eleven Democrats; the opposition consisted of fourteen Republicans and one Democrat.[32] This vote is the sort that led to the tongue-in-cheek assessment of the legislature: "Hague doesn't need a Democratic legislature; the Republicans will always lend him theirs!"[33]

Senate repassage of the bill, as amended, was a formality. On June 9, the upper house concurred in the assembly's amendments by a vote of 16-2. Governor Charles Edison signed the bill the same day.[34] According to the *New Jersey Voter,* Governor Edison signed S. 152 because he thought the fact that Catholic parents paid school taxes but received no services from the public schools created disunity and antagonism in the community.[35] Governor Edison was also a Democrat, and S. 152 was essentially a Democratic bill. The parochial school bus bill, after being considered in five New Jersey legislative sessions, was now scheduled to go into effect on July 1, 1941. The New Jersey Education Code, as amended by S. 152, now read:

> Whenever in any district there are children living remote from any school house, the board of education of the district may make rules and contracts for the transportation of such children to and from school, including the transportation of school children to and from school other than a public school, except such school as is operated for profit in whole or in part.
>
> When any school district provides any transportation for public school children to and from school, transportation from any point in such established school route to any other in such established route shall be supplied to school children residing in such school district in going to and from school other than a public school, except such as operated for profit in whole or in part.[36]

The passage of the parochial school bus bill did not end the controversy. After the bill passed, the New Jersey Taxpayers Association stated, "We believe that many of the legislators who voted for the bill did so only because of 'political expediency' even though they themselves realized that it was not good legislation."[37] The executive director of the New Jersey Taxpayers Association, Arch R. Everson, was also a member of the JOUAM, which, not taking defeat lying down, prepared to resist in the courts.

The Battle Shifts to the New Jersey Courts

In 1941, Ewing Township was a rural Republican district with public school to the eighth-grade level only. Students from that Mercer County community who wished to further their education in a public high school could go either to Pennington High School or Trenton High School. If the students chose to go to high school, the Ewing Board of Education paid their tuition and the cost of their transportation by public carrier, since the township operated no buses to these adjoining districts. On October 20, 1941, the board voted to place pupils attending eligible private and parochial schools on their list of pupils eligible for transportation, in accordance with state board of education rules adopted pursuant to the parochial school bus law, which had gone into effect on July 1 of that year. On November 17, the board authorized reimbursement of fares paid to public carriers by parents of pupils attending Pennington High School, Trenton High School, or the Trenton Catholic schools. This was the same procedure that had been used previously when only students attending public schools had been involved.[38]

On September 21, 1942, the school board voted to continue the same transportation policy and procedures for the 1942–43 school year.[39] A substantial portion of the school year passed uneventfully, but on March 15, 1943, the school board held a special meeting. C. G. Latham, the Ewing Township School District clerk, announced that he had received notice that a suit against the school board would be filed in the New Jersey Supreme Court challenging the board's payment of bus fares to students attending parochial schools. At this time, the Court of Errors and Appeals, rather than the supreme court, was the highest court in the state. The school board decided to retain William Abbotts Jr., who had been a member of the board when the original parochial school bus fare authorization was passed, to represent them in the litigation.[40]

Arch R. Everson, a resident of Ewing Township, was the plaintiff in the suit. Everson indicated that he was bringing the suit as an individual.[41] This claim was only partially correct. Everson, although opposing public support of parochial school transportation, was only nominally the plaintiff; the JOUAM sponsored and paid for the suit.[42] Albert McCay (later assemblyman and senator from Burlington County), counsel to the JOUAM, represented the organization.[43] The lawsuit was therefore a continuation of the legislative struggle over aid to parochial schools, since the JOUAM had been a leading opponent of the parochial school bus bill in the legislature. Roscoe Walker, secretary-treasurer of the state council of the JOUAM, and his successor, Charles Michaelson, directed the lawsuit.[44]

After the JOUAM filed its application for a writ of certiorari with the supreme court, the parties agreed to waive oral argument and have the court reach a decision on the record. The main issue at this time was whether administrative remedies had been pursued. Abbotts argued for the school board that the JOUAM should have pursued action before the commissioner and board of education prior to seeking judicial review. McCay contended that the only issues were constitutional and that since such matters could not be decided by the commissioner or board of education, it was appropriate to bypass those administrative channels and go directly to the courts.[45]

The supreme court granted a writ of certiorari in August 1943. In the meantime, the American Civil Liberties Union (ACLU) became interested in the case. The ACLU had not been a factor during the legislative phase of the struggle over the parochial school bus bill because the New Jersey chapter was largely inactive early in the 1940s.[46] The ACLU interest in the lawsuit, in fact, came from the national office in New York rather than from the New Jersey chapter. Clifford Forster, ACLU staff counsel, wrote to the law firm of Powell and Parker in Mount Holly, New Jersey, on May 18, 1943, to request copies of the briefs filed in the case.[47] McCay was associated with this firm, and the firm's name and Harold Parker's, rather than McCay's, had appeared on the initial papers filed in the supreme court. In his reply to Forster, McCay asked what the position of the ACLU might be in the case.[48] Forster replied that the ACLU opposed use of public funds for transportation to, and social services in, parochial schools but did not commit the ACLU to support the case.[49] By June 24, however, Forster was ready to offer to file an amicus curiae brief in the *Everson* litigation.[50] The ACLU Board of Directors authorized the filing of an amicus brief on July 26.[51] Thus even before it was certain that a writ of certiorari would be granted, the ACLU signed on in support of the JOUAM position in *Everson*.

Once a writ of certiorari was granted, McCay filed a summary of the reasons he thought the parochial school bus law was unconstitutional. McCay listed seven grounds for holding the law void; six of them were based on the New Jersey constitution. The last of the seven reasons was a claim that the parochial school bus law violated the Fourteenth Amendment to the U.S. Constitution.[52] This reason was something of an afterthought. McCay wrote to Roger Baldwin, the executive director of the ACLU, that he had included an allegation that the school bus law violated the Fourteenth Amendment to the U.S. Constitution, but that he doubted he would find support for the claim.[53]

Following McCay's filing of his summary legal arguments, depositions were taken on August 23 in order to establish the facts of the case. These depositions plus the stipulation filed April 27 reveal that the school board reimbursed parents a total of $1263.56 over a year and a half for fares to send their children by public carrier to Trenton parochial schools.[54]

As the parties prepared to file briefs, the ACLU ran into some difficulties. Their first choice to file their amicus brief declined their invitation,[55] so Forster asked McCay to recommend somebody for the task. McCay recommended Joseph Beck Tyler of Camden, who seems to have opposed the 1940 parochial school bus bill for the JOUAM before the assembly Judiciary Committee.[56] The ACLU wanted Tyler to write the brief *pro bono*, but he requested, and got, a fee of $150 plus expenses.[57] McCay and Tyler submitted briefs on behalf of Everson, and Abbotts and John Solan, a New Jersey deputy attorney general, on behalf of the school board.[58]

In September 1944, almost a year after briefs were submitted, the New Jersey Supreme Court held the parochial school bus law unconstitutional by a vote of 2-1. Justice Charles W. Parker wrote the opinion of the court. He was joined by Justice Joseph B. Perskie. Justice Harry Heher dissented. Justice Parker's opinion held that the law violated a portion of the New Jersey constitution providing for a public school fund and requiring that interest from the fund "be annually appropriated to the support of the public free schools, for the equal benefit of all the people of the state."[59] Justice Parker contended that previous decisions of the New Jersey courts required that the law be set aside because it provided aid to nonpublic schools in violation of this constitutional provision.[60] Justice Heher dissented because he viewed the law as providing a service to children rather than a benefit to nonpublic schools. Justice Heher further contended that no proof had been offered that any part of the state school fund had been used for parochial school bus transportation.[61] After the supreme court's decision, parochial school bus transportation came to a halt throughout the state, as it had in Ewing Township following the initial filing of the *Everson* suit.[62]

A sidelight of the *Everson* case is the controversy it aroused within the ACLU. While the case was pending before the New Jersey Supreme Court, the ACLU Board of Directors discussed its policy with regard to the use of public funds for transportation of children to private schools. The ACLU had opposed aid to parochial schools, direct or indirect, in the past. The board asked the Committee on Academic Freedom to consider the matter and make a recommendation to the board. Four alternatives were posed to the committee members. One was to continue the existing policy; another was to draw a line between direct and indirect aid, taking the view that indirect aid (transportation, health, school lunches, school nurses, etc.) should be permitted, but not direct aid to the educational function. Eleven committee members voted to continue existing policy; eight favored adopting the direct/indirect distinction.[63] The ACLU Board of Directors unanimously accepted the recommendation to continue existing ACLU policy.[64] It is not certain that the ACLU board would have accepted a recommendation from the Committee on Academic Freedom that it change its policy to the direct/indirect distinction. A recommendation to that effect failed, however, in the committee by a mere three votes. Should that recommendation have carried in the committee and been accepted by the ACLU board, the subsequent politics of establishment clause litigation would have been somewhat different, although there would no doubt still have been an ample supply of groups willing to take a separationist position on church-state issues.

The School Board Appeals

That the school board would appeal the adverse lower court decision would have seemed to be a foregone conclusion. The Ewing Township School Board, however, was a somewhat reluctant champion of the parochial school bus law. Following the New Jersey Supreme Court's action, a spokesman for the board suggested that since the decision would save the school district money, it was probable that the board would not authorize an appeal.[65] Also, it seems that the *Everson* litigation was a friendly suit aimed at getting a court ruling on the school bus law. Roscoe Walker, secretary-treasurer of the State Council of the JOUAM, wrote to Albert McCay on December 15, 1942, before the lawsuit had been filed in the supreme court, saying that C. G. Latham, the clerk of the board of education, had assured a JOUAM member who had spoken to him that he would cooperate fully.[66] The letter does not specify the nature and extent of the cooperation, but Gilmore Fisher, who became superintendent of schools in Ewing Township while the *Everson* case was in the courts, described the case as a friendly suit,[67] and Frederick Ryan, who became secretary to the school board shortly after Fisher assumed the superintendency, said that it was his impression that the school board had no particular commitment to the parochial school transportation program and would not have been unhappy had Everson prevailed in his case against the board.[68]

The school board's attorney, William Abbotts, however, argued for an appeal of the supreme court ruling. He pointed out that a definitive ruling could be obtained only from the Court of Errors and Appeals and strongly urged the board to authorize an appeal. His arguments convinced the school board, and on October 16, 1944, they authorized Abbotts to proceed.[69] Abbotts appealed the case to the Court of Errors and Appeals in early 1945.

Former judge William H. Speer entered the case on the side of the Ewing

Township Board of Education at this time. Speer was general attorney and director of the New Jersey Public Service Corporation at the time of the *Everson* litigation and was regarded as one of the finest courtroom lawyers in the state,[70] but it is not clear why he became involved in the *Everson* case. The school board might have wanted him because he was an able advocate, but, given the board's lack of enthusiasm for the litigation, it is doubtful that they went out of their way to bring in high-powered legal talent. Indeed, there is no record of any payments by the school board to Speer, only to Abbotts. The pro-busing forces in New Jersey might have suggested that Speer be brought into the case, but no evidence of that has been found.

Albert McCay, who had been elected to the assembly in the 1944 election, once again represented the JOUAM. The ACLU again asked Joseph Beck Tyler to write a brief for them and offered him $100 plus expenses to do so.[71] Once again, the primary issues argued in the case were state issues. A combined total of approximately one page from the parties' main briefs dealt specifically with the Fourteenth Amendment due process issue. The ACLU brief treated the issue of separation of church and state at greater length. Two amicus curiae briefs were filed supporting the position of the Ewing Township Board of Education. One was filed by Deputy Attorney General Joseph Lanigan, acting as an individual. He reportedly was representing the interests of the Roman Catholic Church.[72] The other was by former judge George Tennant, who was thought to be representing the interests of certain Protestant sectarian schools with favorable attitudes toward the school bus law.[73] The amicus briefs were short and added little if anything to the main brief. McCay argued the case on behalf of *Everson*. Both Abbotts and Speer argued the case for the Ewing Township Board of Education.

The litigants did not have to wait as long for a decision this time. The case was argued on May 21, 1945, and on October 15 the Court of Errors and Appeals reversed the lower court decision by a 6-3 vote. Chancellor Luther Campbell wrote the opinion of the court. He accepted dissenting Justice Heher's argument below that there was no proof that any of the state school fund had been used for parochial school bus costs.[74] The attorneys for the school board had relied heavily on this argument in their briefs and oral argument. Chancellor Campbell further contended that use of money from the general state fund, or use of local funds, for parochial school bus transportation was authorized by the statute and that such aid did not amount to gifts to sectarian schools or to individuals. Since education was a public matter, money spent on education could not, by definition, be spent for private purposes; thus money spent on education was spent constitutionally unless a specific constitutional limitation stood in the way, and he found none in the *Everson* case.[75]

Justice Clarence Case wrote a dissenting opinion, in which Justices Frederick Colie and Harold Wells joined, rejecting the notion that use of public funds to provide transportation to parochial schools was a benefit to the child rather than aid to a religious body: "I conclude that the furnishing of transportation to private or parochial schools out of public money is in aid or support of such schools and is in violation of constitutional provisions which prohibit such aid or support."[76] Justice Case found five such provisions of the state constitution that, in his view, the parochial school bus law violated. His minority views were, however, not sufficient to keep the buses from rolling once again for parochial school students.

The day after the *Everson* decision, Clifford Forster of the ACLU wrote to Albert McCay that he was not surprised by the decision but that he regretted it; he expressed the opinion that the religious makeup of the court caused the outcome.[77] One ACLU member was even more explicit in his accusation of Roman Catholic responsibility for the reversal. He named six members of the court (Luther Campbell, Thomas Brogan, Joseph Bodine, Ralph Donges, William L. Dill, and John J. Rafferty) and said four of them seemed indisputably Catholic; he wondered if the other two were also.[78]

The denominational explanation will not bear scrutiny, however. While all three dissenters were Protestants, the majority was composed of two Catholics, two Episcopalians, and two Presbyterians. A political explanation is more plausible. All six members of the majority were Democrats and all had ties of varying degrees of intensity to Mayor Frank Hague of Jersey City, the state's most influential Democrat. Two of the dissenters were Republicans and one was an independent; all three were either unconnected to Mayor Hague or were Hague opponents. Thus what was essentially a Democratic bill was upheld by a court majority consisting entirely of Democrats. This explanation does not assume that overt influence on the court took place; it merely assumes that the judges would have known the political forces at play in the state and might well have been affected by them.

The Case Goes to the Supreme Court of the United States

Forster and McCay began discussing an appeal to the U.S. Supreme Court as soon as the Court of Errors and Appeals handed down its opinion. The day after the decision, Forster wrote to McCay asking him whether he intended to appeal and expressing the view that an appeal would be worth the effort, even though there was not much hope that the Supreme Court would agree to review.[79] McCay initially doubted the possibility of getting a reversal from the Supreme Court because of *Cochran v. Louisiana State Board of Education,* which held that using state funds to provide textbooks for parochial schools did not take property without due process of law.[80] He sought Forster's opinion on the chances for success in Washington, and Forster urged him to appeal on the grounds that things had changed since *Cochran* and that there was nothing to lose.[81] McCay apparently was convinced, for by early December he was seeking an attorney to assist in making the appeal. He did this by writing to firms and lawyers who had appeared in other religion cases.[82] In this way, McCay obtained the services of Challen B. Ellis of the firm of Ellis, Houghton and Ellis, with which former senator Edward R. Burke of Nebraska was associated. The religion case Ellis had previously handled was *Cochran*. Originally somewhat reluctant to take on the *Everson* case, Ellis eventually joined the effort.[83]

A few days after writing to Ellis, McCay wrote a long letter to Roscoe Walker of the JOUAM strongly recommending that the *Everson* decision be appealed to the U.S. Supreme Court and stating that in his opinion there was a chance of winning.[84] The decision to appeal was soon forthcoming. In early February, Chancellor Campbell signed an order permitting an appeal, and on March 4, 1946, the request for a writ of appeal was filed in the federal high court.[85] Early in May the Supreme Court allowed the appeal.

After the U.S. Supreme Court agreed to review the case, both parties intensified their efforts to ready their cases for presentation. Both sides sought to enlist support from groups sympathetic to their positions, and spontaneous offers of support were received. The ACLU, of course, offered to file a brief in support of Everson.[86] The American Jewish Congress expressed interest in filing an amicus brief, but internal disagreement among counsel prevented it from doing so.[87] Briefs from several other organizations were sought, but the only one that materialized was by E. Hilton Jackson on behalf of the General Conference of Seventh-Day Adventists and the Joint Conference Committee on Public Relations of the Southern Baptist Convention, Northern Baptist Convention, and National Baptist Convention. The ACLU filed a brief written by Kenneth Greenawalt, with some help from Whitney North Seymour.[88] Strangely enough, Milton Lasher of the State Council of the JOUAM also filed an amicus brief. It is somewhat unusual that the JOUAM would file an amicus brief in a case that they were sponsoring. It is possible that they did so to mask the fact that they were the motive force behind the case, but there is no documentation to support that notion.

In September, Judge Speer called McCay to say that there might be one or two briefs amicus curiae filed in support of the board of education position and to request his consent to their being filed.[89] Actually, six briefs were ultimately filed in support of Speer's case. These were on behalf of the states of Illinois and Indiana, Louisiana, Massachusetts, Michigan, and New York and for the

National Council of Catholic Men and the National Council of Catholic Women.[90] A team assembled by the National Catholic Welfare Conference and headed by John Courtney Murray, a Jesuit scholar who had considerable knowledge about church-state relations, prepared the last brief.[91]

Judge Speer also had some help on his brief in *Everson*. At the suggestion of the Archdiocese of New York, Speer retained Porter R. Chandler of what was then Davis, Polk, Wardwell, Sunderland and Kiendl to assist him.[92] Chandler was then, and remained for some time, a major legal figure in church-state matters, supporting the position of cooperative arrangements between the two institutions. Kenneth Greenawalt, who wrote the ACLU brief in *Everson,* also remained a major influence on the other side of church-state litigation, supporting strict separation of church and state.

The federal issues that were scarcely mentioned in the New Jersey court briefs, and which were not discussed at all in the state court opinions, now moved to the forefront. The major issues were whether the statute deprived anyone of property without due process of law and whether the law violated the establishment of religion clause of the First Amendment as that provision might be made applicable to the states by the due process clause of the Fourteenth Amendment. Since *Everson* was the first major case of its kind to come before the high court, the briefs discussed these issues fully. Judge Speer and Porter Chandler wrote the board of education's brief, with help from Roger Clisham, a young associate in Chandler's firm. Senator Burke wrote Everson's brief, with assistance from Challen Ellis and Kahl Spriggs, an associate at Ellis, Houghton and Ellis. Oral argument highlighted the arguments made in the briefs. Kenneth Greenawalt, who was at the Supreme Court the day *Everson* was argued, wrote that Senator Burke's argument was excellent, relying extensively on the separation of church and state argument made in the printed brief of the ACLU. E. Hilton Jackson also stressed this argument in his argument for Everson. The justices asked Judge Speer a great many questions, most of them directed at the same issue stressed by Burke and Jackson.[93]

The interest of the justices may have resulted from their uncertainty about how to approach the case. Professor J. Woodford Howard's account of the conference discussion of *Everson*, based on his study of the papers of the justices, indicates that there was a good deal of doubt about how to decide the matter. The justices were in agreement about the desirability of the principle of separation of church and state but found it difficult to agree on how to apply that principle to the parochial school bus transportation case. Only Justices Frankfurter and Rutledge initially voted to invalidate the law. At conference, Justice Rutledge argued for absolute separation of church and state on the grounds that accommodation would lead to aid for things other than transportation and would encourage other religious institutions to seek government aid. Justices

Jackson and Burton eventually switched sides and voted to hold the parochial school bus transportation law void. Justice Murphy, who was both a Catholic and a civil libertarian, had passed at conference but ultimately supported Justice Black's opinion, giving the school board a 5-4 victory.[94]

In his opinion, Justice Black seemed to want to embrace both Justice Rutledge's strict separationist view and the more pragmatic position expressed at conference by Chief Justice Vinson.[95] On the one hand, Justice Black wrote:[96]

> The "establishment of religion" clause of the First Amendment means at least this: Neither a state nor the Federal Government can set up a church. Neither can pass laws which aid one religion, aid all religions, or prefer one religion over another. Neither can force nor influence a person to go to or to remain away from church against his will or force him to profess a belief or disbelief in any religion. No person can be punished for entertaining or professing religious beliefs or disbeliefs, for church attendance or non-attendance. No tax in any amount, large or small, can be levied to support any religious activities or institutions, whatever they may be called, or whatever form they may adopt to teach or practice religion. Neither a state nor the Federal Government can, openly or secretly, participate in the affairs of any religious organizations or groups or vice versa. In the words of Jefferson, the clause against establishment of religion by law was intended to erect "a wall of separation between church and state."

This language could certainly support the conclusion that the parochial school bus law was unconstitutional. Justice Douglas, in fact, announced some years later that he had changed his mind and now thought *Everson* had been wrongly decided.[97] However, Justice Black also wrote that:[98]

> On the other hand, other language of the amendment commands that New Jersey cannot hamper its citizens in the free exercise of their own religion. Consequently, it cannot exclude individual Catholics, Lutherans, Mohammedans, Baptists, Jews, Methodists, Non-believers, Presbyterians, or the members of other faiths, because of their faith, or lack of it, from receiving the benefits of public welfare legislation. While we do not mean to intimate that a state could not provide transportation only to children attending public schools, we must be careful in protecting the citizens of New Jersey against state-established churches, to be sure that we do not inadvertently prohibit New Jersey from extending its general state law benefits to all its citizens without regard to their religious belief.

Everson, therefore, is an equivocal precedent. The opinion of the court contains language that supports both the strict separationist and the accommodationist points of view. Additionally, there seems to have been a good deal of indecision among the justices during the decision process. Two members of the Court changed sides between the conference and the announcement of the decision, and one of the members of the 5-4 majority subsequently announced that he thought the case had been wrongly decided. Despite this apparently hesitant start, *Everson* did establish an important framework for subsequent church-state litigation and there was substantial agreement among the justices. While the Court moved toward an accommodationist position, it included enough strict-separationist language to sustain the *Lemon v. Kurtzman* test that later slowed down the movement toward state aid for parochial schools.[99]

Conclusion

The nature of the legislative controversy over the school bus law, as well as the litigation in the New Jersey courts, was reminiscent of nineteenth-century religious intolerance and conflict. Relations between the major religious groups began to improve after World War II, and it is difficult to imagine a church-state case today involving the sort of secrecy and animosity involved in *Everson*. In this highly charged religious-political context, *Everson* was the first case to hold the establishment of religion clause of the First Amendment applicable to the states through the due process clause of the Fourteenth Amendment. Although it was intended partly to resolve political conflict, *Everson* was not the last word on the subject. Justice Black's opinion set the stage for continued church-state litigation because it had a built-in tension between strict separation and accommodation.

Interest group participation in church-state litigation was much more sophisticated after the *Everson* decision. The JOUAM did not have the resources or legal expertise to put forth a maximum effort to defeat the parochial school bus law, and the ACLU's involvement was also somewhat haphazard. By contrast, the Archdiocese of New York and the National Catholic Welfare Conference effectively mobilized their strengths, bringing Porter Chandler and John Courtney Murray into the case on the side of the Ewing Township Board of Education. Heartened by the "wall of separation" rhetoric and disturbed by the approval of busing, the separationist forces were not to be as disorganized in the future. They were to be represented by Protestants and Other Americans United for Separation of Church and State, formed shortly after *Everson,* in direct response to that decision. That organization, along with others that emerged later, subsequently took the lead in challenging attempts to extend state aid to parochial schools.

Everson continues as a major influence on both church-state law and church-state relations in the United States. A better understanding of the history of the *Everson* case and the process by which it was decided is helpful, especially as the issues it raised fifty years ago remain a matter of public debate in legislatures and in the courts. Justice Rutledge was quite right, then, when he wrote in his *Everson* dissent, "This is not therefore just a little case over bus fares."[100]

Notes

Portions of the first section of this chapter, dealing with the legislative history of the parochial school bus bill, originally appeared in the article "Remote from the Schoolhouse," *New Jersey History* 99 (Spring/Summer 1981): 49–65, and are reprinted here with permission of the New Jersey Historical Society.

1. *Everson v. Board of Education,* 330 U.S. 1 (1947).
2. E.g., *Cochran v. Louisiana State Board of Education*, 281 U.S. 370 (1930).
3. Leo Pfeffer, *God, Caesar, and the Constitution* (Boston: Beacon Press, 1975), 257–58.
4. Richard E. Morgan, *The Politics of Religious Conflict* (New York: Pegasus, 1968), 110; *Judd v. Board of Education*, 278 N.Y. 200 (1938); Anson Phelps Stokes, *Church and State in the United States,* rev. ed. (New York: Harper & Row, 1964), 425–27.
5. New Jersey, *Laws of New Jersey, 1903 (Special Session)*, chap. 1, sec. 117.
6. For a more detailed description of the legislative history of the parochial school bus bill, see Daryl R. Fair, "Remote from the Schoolhouse: The Passage of the New Jersey Parochial School Bus Bill," *New Jersey History* 99 (Spring/Summer 1981): 49–65.
7. The other four were James K. Allardice of Ocean County, Clifford R. Powell of Burlington County, Thomas D. Taggart Jr. of Atlantic County, and Homer C. Zink of Essex County.
8. Carteret, "Joint Session Idea No Joke," *Newark Sunday Call*, 23 March 1941, 10; New Jersey, *Journal of the Senate, 1941*, 254, 263.
9. John Higham, *Strangers in the Land* (New York: Atheneum, 1973), 173–75; letter from Charles H. Michaelson, former secretary-treasurer, State Council of the JOUAM of New Jersey, to the author, 16 January 1975.
10. "School Bus Bill Passage Is Urged," *Newark Evening News*, 7 April 1941, 7; New Jersey, *New Jersey Legislative Index, 1941*, 195.
11. "Vote Likely on Bus Bill," *Newark Evening News*, 8 April 1941, 6.
12. "Nutley Board Discusses Bill," *Newark Evening News*, 17 April 1941, 42.
13. "History of New Jersey 'Bus Bill' Compiled," *Catholic News*, 25 October 1941, 1.
14. "School Bus Bill Hearing May 2," *Newark Evening News*, 22 April 1941, 22.
15. "Holds Bus Bill Must Be Aired," *Newark Sunday Call*, 20 April 1941, 12; "School Bus Views Aired," *Newark Evening News*, 3 May 1941, 2.
16. Dayton D. McKean, *Pressures on the Legislature of New Jersey* (New York: Columbia University Press, 1938), 102-3, 119, 125–26.
17. "School Bus Bill Passage Is Urged," 7; "City Commission Favors Bus Bill," *Newark Evening News*, 10 April 1941, 4; "School Bus Views Aired," *Newark Evening*

News, 3 May 1941, 2; "Bus Bill Release Asked by K. of C.," *Newark Sunday Call*, 11 May 1941, 2; "Student's Bus Bill," *Newark Evening News*, 4 April 1941, 18; "Is It Good Legislation?" *New Jersey Voter* 4 (July 1941): 17; "Saturday's Siren," *Jersey Journal*, 9 October 1943, found in the American Civil Liberties Union Archives, Firestone Library, Princeton University, vol. 2516, 163 (hereafter ACLU Archives).

18. "School Bus Views Aired," 7.

19. Carteret, "Stories of Legislators on Adjournment Vary," *Newark Sunday Call*, 4 May 1941, 7.

20. "History of New Jersey 'Bus Bill' Compiled," 1; "Sacerdotal Mass to Celebrate Anniversary of Dr. Glover," *Newark Evening News*, 2 May 1941, 16; "City USO Picks Treasurer; Catholics Name Matthews," *Newark Evening News*, 20 May 1941, 14; "Bus Bill Gets Assembly O.K.," *Newark Evening News*, 4 June 1941, 4.

21. "Murphy Asks Vote on School Bus Bill," *Newark Evening News*, 2 May 1941, 2.

22. Carteret, "Vote Reform Programs Doomed But GOP Hopes for Some Gains," *Newark Sunday Call*, 13 April 1941, 5.

23. "Women in Politics," *Newark Evening News*, 23 April 1941, 19; "Women in Politics," *Newark Evening News*, 28 May 1941, 23.

24. "Bus Bill Release Asked by K. of C.," 2.

25. "Parochial Bus Bill Amended," *Newark Evening News*, 20 May 1941, 8.

26. "Women in Politics," 28 May 1941, 23.

27. "Assembly Caucus to Get Bus Bill," *Newark Evening News*, 3 June 1941, 17.

28. "History of New Jersey 'Bus Bill' Compiled," 1.

29. "Bus Bill Gets Assembly O.K.," *Newark Evening News*, 4 June 1941, 4.

30. New Jersey, *Minutes of the General Assembly, 1941*, 846–48.

31. Carteret, "Stories of Legislators on Adjournment Vary," 7.

32. New Jersey, *Minutes of the General Assembly, 1941*, 848.

33. Letter from Richard Connors to the author, 6 January 1975.

34. "Parochial Bus Bill Now Law," *Newark Evening News*, 10 June 1941, 11.

35. "Is It Good Legislation?" 17.

36. New Jersey, *Laws of New Jersey, 1941*, chap. 191, sec. 1

37. "School Bus Bill Becomes Law," *NJTA Taxegram*, 16 June 1941, 107.

38. *Everson v. Board of Education, Records and Briefs*, 10 New Jersey Supreme Court 29 (1943).

39. Ewing Township Board of Education, Minutes, 21 September 1942.

40. Ewing Township Board of Education, Minutes, 15 March 1943.

41. "Liberties Union Assails Bus Bill," *Newark Evening News*, 6 October 1943, 19.

42. Letter from Albert McCay to Philip S. Irons Jr., 1 March 1946, in Albert McCay's file on the *Everson* case, Parker, McCay & Criscuolo, Mount Holly, N.J. (hereafter "McCay file").

43. Letter from Charles H. Michaelson to the author, 16 January 1975.

44. The McCay file contains many letters to and from Walker and Michaelson concerning the lawsuit.

45. "First Test Made on School Rides," *Newark Evening News*, 5 April 1943, 2.

46. Letter from Roger Baldwin to Franz Boas, 14 April 1941, ACLU Archives, vol.

2335, 154; letter from Archey D. Ball to Mrs. M. B. Milner, 19 September 1941, ACLU Archives, vol. 2335, 189; letter from Jerome C. Eisenberg to Mrs. Lucille B. Milner, 12 June 1941, ACLU Archives, vol. 2335, 173; letter from Archey D. Ball to Roger Baldwin, 26 June 1941, ACLU Archives, vol. 2335, 181.

47. Letter from Clifford Forster to Harold Parker, 18 May 1943, ACLU Archives, vol. 2755, 35.

48. Letter from McCay to Forster, 11 June 1943, ACLU Archives, vol. 2755, 36–37.

49. Letter from Forster to McCay, 16 June 1943, ACLU Archives, vol. 2755, 38.

50. Letter from Forster to McCay, 24 June 1943, ACLU Archives, vol. 2755, 40.

51. ACLU Archives, vol. 2755, 44.

52. *Everson v. Board of Education, Records,* 1785 Court of Errors and Appeals 13–15 (1945).

53. Letter from McCay to Roger Baldwin, 24 August 1943, ACLU Archives, vol. 2755, 51.

54. *Everson v. Board of Education, Records and Briefs,* 10 New Jersey Supreme Court 28–36 (1943).

55. Letter from Forster to Raymond Wise, 26 July 1943, ACLU Archives, vol. 2755, 45, 47.

56. Letter from McCay to Joseph Beck Tyler, 17 June 1940, McCay file; Joseph Beck Tyler, "In re Assembly Bill 123," McCay file. McCay's letter to Forster about Tyler gives the impression that Tyler spoke at the hearings on S. 152 in 1941; letter from McCay to Forster, 2 September 1943, ACLU Archives, vol. 2755, 53.

57. Letter from Forster to Tyler, 8 September 1943; letter from Tyler to Forster, 7 September 1943; letter from Forster to Tyler, 8 September 1943; ACLU Archives, vol. 2755, 54–56.

58. *Everson v. Board of Education,* 132 N.J.L. 98 (1944).

59. *Everson v. Board of Education,* 132 N.J.L. 99.

60. *Everson v. Board of Education,* 132 N.J.L. 100–101.

61. *Everson v. Board of Education,* 132 N.J.L. 102, 105.

62. "School Bus Plea Studied," *Newark Evening News,* 22 May 1944, 4; Ewing Township Board of Education, Minutes, 20 March 1944.

63. Memorandum from James M. O'Neill, chair of the Committee on Academic Freedom, to ACLU Board of Directors, 21 December 1944, ACLU Archives, vol. 2755, 99–100.

64. Memorandum from O'Neill to members of the Committee on Academic Freedom, 5 January 1945, ACLU Archives, vol. 2755, 98.

65. "Plea Is Likely on Bus Riding," *Newark Evening News,* 14 September 1944, 3.

66. Letter from Roscoe Walker to Albert McCay, 15 December 1942, McCay file.

67. Letter from Gilmore Fisher to the author, 20 March 1975.

68. Frederick Ryan, interview by author, 11 November 1974.

69. Ewing Township Board of Education, *Minutes,* 16 October 1944.

70. Obituary of William H. Speer, *Newark Evening News,* 8 July 1959, 33.

71. Letter from Forster to Tyler, 2 January 1945, ACLU Archives, vol. 2700, 127.

72. Letter from Tyler to Forster, 18 May 1945, ACLU Archives, vol. 2700, 149; letter from McCay to Forster, 24 May 1945, ACLU Archives, vol. 2700, 157.

73. Letter from McCay to Forster, ACLU Archives, vol. 2700, 157.

74. *Everson v. Board of Education*, 133 N.J.L. 350, 351–52 (1945).

75. *Everson v. Board of Education*, 133 N.J.L. 354–55.

76. *Everson v. Board of Education*, 133 N.J.L. 362.

77. Letter from Forster to McCay, 16 October 1945, ACLU Archives, vol. 2700, 161.

78. Letter from S. S. Neiss to American Civil Liberties Union, 16 October 1945, ACLU Archives, vol. 2700, 163.

79. Letter from Forster to McCay, 16 October 1945, ACLU Archives, vol. 2700, 161.

80. *Cochran v. Louisiana State Board of Education,* 281 U.S. 370 (1930).

81. Letter from McCay to Forster, 17 October 1945, ACLU Archives, vol. 2700, 165; letter from Forster to McCay, 26 October 1945, ACLU Archives, vol. 2700, 167.

82. Letter from McCay to Dudley, Duvall and Dudley, 8 December 1945, ACLU Archives, vol. 2700, 176; letter from McCay to Challen B. Ellis, 8 December 1945, ACLU Archives, vol. 2700, 177–79.

83. Letter from Ellis to McCay, 16 January 1946, McCay file; letter from Ellis to McCay, 19 February 1946, McCay file.

84. Letter from McCay to Roscoe Walker, 11 December 1945, ACLU Archives, vol. 2700, 181–83.

85. "Parochial Buses to Supreme Court," *Newark Evening News*, 5 February 1946, 2; *Everson*, 330 U.S. 1 (1947), *U.S. Supreme Court Records and Briefs*.

86. Letter from Forster to Ellis, 7 May 1946, ACLU Archives, vol. 2755, 137.

87 Letter from McCay to Ellis, 7 May 1946, ACLU Archives, vol. 2755, 137; letter from McCay to Forster, 19 September 1946, ACLU Archives, vol. 2755, 168; letter from Frederick E. Robin to Ellis, 12 November 1946, ACLU Archives, vol. 2755, 199.

88. Letter from Whitney North Seymour to Forster, 18 October 1946, ACLU Archives, vol. 2755, 188.

89. Letter from McCay to Ellis, 23 September 1946, ACLU Archives, vol. 2755, 171.

90. *Everson v. Board of Education*, 330 U.S. 2–3.

91. Jo Renée Formicola, "Everson Revisited: 'This Is Not . . . Just a Little Case over Bus Fares,'" *Polity* 28, no. 1 (Fall 1995).

92. Letter from Porter R. Chandler to the author, 14 February 1975.

93. Letter from Kenneth Greenawalt to Nannette Dembitz, 25 November 1946, ACLU Archives, vol. 2755, 200–201.

94. J. Woodford Howard, "On the Fluidity of Judicial Choice," *American Political Science Review* 62 (1968): 54.

95. Howard, "Fluidity of Judicial Choice," 54.

96. *Everson v. Board of Education*, 330 U.S. 15–16.

97. *Engel v. Vitale*, 370 U.S. 421, 443 (1962).

98. *Everson v. Board of Education,* 330 U.S. 16–17.

99. *Lemon v. Kurtzman,* 403 U.S. 602 (1971). *Lemon* held that to be constitutional, a state law aiding parochial schools in some way had to have a secular purpose and a primary effect that neither advanced nor inhibited religion and it could not involve excessive entanglement of government and religion.

100. *Everson v. Board of Education*, 330 U.S. 57.

2

Everson and the Command of History:
The Supreme Court, Lessons of History, and Church-State Debate in America

Daniel L. Dreisbach

Few opinions of the U.S. Supreme Court have generated more commentary from diverse disciplines than *Everson v. Board of Education* (1947). This discussion has engaged some of the nation's most thoughtful scholars of law, history, politics, education, and religion. The Court's ruling revived questions about the historical, prudential, and constitutional role of religion in American public life; theories of constitutional interpretation; and the place of private, religious education in a free and pluralistic society. In particular, it provoked energetic debate on the propriety of contributing public funds to parochial schools or to the children who attend them. These were issues of profound interest to American society at midcentury, and they continue to agitate the public mind.

Legal and academic attention is appropriately focused on *Everson*. This case, as Gerard V. Bradley remarked, "effectively opened the modern era of church-state jurisprudence."[1] In an influential essay entitled "Everson v. Board of Education: A Product of Judicial Will," noted constitutional scholar Paul G. Kauper observed that *Everson* "stands as a key decision in laying the foundation for judicial review of all governmental practices supportive of religion. The beginning of an impressive and influential body of case law, it nationalized the restrictions embodied in the establishment clause of the first amendment and opened up a new and comprehensive surveillance of state and local laws and practices dealing with religious matters."[2] The word "landmark" is used promiscuously in discussions of constitutional case law; it is, however, appropriately used to describe *Everson*. The case not only incorporated the First Amendment nonestablishment guarantee into the Fourteenth Amendment due process of law clause, thereby holding the prohibition on establishment against the states, but also marked the first time the Supreme Court gave an authoritative interpretation of the nonestablishment principle. It is, in short, a defining First Amendment religion case. Any informed discussion of the constitutional prohibition on "an establishment of religion" must contend with the reasoning and holding of *Everson v. Board of Education.*

In the fifteen years or so I have studied American church-state relations—as a congressional aide, graduate student, public interest lawyer, and academic—I recollect few discussions of the First Amendment religion provisions in which *Everson* was not mentioned. In virtually all these discussions of *Everson*, the primary focus was on the Court's sweeping separationist pronouncement, rooted in its reading of history, rather than on the narrow legal holding. It is significant, indeed, that the *Everson* Court's interpretive approach and rhetoric often overshadow the holding in discussions among scholars and lawyers. This chapter examines the Court's historical interpretive approach. The Court's reading of history, which the justices maintained mandated a strict separationist interpretation of the First Amendment nonestablishment principle, is briefly summarized. Attention is then turned to a critique of the historical assertions buttressing the Court's analysis. This is followed by a survey of the voluminous secondary literature generated by the *Everson* decision. This section identifies leading scholars and works that have shaped a vital debate on the Court's use of history and places this continuing discussion in a historical and legal context. This constitutional dispute is one of the most bitterly contested of the last half century. A concluding section offers observations on the promises and problems of the Supreme Court's reliance on history to inform its church-state pronouncements.

While much that has been written on *Everson* has focused on the Court's controversial use of history and separationist pronouncements, the decision is important because of its implications for the role of religion in public life and the future of American education, both public and private. Nothing less than the content and sponsorship of education is at stake. Indeed, the Court's version of history and the separationist construction of the First Amendment that it purportedly buttresses laid a foundation for the released-time cases that soon followed, the school prayer cases in the early 1960s, the continuing controversies over religious expression and instruction in public schools, and the multitude of disputes involving public financial assistance for private religious schools or their pupils. These controversies raise fundamental questions about the role of religion in education and the place of private schools in an increasingly secular, pluralistic society. Thus the debate provoked by the *Everson* Court's use of history is less about the past than it is about the future.

Everson and the Command of History

The most enduring and poignant legacy of *Everson v. Board of Education*—more important than the legal holding—is the lavish use of separationist rhetoric in both the majority and minority opinions. In this regard, there was a remarkable lack of confrontation between the majority and minority opinions. In defining the nonestablishment provision, Justice Hugo L. Black, writing for a slender majority of five justices, declared: "Neither a state nor the Federal Government can set up a church. Neither can pass laws which aid one religion, aid all religions, or prefer one religion over another. . . . No tax in any amount, large or small, can be levied to support any religious activities or institutions, whatever they may be called, or whatever form they may adopt to teach or practice religion. . . . In the words of Jefferson, the clause against establishment of religion by law was intended to erect 'a wall of separation between church and State. . . . That wall must be kept high and impregnable. We could not approve the slightest breach."[3] In even more sweeping terms, Justice Wiley B. Rutledge asserted in a minority opinion that the First Amendment's purpose was "to uproot" all religious establishments and "to create a complete and permanent separation of the spheres of religious activity and civil authority by comprehensively forbidding every form of public aid or support for religion."[4] Despite the unequivocal separationist rhetoric, a divided Court upheld the constitutionality of state reimbursements to parents for money expended in the transportation of their children to and from parochial schools, rejecting the minority contention that the tax supported program constituted an "establishment of religion" in violation of the First Amendment.[5]

Many constitutional scholars have noted that while Justice Black's majority opinion upheld the use of public funds for the transportation of parochial school pupils and the dissenters thought the challenged state program was unconstitutional, the historical analysis and separationist rhetoric used in both the majority and minority opinions were essentially the same except for the final judgment. Indeed, one of the most perplexing aspects of *Everson* is the absence of disagreement between the majority and minority opinions regarding a separationist perspective and underlying historical assumptions. Justice Black, for the Court, and Justices Robert H. Jackson, Wiley B. Rutledge, Felix M. Frankfurter, and Harold H. Burton, in dissent, were unanimous in their reliance on the contributions of Jefferson and Madison to the bitter disestablishment struggle in revolutionary Virginia and their conclusion that this history buttressed a strict separationist construction of the First Amendment nonestablishment provision.[6] The dissenting justices were struck by the apparent inconsistency between the majority's separationist rhetoric and its accommodationist holding. Justice Jackson remarked sardonically that "the undertones of the opinion, advocating complete and uncompromising separation of Church from State, seem utterly discordant with its conclusion yielding support to their commingling in educational matters. The case which irresistibly comes to mind as the most fitting precedent is that of Julia who, according to

Byron's reports, 'whispering "I will ne'er consent,"—consented.'"[7] Even Justice Black in *McCollum v. Board of Education* (1948) noted that both the majority and minority *Everson* opinions "agreed that the First Amendment's language, properly interpreted, had erected a wall of separation between Church and State."[8] The Court's unanimous endorsement of a strict separationist interpretation of the First Amendment is arguably the most significant aspect of *Everson*, not the differing conclusions reached on the facts of the case. Accordingly, it is appropriate to regard the historical analysis and rhetoric of both the majority and minority opinions as essentially the same and to subject both to similar scrutiny and criticism.

The Court contended that its strict separationist construction of the First Amendment was rooted in, indeed compelled by, the "command of history, not the preference of the justices."[9] In the years since *Everson*, if there has been one constant in the confused arena of church-state law, it is that jurists and commentators—regardless of their legal opinion—consistently have appealed to history to buttress their respective interpretations of the First Amendment ban on religious establishment.[10] Justice Black opined that the Court should construe the Constitution "in the light of its history and the evils it was designed forever to suppress."[11] Justice Rutledge similarly observed:

> No provision of the Constitution is more closely tied to or given content by its generating history than the religious clause of the First Amendment. It is at once the refined product and the terse summation of that history. The history includes not only Madison's authorship and the proceedings before the First Congress, but also the long and intensive struggle for religious freedom in America, more especially in Virginia, of which the Amendment was the direct culmination. In the documents of the times, particularly of Madison, who was leader in the Virginia struggle before he became the Amendment's sponsor, but also in the writings of Jefferson and others and in the issues which engendered them is to be found irrefutable confirmation of the Amendment's sweeping content.[12]

In view of these pronouncements, the Court could hardly have applied a different interpretive approach in *Everson* and subsequent church-state cases. In construing the First Amendment, the Court purported to enter the minds and divine the intentions of the constitutional framers. This interpretive approach, as well as the Court's separationist rhetoric, laid the foundations for subsequent church-state jurisprudence.[13] As Laurence H. Tribe observed: "Whether the Black-Rutledge version is accurate history has been disputed vigorously off the Court, . . . what is indisputable is that, with remarkable consensus, later Courts accepted the perspective of these Justices as historical truth."[14]

The Court confirmed its strict separationist orientation in *McCollum v. Board of Education* (1948), decided the following term. Building on the historical and separationist foundations laid in *Everson*, the *McCollum* Court held that an Illinois released-time program that permitted religious instruction at private expense in public school facilities during regular school hours violated the First Amendment nonestablishment provision. In some respects, the *McCollum* decision was even more significant than *Everson*. The narrow 5-4 decision in *Everson* gave way to an 8-1 majority, thereby solidifying a strict separationist bloc on the Court. More significantly, *McCollum* differed from *Everson* in that minimal funds from the public treasury were expended in the challenged released-time program. *Everson*, however, was an essential precursor to *McCollum*. In any case, much criticism in the late 1940s and 1950s of the Supreme Court's church-state jurisprudence was directed at both *Everson* and *McCollum*.

The Supreme Court as Historian

Critics challenged *Everson* on both historical and normative grounds. The focus here is on the Court's historical analysis. "[T]he Supreme Court," Professor Tribe noted, "has occasionally assumed the role of constitutional historian to seek guidance in the origins and original meanings of the religion clauses. For nearly thirty years Justices Black and Rutledge served as the chief chroniclers of these investigations."[15] Both the majority and minority in *Everson* contended that a separationist construction of the First Amendment nonestablishment provision was compelled by American history. In particular, the Court appealed to selected events in revolutionary Virginia and to the words and deeds of Thomas Jefferson and James Madison, not only because they led the dramatic disestablishment struggle in their native commonwealth, but also because their idea of the proper church-state arrangement was thought to be expressive of the purposes of the First Amendment religion provisions.[16] The Court referenced Jefferson's "Bill for Establishing Religious Freedom" and Madison's "Memorial and Remonstrance," which the justices argued gave content and meaning to the First Amendment.[17] These documents were viewed as uncompromising manifestos for an absolute separation between church and state. Justice Black, for the majority, argued that "the First Amendment, in the drafting and adoption of which Madison and Jefferson played such leading roles, had the same objective and were intended to provide the same protection against governmental intrusion on religious liberty as [Jefferson's] Virginia statute [for establishing religious liberty]."[18] While giving greater attention to Madison, Justice Rutledge in dissent similarly remarked that the great documents of the "Virginia struggle for religious liberty . . . became warp and woof of our constitutional tradition" of church-state separation.[19] In this history,

Rutledge concluded, was "found irrefutable confirmation of the [First] Amendment's sweeping content."[20] The justices maintained that the historical and constitutional understanding of "establishment of religion" included not only a formal recognition of, and legal preference for, one particular church or denomination but also every form of public aid or encouragement for religious objectives. As the principal organizing theme of its decision, the *Everson* Court invoked the celebrated metaphor Jefferson coined in an address to the Danbury Baptist Association on New Year's Day, 1802:[21] "In the words of Jefferson, the [First Amendment] clause against establishment of religion by law was intended to erect 'a wall of separation between church and State'. . . . That wall," the *Everson* Court declared, "must be kept high and impregnable. We could not approve the slightest breach."[22]

Critics countered that neither constitutional text nor the American experience dictates a strict separation between church and state. A recurring theme advanced by the Court's detractors is that *Everson* promulgated a distorted version of history to buttress a strict separation, no-aid-to-religion construction of the First Amendment. "There is no substantial evidence," Professor Kauper remarked, "to indicate that the no-establishment phrasing [of the First Amendment] was generally understood to convey a meaning that could be equated with the Virginia Bill of Religious Liberty or with Madison's views or with the interpretation placed on it in *Everson*."[23] Gerard V. Bradley reported that "the Court has resolutely, even proudly, rejected the most accessible, standard of definitions" of the First Amendment prohibition. He further argued:

> Modern dictionaries define *establishment* as a state church, such as the Church of England or Church of Scotland. Traditional legal sources are in accord. Blackstone said that "by establishment of religion is meant the setting up or recognition of a state church, or at least the conferring upon one church of special favors and advantages which are denied to others." The *Everson* Court, however, expressly eschewed "narrow interpretations" such as the mere prohibition of a "national church" or "no sect preference." It also rejected the modest option of simply outlawing some cluster of discreet, too cozy, relations between church and state falling short of a "state church," like that now prevailing in England.[24]

In perhaps the most influential article written on *McCollum*, the late dean of American constitutional scholars, Edward S. Corwin, unambiguously took issue with the Court: "What the 'establishment of religion' clause of the First Amendment does, and *all that it does, is to forbid Congress to give any religious faith, sect, or denomination a preferred status*."[25] Corwin rebuked the Court in strikingly strong language for playing fast and loose with historical evidence: "The historical record shows beyond peradventure that the core idea of 'an establishment of religion' comprises the idea of *preference*; and that any act of public authority favorable to religion in general cannot, without manifest falsification of history, be brought under the ban of that phrase. Undoubtedly the Court has the right to make history, as it has often done in the past; but it has no right to *remake* it."[26] This view has come to be known as the "no preference" theory, or nonpreferentialism.[27]

Critics have sought to discredit the Court's "near blind faith that the opinions" of Jefferson and Madison "accurately reflect the purpose and intent of the framers and ratifiers" of the First Amendment.[28] They have rejected the notion that Jefferson and Madison were zealous advocates of a pervasive separation of the spheres of religious activity and civil authority.[29] Madison's "Memorial and Remonstrance," they have countered, opposed the use of public monies for the *discriminatory* and unequal advancement of *one* religion,[30] while Jefferson's "Bill for Establishing Religious Freedom" was designed, in general, to codify the expanding scope of religious liberties increasingly available in Virginia. Indeed, Jefferson's bill, as the eminent legal historian Mark DeWolfe Howe observed, did not "in its enacting clauses explicitly prohibit establishment."[31] These documents, critics have thus concluded, were not briefs for an absolute separation of religion and the civil state.

Some of *Everson*'s detractors have argued that even if it is conceded that Jefferson and Madison were ardent separationists, confirmed by the religious-freedom bill and the "Memorial and Remonstrance," there is little evidence that these views found equivalent expression in the First Amendment. While Madison may have wanted the First Amendment to embody a disestablishment principle like that he had campaigned for in Virginia, keen opposition in the First Congress to such an arrangement forced him to make substantial compromises. Despite the impression left by the *Everson* Court, "Madison did not carry the country along with Virginia's sweeping separation of churches from the state: indeed, the country in some degree carried him."[32] Therefore, the modern Court has inappropriately limited its historical investigation to the presumed ambitions of Madison.[33] Rather, judicial inquiries into the original understanding of the First Amendment should consider the views of the majority of the First Congress that apparently diluted Madison's "sweeping" intentions. The *Everson* Court failed to consider the possibility that Jefferson and Madison, instrumental as they were in formulating American church-state doctrine, embraced views on church-state separation decidedly more radical than those of a majority of their contemporaries. The *Everson* Court, it is argued, distorted the intentions of the First Congress by elevating a minority opinion (the arguably radical separationist views of Jefferson and Madison) to a central position in their historical analysis of the original understanding of the First Amendment religion provisions. Thus, even if Jefferson and Madison sought to foster sweeping church-state separation in both the state and federal settings, it does not necessarily follow that such a vision was enshrined in the First Amendment.

Critics also question the Court's reliance on Virginia's disestablishment movement as a precursor to, or model for, the church-state arrangement set forth in the First Amendment.[34] There are obvious reasons why the struggle in Virginia is given extensive coverage in judicial and scholarly accounts of the development of church-state relationships in America. "No doubt historians focus their attention on the Virginia story," Leonard W. Levy observed, "because the sources are uniquely ample, the struggle was important and dramatic, and the opinions of Madison . . . and of Jefferson were fully elicited." While concurring with the *Everson* ruling, Levy cautioned that if the "object is to understand what was meant by 'an establishment of religion' at the time of the framing of the Bill of Rights, the histories of the other states are equally important, notwithstanding the stature and influence of Jefferson and Madison as individuals."[35] Most states in the founding era retained various forms of religious establishment, including state churches and religious test oaths for officeholders. Furthermore, if the object is to ascertain the original understanding of the First Amendment, as framed by the First Congress and ratified by the states, then attention must be devoted to the views of all members of the First Congress, not just Madison, and to the views of delegates at state ratifying conventions. "Not a word of the state-by-state process of ratification is spoken in *Everson*," lamented Gerard V. Bradley. "In fact, one would think from the [*Everson*] opinions that the First Amendment was rendered operative by House approval, if not by the simple act of Madison's penmanship."[36]

Conspicuous by its omission is an analysis by the Court of the recorded debates in the First Congress on the framing of the First Amendment. Conventional rules of interpretation suggest that the interpretation of a constitutional provision begin with an examination of the text and the deliberations of the body that drafted and adopted it. Significantly, both Justices Black and Rutledge in their respective *Everson* opinions devoted considerable space to recounting the dramatic church-state controversy in revolutionary Virginia, yet they virtually ignored the legislative history of the First Amendment religion provisions.[37] The interpretation of the First Amendment was, after all, at issue in *Everson*. It would seem that the legislative history of the First Amendment, not the disestablishment battles in Virginia, should have been the focus of the Court's historical review.[38] Opponents speculate that the Court disregarded the text and legislative history of the First Amendment because they failed to support the Court's separationist prepossessions.

Critics also reject the *Everson* Court's invocation of Jefferson's "wall of separation" metaphor as an organizing theme of church-state jurisprudence.[39] Interestingly, some of the harshest criticisms of the Court's use of the metaphor have emanated from the Court itself. The *McCollum* majority, citing *Everson*, similarly found the metaphor irresistible, elevating it to an authoritative gloss on the First Amendment. A dissenting Justice Stanley F. Reed denounced the Court's reliance on the metaphor. "A rule of law," he protested, "should not be drawn from a figure of speech."[40] Over a decade later, in the first school prayer case, Justice Potter Stewart similarly cautioned his judicial brethren. The Court's task in resolving complex constitutional controversies, he opined, "is not responsibly aided by the uncritical invocation of metaphors like the 'wall of separation,' a phrase nowhere to be found in the Constitution."[41] Justice Robert H. Jackson quipped that, absent sure "legal guidance" in this matter, the justices "are likely to make the legal 'wall of separation between church and state' as winding as the famous serpentine wall designed by Mr. Jefferson for the University he founded."[42] Chief Justice William H. Rehnquist, perhaps the most vociferous critic of the "wall," concluded:

It is impossible to build sound constitutional doctrine upon a mistaken understanding of constitutional history, but unfortunately the Establishment Clause has been expressly freighted with Jefferson's misleading metaphor for nearly 40 years. Thomas Jefferson was of course in France at the time the constitutional Amendments known as the Bill of Rights were passed by Congress and ratified by the States. His letter to the Danbury Baptist Association was a short note of courtesy, written 14 years after the Amendments were passed by Congress. He would seem to any detached observer as a less than ideal source of contemporary history as to the meaning of the Religion Clauses of the First Amendment. . . .

There is simply no historical foundation for the proposition that the Framers [of the First Amendment] intended to build the "wall of separation" that was constitutionalized in *Everson.*

Notwithstanding the absence of a historical basis for this theory of rigid separation, the wall idea might well have served as a useful albeit misguided analytical concept, had it led this Court to unified and principled results in Establishment Clause cases. The opposite, unfortunately, has been true; in the 38 years since *Everson* our Establishment Clause cases have been neither principled nor unified. Our recent opinions, many of them hopelessly divided pluralities, have with embarrassing candor conceded that the "wall of separation" is merely a "blurred, indistinct, and variable barrier," which "is not wholly accurate" and can only be "dimly perceived." *Lemon v. Kurtzman,* 403 U.S. 602, 614 (1971); *Tilton v. Richardson,* 403 U.S. 672, 677-678 (1971); *Wolman v. Walter,* 433 U.S. 229, 236 (1977); *Lynch v. Donnelly,* 465 U.S. 668, 673 (1984).

Whether due to its lack of historical support or its practical unworkability, the *Everson* "wall" has proved all but useless as a guide to sound constitutional adjudication. . . . [N]o amount of repetition of historical errors in judicial opinions can make the errors true. The "wall of separation between church and State" is a metaphor based on bad history, a metaphor which has proved useless as a guide to judging. It should be frankly and explicitly abandoned.[43]

It is unfortunate that figures of speech designed to simplify and liberate thought end often by trivializing or enslaving it. Therefore, as Justice Benjamin Cardozo counseled, "[m]etaphors in law are to be narrowly watched."[44]

Another criticism of *Everson* frequently raised in nonpreferentialist literature concerns the nationalization of the First Amendment. The federal Constitution provided for a national government of limited authority and strictly delegated, enumerated powers only. Those powers not explicitly entrusted to the federal government were assumed to be reserved to the individual or the states (so far as they legitimately resided in any governmental authority). Since no power in matters pertaining to religion was explicitly delegated to the federal government by the Constitution, the federal regime had no jurisdiction over religion, and each state was free to define its own church-state arrangements. Similarly, the First Amendment not only explicitly prohibited the federal legislature from making laws respecting "an establishment of religion" but also implicitly denied the federal regime the authority to interfere with existing state religious practices and establishments. Therefore, as a matter of federalism, the First Amendment altered nothing in matters pertaining to federal involvement with religion; it simply made explicit that which was already understood in the federal arrangement. In other words, the First Amendment affirmed the principle of federalism; and by restraining the federal government, the states were free to establish or disestablish a state church, or to discriminate against one sect in particular. As Edward S. Corwin observed, "the principal importance of the [first] amendment lay in the separation which it effected between the respective jurisdictions of state and nation regarding religion, rather than in its bearing on the question of the separation of church and state."[45] The *Everson* Court, critics complained, turned this principle on its head by incorporating (or nationalizing) the nonestablishment provision into the word "liberty" in the Fourteenth Amendment due process of law clause, thereby making the First Amendment ban on "an establishment of religion" applicable to the states. Professor Corwin was among those who argued that "the Fourteenth Amendment does not authorize the Court to substitute the word 'state' for 'Congress' in the ban imposed by the First Amendment on laws 'respecting an establishment of religion.'"[46] Opponents challenged the legitimacy of incorporation on a variety of grounds, including the Court's textual and historical interpretation of the Fourteenth Amendment. There is no question that incorporation marked a radical departure from the original understanding of the First Amendment; whether it accorded with the designs of those who framed and ratified the Fourteenth Amendment is a subject of great debate.[47]

In the half century since *Everson*, the Supreme Court has continued to rely on a version of history invoked by Justices Black and Rutledge. Critics, such as Mark DeWolfe Howe, have contended that the Court recounted American history, "not in order to tell accurately the story of the past, but in order to legitimate its own judgment of policy."[48] While critics have generally agreed that history is useful, if not crucial, to a legitimate understanding of the First Amendment, they have complained that the Court promulgated a fundamentally flawed, "simplistic and largely fictionalized version of American history."[49] Although critics have disagreed about whether or not the Court's misreading of history was inadvertent, there has been broad agreement that the Court was attracted to a selective, erroneous version of history in order to buttress the justices' ideological predilection for an absolute separation between church and state. In a powerful and influential critique of the Court's history, Professor Howe commented on the role of historian assumed by the Court:

> In recent years the Court has decided a number of important cases relating to church and state and, in each of the cases, has alleged that the command of history, not the preference of the justices, has brought the Court to its decision. I believe that in the matters at issue the Court has too often pretended that the dictates of the nation's history, rather than the mandates of its own will, compelled a particular decision. By superficial and purposive interpretations of the past, the Court has dishonored the arts of the historian and degraded the talents of the lawyer. Such dishonoring and degrading may not be of large moment when the history that the Court manipulates is merely 'legal history'—the story, that is, of the law's internal growth and development. When, however, the Court endeavors to write an authoritative chapter in the intellectual history of the American people, as it does when it lays historical foundations beneath its readings of the First Amendment, then any distortion becomes a matter of consequence.[50]

The appropriate use and interpretation of history has emerged as one of the most contested aspects of modern church-state jurisprudence. Briefs filed in church-state cases, as well as judicial pronouncements, are replete with historical analyses. This is a legacy of the interpretive approach adopted in *Everson*. The Court's extensive and continuing reliance on history to inform its interpretation of the First Amendment religion provisions invites further historical inquiry. Insofar as the Court has relied on an erroneous version of "history" to construct church-state doctrine, its legal pronouncements lack analytical merit and legitimacy.[51] As Justice Rehnquist opined in *Wallace v. Jaffree:* "It is impossible to build sound constitutional doctrine upon a mistaken understanding of constitutional history."[52] Furthermore, the Court has formulated its analysis in such absolute, strict separationist terms that to document just one error or exception undermines the credibility of the Court's entire separationist position.[53] Thus review of the historical record casts light on the legitimacy of the Court's church-state jurisprudence in a long line of cases starting with *Everson.*

The section that follows charts the debate provoked by the *Everson* Court's version of history. Influential commentators who shaped that debate are identified, and the debate is placed in the context of church-state controversies in the second half of the twentieth century.

A Debate on the Court's Version of History

The profound legal and policy implications of *Everson v. Board of Education* were recognized long before the Court handed down its ruling, and thus the decision was eagerly awaited by legal scholars, school administrators, and religious leaders. The Court's opinion was prominently reported in the national media and intensely scrutinized in academic and professional journals.[54] The *Everson* decision and its immediate progeny were followed by several popular and academic treatises either challenging or substantiating the accuracy of the Court's use of history and interpretation of the intentions of the constitutional draftsmen. The debate set forth in this literature, frequently generating more heat than light, has become one of the most controversial in American constitutional law. Significantly, this debate has engaged some of the most thoughtful and creative scholars in diverse disciplines, including law, politics, history, education, and religion.

The seminal critique of the *Everson* Court's use of history was James Milton O'Neill's *Religion and Education under the Constitution* (1949). O'Neill, a professor of speech at Brooklyn College (formerly on the faculties of Dartmouth College, University of Wisconsin, and University of Michigan), with devastating effect methodically and logically exposed the poverty of the Court's version of history. "To my mind," O'Neill warned, "the greatest threat to our civil liberties in recent times is to be found in Justice Rutledge's argument in the minority opinion in the Everson case and in the Supreme Court decision in the McCollum case."[55] The simple but essential question before the Court in both cases was the meaning of the First Amendment phrase "an establishment of religion." O'Neill argued that the Court, misinterpreting Madison, Jefferson, and judicial precedents, erroneously concluded that there was a "great constitutional American principle of complete separation of Church and State. There is no such great American principle and there never has been."[56] Rather, O'Neill's thesis was "that the words 'establishment of religion' meant to Madison, Jefferson, the members of the First Congress, the historians, the legal scholars, and substantially all Americans who were at all familiar with the Constitution until very recent years, *a formal, legal union of a single church or religion with government, giving the one church or religion an exclusive position of power and favor over all other churches or denominations.*"[57] The impact of O'Neill's book on legal debate in the wake of *Everson* was immediate and profound. While his treatise was still in manuscript form, O'Neill shared it with attorneys for the Champaign, Illinois, Board of Education who drew liberally on the work in drafting their briefs in *McCollum v. Board of Education.* The book was given a chilly reception by O'Neill's colleagues at the American Civil Liberties Union, where he served as chairman of the Committee on Academic Freedom. Although nearly a half-century old, *Religion and Education under the Constitution* is still widely regarded as a leading manifesto for the nonpreferentialist position.

Similarly compelling critiques of the Court's historical analysis and normative assertions were Wilfrid Parsons's *First Freedom: Considerations on Church and State in the United States* (1948) and Joseph H. Brady's *Confusion Twice Confounded: The First Amendment and the Supreme Court* (1954). Father Parsons was a political scientist on the faculties of Georgetown University and the Catholic University of America. Monsignor Brady was a professor of history and head of the Department of Social Studies at Seton Hall University. A symposium on "Religion and the State" in Duke University's *Law and Contemporary Problems* included insightful commentary by, among others, Edward S. Corwin, Charles Fahy, Alexander Meiklejohn, and John Courtney Murray.[58] Corwin's seminal contribution, "The Supreme Court as National School Board," expertly challenged the *McCollum* ruling, and by extension *Everson* before it, on multiple legal grounds, including standing, incorporation, and historical and textual interpretation of the First Amendment. "Undoubtedly the Court has the right to make history, as it has often done in the past," Corwin observed tartly, "but it has no right to *make it up.*"[59] Corwin's commentary remains among the most influential written on the subject.[60]

The *Everson* Court was not without its defenders in the face of this broadside attack on its version of history. The two most important early apologia for the Court's history were R. Freeman Butts's *American Tradition in Religion and Education (*1950) and Conrad Henry Moehlman's *Wall of Separation between Church and State: An Historical Study of Recent Criticism of the Religious Clause of the First Amendment* (1951). Butts, a distinguished professor of education at the Teachers College, Columbia University and a respected scholar of American public education, concurred with the separation principle in education most forcefully articulated in the dissenting *Everson* opinions of Justices Rutledge and Jackson. His goal was to demonstrate through authentic historical evidence that America embraced a constitutional tradition of separation in which the First Amendment prohibition on an "establishment of religion" "means that there shall be no legal connection between the state and any one or all churches and, further, that this does *not* mean state hostility toward religion but is the basic *condition* of genuine religious freedom."[61] Moehlman, a professor of church history at Colgate-Rochester Divinity School, dedicated his work to Eleanor Roosevelt, who was in the midst of a bitter exchange with Cardinal Spellman, and to the "Supreme Court of the United States for its unanimous defense of the principle of separation of church and state imbedded in the religious clause of the First Amendment."[62] Like Butts, on whose work he liberally drew, Moehlman was moved by an opposition to religious instruction in public schools, public financing for parochial schools, and, most immediately, the nonpreferentialists' assault on the Court's separationist construction of the First Amendment. Moehlman wrote his book "to present in detail the historical background, the significance, and subsequent development of the religious clause of the First Amendment; and to show why the Roman Catholic tradition of the union of church and state is antithetical to the American emphasis upon governmental neutrality in religious matters."[63] Both Butts and Moehlman viewed O'Neill as their most dangerous adversary because, in the words of Moehlman, his "novel thesis has . . . become the basis of Roman Catholic action in the United States."[64] Frank Swancara, an ardent secularist and strident polemicist, wrote *The Separation of Religion and Government: The First Amendment, Madison's Intent, and the McCollum Decision: A Study of Separationism in America* (1950) to rebut the bitter criticism of "[s]ome religionists, mostly Catholic," who had denounced recent separationist pronouncements of the Supreme Court.[65] Published by the Freethought press, Truth Seeker, and endorsed by the National Liberal League, Swancara's screed unabashedly praised the Court for rebuffing illiberal sectarian forces (i.e., religionists) that sought to undermine the "wall of separation." "It is to the glory of Justices Black, Frankfurter, and Rutledge," wrote Swancara, "that their opinions in the *McCollum* and *Everson* cases, so long as they remain authoritative, will, as a *Magna Carta* of Freedom from Religion, do much to minimize such forms of 'debasing tyranny' as have been practiced by political religionists in the past."[66] Although not written specifically in response to *Everson* and *McCollum*, the most comprehensive, thoughtful, and influential treatise of the decade defending the separationist principle was Leo Pfeffer's *Church, State, and Freedom* (1953; rev. ed. 1967). No individual of the twentieth century has left a more distinct imprint on American church-state jurisprudence than Leo Pfeffer.[67] A longtime legal counsel for the American Jewish Congress, Pfeffer was a prolific scholar and zealous advocate whose strict separationist views, more than any other commentator's, informed the Supreme Court's reasoning on church-state relations.[68] *Church, State, and Freedom* is a classic separationist text and has had considerable influence in legal and academic communities over the last half century.

Butts, Moehlman, and other apologists for the *Everson* Court agreed that the First Amendment should be interpreted in the light of its history and the purposes for which it was framed. They were also in general agreement on the following assertions: first, Jefferson and Madison advocated a strict separation between religion and civil government (that is, they disapproved of not only a formal ecclesiastical establishment but also every other form of state aid or encouragement for religious objectives); second, they successfully implemented this separationist policy in their native commonwealth during the tumultuous decade following independence; and third, the Virginia experiment was the model for church-state relations adopted in the First Amendment. Therefore, Jefferson and Madison were the principal architects of the U.S. Constitution's strict separationist approach to church-state relations. Significantly, evidence for the claim that the two Virginians were ardent separationists came largely from pronouncements made in the Virginia disestablishment struggle (such as Jefferson's "Bill for Establishing Religious Freedom" and Madison's "Memorial and Remonstrance") or from statements made after they had left public office (such as Madison's "Detached Memoranda"). *Everson*'s critics have contended that the relevant guides to the original design and purposes of the First Amendment are public statements made and actions taken at the time the amendment was written and ratified (especially statements made in an official capacity and upon which others engaged in framing the First Amendment may have relied), not what happened years earlier in the course of a state legislative struggle or what was said years later in reflections on past actions.

Two published exchanges in the early 1950s presented clearly articulated, sharply contrasting views of the historical issues raised in *Everson* and *McCollum*. Opposing perspectives occasioned by the *McCollum* decision were ably presented by T. Raber Taylor and Conrad Henry Moehlman in the April 1952 issue of the *American Bar Association Journal*.[69] In the pages of the *Buffalo Law Review*, the two intellectual giants of this contest, James M. O'Neill and Leo Pfeffer, faced off in a fascinating and lively debate that explored the historical understanding of the First Amendment ban on religious establishment.[70] The wider debate evidenced by this literature from the late 1940s and 1950s pitted those, on the one side, who viewed the Court's endorsement of a high and impregnable "wall of separation" as little more than a shibboleth of doctrinaire secularism in public life (tending to exclude religion from the public marketplace of ideas), against those, on the other side, who believed that religious instruction in public schools and public funding of parochial education threatened public education as a vital "symbol of our secular unity" and a "powerful agency for promoting cohesion among a heterogeneous democratic people."[71] Unfortunately, the latter typically viewed Catholics as the source of this threat and often employed thinly veiled anti-Catholic rhetoric.[72]

The Supreme Court's controversial school prayer decisions in the early 1960s banning state-sponsored prayer and Bible reading in public schools occasioned a second wave of scholarship critical of the historical and jurisprudential foundations laid in *Everson*.[73] Most prominent among the works revisiting historical themes were Chester James Antieau, Arthur T. Downey, and Edward C. Roberts, *Freedom from Federal Establishment: Formation and Early History of the First Amendment Religion Clauses* (1964), and Charles E. Rice, *The Supreme Court and Public Prayer: The Need for Restraint* (1964). Like the pioneering nonpreferentialist scholars O'Neill, Parsons, and Brady, both Professors Antieau and Rice were Roman Catholics. Another influential work highly critical of the Court's use of history in church-state cases was Mark DeWolfe Howe's *Garden and the Wilderness: Religion and Government in American Constitutional History* (1965).[74] Howe, a Harvard University legal historian, noted that a century and a half before Jefferson penned the Danbury Baptist letter, the colonial champion of religious liberty, Roger Williams, erected a "wall of separation" to achieve a much different end than Jefferson's "wall." Williams's earlier, lesser known, and essentially theological expression was used in stark contrast to Jefferson's later and primarily political version informed by the Enlightenment. Williams believed a "wall of separation" was necessary to safeguard the garden of the church (and religious truth) from the rough and corrupting hand of civil government. Jefferson, in contrast, arguably viewed the "wall" as a device to protect the secular polity from ecclesiastical depredations and incursions or to protect civil society from sectarian strife. Howe concluded that "if the First Amendment codified a figure of speech[,] it embraced the believing affirmations of Roger Williams and his heirs no less firmly than it did the questioning doubts of Thomas Jefferson and the Enlightenment."[75] The Supreme Court, he lamented, had drawn only on the Jeffersonian construction of the "wall." Howe's provocative essay remains a frequently cited work in church-state literature.[76]

The Supreme Court's reliance on historical analysis in church-state cases has waxed and waned in the years since *Everson*. In the early 1960s and even into the 1970s, reeling from the severe criticism of its use of history in *Everson*, the Court retreated slightly from its extensive reliance on history. For example, a cautious, if not apologetic, Justice William Brennan wrote in the 1963 school prayer case: "A too literal quest for the advice of the Founding Fathers upon the issues of these cases seems to me futile and misdirected. . . . [O]ur use of the history of their [Jefferson's and Madison's] time," Brennan continued, "must limit itself to broad purposes, not specific practices."[77] The debate surrounding the *Everson* Court's version of history and the prudential and constitutional role of religion in American public life was revived, once again, in the late 1970s and 1980s in the wake of the reemergence of a religious right and controversial Supreme Court decisions on religion and education, legislative chaplains, public expressions of faith, and public displays of religious symbols.

Perhaps chastened by new scholarship challenging the separationist version of history and fortified by Republican judicial appointees more open to the nonpreferentialist perspective, in the early 1980s the Court returned to a decidedly historical approach in several highly publicized church-state decisions. In *Marsh v. Chambers* (1983), for example, the Court upheld the maintenance of a state-supported legislative chaplain who opened each session with prayer because this religious practice was deeply embedded in the national tradition and was accepted as a constitutional practice at the time the religion clauses were drafted and enacted.[78] As an alternative to the *Lemon* tripartite test in nonestablishment analysis,[79] the Court employed a historical test that explicitly analyzed the language, objectives, and history of the Constitution.[80] Once again, the Court invited scrutiny of the history of the constitutional provisions governing church-state relations as a result of its own reliance on a decidedly historical analysis. Significantly, the version of history adopted in *Marsh* was more compatible with the nonpreferentialist position than with the strict separationist version embraced in *Everson*. Consequently, in an ironic twist, some of the harshest critics of the Court's use of history in the 1980s were counterrevisionists who aligned themselves with the separationist history presented in *Everson* and *McCollum*.

The most influential nonpreferentialist contributions to the debate concerning the history of the First Amendment were Michael J. Malbin's monograph on the debates in the First Congress, *Religion and Politics: The Intentions of the Authors of the First Amendment* (1978); James McClellan's essay "The Making and the Unmaking of the Establishment Clause";[81] and Robert L. Cord's treatise *Separation of Church and State: Historical Fact and Current Fiction* (1982). Cord's fastidiously researched, richly documented critique of *Everson*, in the tradition of James M. O'Neill, argued that the Court manifestly manipulated the historical record and negated every conventional canon of sound construction. *Separation of Church and State* is perhaps the most discussed and referenced study of the last two decades exploring the historical understanding of the constitutional provisions governing church-state relations. Cord's treatise received praise from both sides of the political aisle. "Robert Cord's illuminating contribution to the continuing debate on the meaning of the First Amendment's establishment clause," Senator Daniel Patrick Moynihan (D-N.Y.) remarked, "is a model of careful research, incisive analysis and lucid exposition. If we are ever to regain the course the Founding Fathers charted through these stormy seas, it will be because the scholarly navigation of Professor Cord and his peers has shown beyond dispute just where and how we went astray."[82] William F. Buckley described it as a *tour de force* that, without polemics and ideological cant, "clearly, brilliantly, and definitively . . . deprives the secularists of their historical pedigree, leaving them exposed as mere ideologues."[83] Separationist detractors, such as Leonard W. Levy, derisively dismissed it as "[m]ostly historical fiction masquerading as scholarship."[84] Cord, a Distinguished University Professor at Northeastern University, along with Malbin and McClellan, revived and redefined the church-state debate in the early 1980s. Even their severest critics were forced to contend with their arguments, and their scholarship did not go unnoticed by the Supreme Court. Indeed, this revisionist history found a receptive audience among the federal judiciary, including several justices of the Supreme Court. In a 1983 case challenging an Alabama statute authorizing a "moment of silence" in public schools for meditation or voluntary prayer, a federal district judge boldly repudiated the *Everson* Court's version of history and overruled two decades of legal precedents regarding school prayer.[85] This nonpreferentialist revision of judicial doctrine was quickly overturned by higher federal courts, despite an impassioned dissenting opinion from then Associate Justice Rehnquist challenging the Court's separationist version of history.[86]

By the mid- to late 1980s still another generation of revisionist scholarship had emerged. Among the more important works challenging the separationist history according to *Everson* were Gerard V. Bradley, *Church-State Relationships in America* (1987); Norman DeJong, with Jack Van Der Slik, *Separation of Church and State: The Myth Revisited* (1985); Daniel L. Dreisbach, *Real Threat and Mere Shadow: Religious Liberty and the First Amendment* (1987); and Rodney K. Smith, *Public Prayer and the Constitution: A Case Study in Constitutional Interpretation* (1987).[87]

Defenders of the separationist view advanced by the *Everson* Court and Leo Pfeffer were not silent. They, too, produced several widely discussed volumes. These works not only championed the separationist perspective but also attempted to discredit the nonpreferentialist school that was attracting a growing following in the academic community and in the judicial ranks. Most prominent among these separationist works were Robert S. Alley, *School Prayer: The Court, the Congress, and the First Amendment* (1994); R. Freeman Butts, *Religion, Education, and the First Amendment: The Appeal to History* (People for the American Way, January 1986); Leonard W. Levy, *The Establishment Clause: Religion and the First Amendment* (1986; rev. ed. 1994); Robert L. Maddox, *Separation of Church and State: Guarantor of Reli-*

gious Freedom (1987); William Lee Miller, *The First Liberty: Religion and the American Republic* (1986); and John M. Swomley, *Religious Liberty and the Secular State: The Constitutional Context* (1987). *The Establishment Clause,* by Pulitzer Prize–winning author Leonard W. Levy, is the most scholarly exposition of the separationist thesis and an angry refutation of the nonpreferentialist brief. In a 1992 concurring opinion, which relied heavily on Levy's book, Justice David Souter heartened separationists by stating that he found "in the history of the [no establishment of religion] Clause's textual development a . . . powerful argument supporting the Court's jurisprudence following *Everson.*"[88]

This critical debate initiated by the *Everson* and *McCollum* decisions shows few signs of receding.[89] The Supreme Court has never authoritatively repudiated or corrected the version of history relied on in *Everson*. For as long as *Everson* and its progeny remain good law, the historical debate over the prudential and constitutional role of religion in American public life will, no doubt, continue to provoke controversy.

The participants in this debate have been keenly aware that this is not simply a debate about the past; rather, this is a debate about the future. In particular, the debate has had profound implications for American education. This is evident from the titles of the seminal works by Professors O'Neill and Butts. It is no coincidence that some of the principal discussants have been educators active in shaping education policy. Indeed, many have been drawn to this bitterly contested matter because of their concern for the future of public education or private religious schools. (Interestingly, those most vocal in the debate over the Court's use of history have been educators, lawyers, and political scientists, and not trained historians.) The most immediate impact of the *Everson* decision was on the use of public funds for private religious schools. The Court's chief defenders ardently championed secular public education, and many argued that parochial schools undermined social cohesion in a democratic, pluralistic community. Accordingly, they interpreted the Court's separationist rhetoric broadly and sought to use *Everson* to deny public funds for private schools. Opponents, however, were eager to exploit the narrow opening in the Court's decision permitting the use of state funds to benefit private-school pupils. *McCollum* made clear that the *Everson* Court's analysis also had implications for religious activity in *public* schools. Among the public school practices litigated in the following five decades were released time for religious instruction, prayer and Bible reading, moments of silence, graduation prayers, and student-initiated religious clubs. The analytical and rhetorical foundations laid in *Everson* shaped other aspects of religion in public life, but it was in the field of education that *Everson*'s impact was most immediately and profoundly felt.

Conclusion: The Supreme Court and the Uses of History

"A page of history is worth a volume of logic," Justice Oliver Wendell Holmes opined.[90] Few commentators deny the importance of understanding the historical factors that give content and meaning to constitutional text and principles, if for no other reason than to avoid repeating the mistakes of the past. History, in short, provides perspective and context for constitutional questions. If Justice Holmes was correct, then there is great advantage in frequent reference to our past.

However, the *Everson* Court's reliance on a problematic version of history, followed by revisionist and counterrevisionist critiques of that history, raises difficult questions concerning the appropriate uses of history in constitutional interpretation. Does history provide an essential or useful guide to the interpretation of constitutional provisions framed more than two centuries ago? If so, what history should be referenced? This question is pertinent given the charge that "[b]y omitting any historical facts that ran counter to the impregnable wall thesis, all the opinions in *Everson* display a fallacious history by omission that should no longer be allowed to pass for an adequate, scholarly, or even fair scrutiny in search of the establishment clause's prohibitions."[91] Where should scholars and jurists look in order to ascertain the original understanding of constitutional provisions governing church-state relations? What weight, if any, should be given to the thought of Madison, Jefferson, the entire First Congress, or delegates to state ratifying conventions and electors of those delegates? What attention should be given to church-state relations in the Old World or in the American colonial experience? What are we to make of a history that does not reflect one coherent original understanding of a constitutional model for church-state relations? The Constitution, Elizabeth B. Clark reminds us, "was assented to by motley groups of citizens; and socially, religiously, and regionally diverse thought went into its making. By the standards of good history, then," the pursuit of original intent and "the attempt to depict a single true meaning or intent, is a questionable enterprise."[92] What are we to make of the fact that the historical record is rarely free of ambiguity, and many church-state controversies we confront today were not anticipated by the founding generation? Is the history of the framing of the First Amendment even relevant, Professor Tribe asked, when dealing with "questions, like the permissibility of various practices in public schools, that the Framers could not have contemplated?"[93]

The use of historical arguments in the adversarial environment of litigation is fraught with dangers. Can the history recounted by lawyers (including Supreme Court justices) be trusted, or should it always be viewed skeptically as "law office history"?[94] Arthur Sutherland sagely pondered "whether the lawyer who ventures to write of the past, recent or remote, is characteristically an advocate of some disputed cause, selecting for his comment only those past records which favor his side."[95]

The Supreme Court frequently appeals to the supposed "command of history" in controversial cases. Justices are relieved of accountability if their decisions are dictated, not by their own prepossessions, but by the will of Jefferson, Madison, or some other icon of the founding era. By appealing to history, the Court is claiming "a degree of detachment or objectivity, whereas when history is not used the Court may be viewed as a committed participant either for or against religion."[96] The justices are also drawn to history, one suspects, when they are uncertain of the propriety of their position or when they depart from paths of convention. Invocation of Jefferson or Madison gives an appearance of legitimacy to uncertain or unconventional positions. As Professor Sutherland observed: "Having so decided something, [Supreme Court justices] must feel the desire of all mankind to demonstrate that they decided rightly, and like all the rest of us seek supporting testimony in man's past experience."[97] The *Everson* Court, for example, may have embraced Jefferson's "wall of separation" thinking it would legitimize the Court's strict separationist stance (despite the fact that the metaphor is not found in the Constitution and was written more than ten years after the First Amendment by a man who was not a member of the Constitutional Convention or First Congress).[98]

The intense public debate that has accompanied the Court's version of history should not surprise us. "The history of any subject which has a volatile contemporary life will be politically charged, and this is especially true in the study of church-state relations, where history has the power to decide issues."[99] The tendency of those with a political agenda "to ignore historical complexity in favor of persuasive simplicity will be great,"[100] as will be the temptation to arrange historical data, or even twist or suppress the past, to serve present political purposes. It is, perhaps, basic to human nature to want "to arrange our data so as most convincingly to persuade."[101] Justices apparently are no more immune to this temptation than are lawyers and the rest of humankind. The complexity and ambiguity often inherent in historical inquiry make it difficult to foreclose such manipulations of the historical record. Defenders of historical inquiry in constitutional interpretation often argue that the "command of history" serves to control the discretionary power of judges to make policy according to personal preferences.[102] If, however, "history" may be manipulated in any direction, then unrestrained judicial activism is possible under the cloak of adherence to "original intent" (that is, judges selectively recount history to advance their own prepossessions).[103]

Everson's critics allege that the Court perpetuated a profoundly flawed version of history in order to buttress its strict separationist predilections. As

Professor Howe reminded us, when "the Court endeavors to write an authoritative chapter in the intellectual history of the American people, as it does when it lays historical foundations beneath its readings of the First Amendment, then any distortion becomes a matter of consequence." Misreadings of history become "synthetic strands" woven "into the tapestry of American history" and corpus of American law.[104] This raises a question of great moment: when legal "precedents seem to be based on [a] misreading of history, how should judges balance the new, apparently correct historical account with the demands of *stare decisis*?"[105] As Professor Howe observed, "a great many Americans—lawyers and non-lawyers alike—tend to think that because a majority of the justices have the power to bind us by their law they are also empowered to bind us by their history. Happily that is not the case. Each of us is entirely free to find his history in other places than the pages of the *United States Reports*."[106] Justice Rehnquist, more to the point, succinctly stated that "*stare decisis* may bind courts as to matters of law, but it cannot bind them as to matters of history."[107] The Supreme Court's continuing reliance on the historical foundations laid in *Everson* to inform its separationist interpretation of the First Amendment invites further historical inquiry. Insofar as the Court relied on an erroneous version of "history" to construct church-state doctrine, its legal analysis lacks analytical merit and legitimacy.

Beginning with *Everson*, an examination of American history became a seemingly inescapable feature of discourse on church-state law. The interpretive approach and separationist rhetoric embraced by the *Everson* Court laid the foundation for subsequent church-state jurisprudence. Indeed, the profound impact of *Everson* cannot be measured apart from its interpretive methodology and rhetoric. The allegation that the *Everson* Court ignored aspects of the past that conflicted with its separationist biases and misconstrued those pages of history it chose to report, including Jefferson's "wall" metaphor, has since 1947 sustained a lively debate about the historical, prudential, and constitutional role of religion in American public life. For as long as *Everson* and its progeny inform church-state case law and Americans care about relationships between religion and civil government, the historical understanding of the constitutional provisions governing church-state relations will remain a subject of intense scrutiny and energetic debate.

Notes

1. Gerard V. Bradley, *Church-State Relationships in America* (Westport, Conn.: Greenwood Press, 1987), 1.

2. Paul G. Kauper, "Everson v. Board of Education: A Product of the Judicial Will," *Arizona Law Review* 15 (1973): 307. See also Paul G. Kauper, "The Supreme

Court and the Establishment Clause: Back to *Everson*," *Case Western Reserve Law Review* 25 (1974): 107–29 (arguing that the sweeping separationist, no-aid rhetoric of *Everson* informed four 1973 Supreme Court decisions concerning the constitutionality of state programs that aid church-affiliated educational institutions).

3. *Everson v. Board of Education*, 330 U.S. 1, 15–16, 18 (1947).

4. *Everson v. Board of Education*, 330 U.S. at 31–32 (Rutledge, J., dissenting).

5. See Barbara A. Perry, "Justice Hugo Black and the 'Wall of Separation between Church and State,'" *Journal of Church and State* 31 (1989): 60 ("Although his decision . . . reached a rather astonishing accommodationist result, Black's opinion for a narrow five-man majority is in fact a ringing defense of the principle of strict separation between religion and government."); Gregg Ivers, *To Build a Wall: American Jews and the Separation of Church and State* (Charlottesville: University Press of Virginia, 1995), 24 ("But what baffled the plaintiffs, as well as later commentators, most about Justice Black's conclusion in *Everson* was its inconsistency with the analysis of the establishment clause that he set forth in the first thirteen pages of the Court's fifteen-page majority opinion. . . . Indeed, the conceptual dissonance between Justice Black's interpretation of the clause and his subsequent argument that the *Everson* case did not in fact involve the use of public funds for private religious purposes could hardly escape notice.").

6. See Leo Pfeffer, "Church and State: Something Less than Separation," *University of Chicago Law Review* 19 (1951): 1 ("All the Justices also agreed that the First Amendment was to be given a broad interpretation and that its intent was not merely to prohibit the establishment of a state church but to preclude any governmental aid to religious groups or dogmas."); Bradley, *Church-State Relationships in America,* 2 ("The various opinions in *Everson*, especially that of Justice Wiley Rutledge, are steeped in historical detail, but each traverses the same path, draws the same conclusions."); Leonard W. Levy, *The Establishment Clause: Religion and the First Amendment* (New York: Macmillan, 1986), 124 ("The dissenting justices in the *Everson* case, while disagreeing with the majority on the question whether the 'wall of separation' had in fact been breached by the practice at issue, concurred with the majority on the historical question of the intentions of the framers and the meaning of the establishment clause."); Ivers, *To Build a Wall,* 25 ("The *Everson* dissenters . . . agreed with Justice Black's interpretation of the establishment clause, notably his conclusion that the limits it placed on government's power to support or aid private religion applied to state as well as federal laws."); John T. Valauri, "*Everson v. Brown*: Hermeneutics, Framers' Intent, and the Establishment Clause," *Notre Dame Journal of Law, Ethics, and Public Policy* 4 (1990): 665 ("The *Everson* dissenters fully accept Justice Black's establishment clause history.").

7. *Everson v. Board of Education*, 330 U.S. at 19 (Jackson, J., dissenting).

8. *McCollum v. Board of Education,* 333 U.S. 203, 211 (1948).

9. Mark DeWolfe Howe, *The Garden and the Wilderness: Religion and Government in American Constitutional History* (Chicago: University of Chicago Press, 1965), 4.

10. Book Note, *Harvard Law Review* 97 (1984): 1509. See also Robert L. Cord and Howard Ball, "The Separation of Church and State: A Debate," *Utah Law Review* 1987

(1987): 896 ("To answer [church-state] questions, the United States Supreme Court, without deviation, has looked to American history. If anything about Supreme Court church-state decisions is clear, it is the Court's consistent appeal to the intentions of the Founding Fathers, especially those of James Madison and Thomas Jefferson. . . . [S]ince 1947 when the United States Supreme Court initially provided a comprehensive definition of the first amendment's establishment clause in *Everson v. Board of Education*, the Court, playing historian, has represented itself as having fashioned church-state law in accordance with and faithful to the intentions of the Framers of the Constitution and the first amendment.").

11. *Everson v. Board of Education*, 330 U.S. at 14–15.

12. *Everson v. Board of Education*, 330 U.S. at 33–34 (Rutledge, J., dissenting) (footnotes omitted).

13. See Elizabeth B. Clark, "Church-State Relations in the Constitution-Making Period," in *Church and State in America: A Bibliographical Guide: The Colonial and Early National Periods*, ed. John F. Wilson (Westport, Conn.: Greenwood Press, 1986), 151 ("In the nearly forty years since *Everson*, the Court's historical method and doctrine of absolute separation have remained keystones of federal adjudication on church-state matters.").

14. Laurence H. Tribe, *American Constitutional Law*, 2d ed. (Mineola, N.Y.: Foundation Press, 1988), 1160 (footnote omitted).

15. Tribe, *American Constitutional Law,* 1159 (footnotes omitted).

16. Comment, "The Supreme Court, the First Amendment, and Religion in the Public Schools," *Columbia Law Review* 63 (1963): 79. See also editors' preface to *The Virginia Statute for Religious Freedom: Its Evolution and Consequences in American History*, ed. Merrill D. Peterson and Robert C. Vaughan (New York: Cambridge University Press, 1988), x ("The [Supreme Court] justices were much influenced in their understanding of the First Amendment by their understanding of the Virginia Statute for Religious Freedom and the circumstances that had produced it."); A. E. Dick Howard, "The Supreme Court and the Serpentine Wall," in *The Virginia Statute for Religious Freedom,* 315 ("Tracing the events in Virginia that led to Madison's drafting of the 'Memorial and Remonstrance' and to the enactment of Jefferson's Bill for Establishing Religious Liberty, [Justice] Black concluded [in *Everson*] that the First Amendment was meant to provide 'the same protection against governmental intrusion on religious liberty as the Virginia statute.'") (quoting *Everson v. Board of Education,* 330 U.S. at 13); Arlin M. Adams and Charles J. Emmerich, "A Heritage of Religious Liberty," *University of Pennsylvania Law Review* 137 (1989): 1572 n. 54 ("No other historical episode has influenced the Supreme Court's interpretation of the religion clauses more than the Virginia struggle. References to it abound in the Justices' opinions in religious liberty cases."); Gerard V. Bradley, "Imagining the Past and Remembering the Future: The Supreme Court's History of the Establishment Clause," *Connecticut Law Review* 18 (1986): 832 ("Justice Black essentially reduced the religion clauses to a federal codification of Thomas Jefferson's 'Bill for Establishing Religious Freedom,' the denoue-

ment of the 1784–85 Virginia controversy over public stipends for Protestant clergymen.").

17. For a list of state and federal judicial opinions that cite these documents, see Daniel L. Dreisbach, "Thomas Jefferson and Bills Number 82–86 of the Revision of the Laws of Virginia, 1776–1786: New Light on the Jeffersonian Model of Church-State Relations," *North Carolina Law Review* 69 (1990): 173–75 nn. 77–83. Justice Rutledge thought the "Remonstrance" was sufficiently important that he appended it to his *Everson* opinion. *Everson v. Board of Education*, 330 U.S. at 63–72 (appendix to opinion of Rutledge, J., dissenting). See also *American Jewish Congress v. City of Chicago*, 827 F. 2d 120, 136 (7th Cir. 1987) (Easterbrook, C. J., dissenting) (noting that the Supreme Court has relied on the "Memorial and Remonstrance" "too many times to count"). A. E. Dick Howard opined that "[t]he United States Supreme Court has taken the Virginia Bill [for Religious Freedom] and the First Amendment to be coextensive and has acknowledged the intended wall of separation implicit in both." Howard, *Commentaries on the Constitution of Virginia*, 2 vols. (Charlottesville: University Press of Virginia, 1974), 1:293; Marvin K. Singleton, "Colonial Virginia as First Amendment Matrix: Henry, Madison, and Assessment Establishment," *Journal of Church and State* 8 (1966): 344–64.

18. *Everson v. Board of Education*, 330 U.S. at 13.

19. *Everson v. Board of Education*, 330 U.S. at 39 (Rutledge, J., dissenting).

20. *Everson v. Board of Education*, 330 U.S. at 34 (Rutledge, J., dissenting).

21. For an extensive examination of the origins and use of Jefferson's "wall of separation" metaphor, see Daniel L. Dreisbach, "'Sowing Useful Truths and Principles': The Danbury Baptists, Thomas Jefferson, and the 'Wall of Separation,'" *Journal of Church and State* (forthcoming).

22. *Everson v. Board of Education*, 330 U.S. at 16, 18. Critics have noted that it is surprising that the Supreme Court elevated Jefferson's letter to virtual constitutional status since, as the American minister to France from 1785 to 1789, Jefferson did not participate in either the Constitutional Convention or the First Congress. The latter drafted the First Amendment in the summer of 1789. Also, Gerard V. Bradley has raised the question: "if the wall of separation metaphor was first used in 1802 (as the Court admits it was), how could its meaning be apparent to the 1788 conventioneers who demanded nonestablishment or to the state legislators who ratified that stricture in 1790?" Bradley, *Church-State Relationships in America*, 142–43 (endnote omitted).

23. Kauper, "A Product of the Judicial Will," 318.

24. Bradley, *Church-State Relationships in America*, 3 (emphasis in the original) (endnotes omitted).

25. Edward S. Corwin, "The Supreme Court as National School Board," *Law and Contemporary Problems* 14 (1949): 10 (emphasis in original).

26. Corwin, "Court as School Board," 20 (emphasis in original).

27. The nonpreferentialist view espoused by *Everson*'s critics is challenged on historical grounds by Levy, *Establishment Clause*, 91–119; and Douglas Laycock, "'Nonpreferential' Aid to Religion: A False Claim about Original Intent," *William and Mary Law Review* 27 (1986): 875–923. For a rebuttal of Laycock's historical analysis, see

Rodney K. Smith, "Nonpreferentialism in Establishment Clause Analysis: A Response to Professor Laycock," *St. John's Law Review* 55 (1991): 245–71.

28. Nancy H. Fink, "The Establishment Clause according to the Supreme Court: The Mysterious Eclipse of Free Exercise Values," *Catholic University Law Review* 27 (1978): 216.

29. Critics have noted, for example, that the Court ignored, among other things, both Jefferson's and Madison's involvement in religious proclamations and the fact that Jefferson apparently framed, and Madison sponsored in the Virginia legislature, a legislative package that included, in addition to Jefferson's celebrated "Bill for Establishing Religious Freedom," "A Bill for Punishing Disturbers of Religious Worship and Sabbath Breakers" and "A Bill for Appointing Days of Public Fasting and Thanksgiving."

30. Advocates of this view point to the third paragraph of the "Memorial and Remonstrance" in which Madison argued: "Who does not see that the same authority which can establish Christianity, *in exclusion of all other Religions, may establish with the same ease any particular sect of Christians, in exclusion of all other Sects?* [T]hat the same authority which can force a citizen to contribute three pence only of his property for the support of any *one establishment*, may force him to conform to any other establishment in all cases whatsoever?" James Madison, "Memorial and Remonstrance," in *The Papers of James Madison*, ed. Robert A. Rutland, et al. (Chicago: University of Chicago Press, 1973), 8:300 (emphasis added). According to Corwin, these words show that "Madison's conception of an 'establishment of religion' in 1785 was precisely . . . *a religion enjoying a preferred status.*" Corwin, "Court as School Board." 10 (emphasis in original). In a biting critique of *Everson*, John Courtney Murray opined: "I suspect that the Court was really saying that Madison's idea *should* have been the idea of the First Amendment, whether it actually was or not." Murray, "Law or Prepossessions?" *Law and Contemporary Problems* 14 (1949): 28.

31. Howe, *Garden and Wilderness,* 44. James M. O'Neill similarly rejected the notion that Jefferson's bill advocated strict separation: "[T]he attempt to get from it any support for the thesis that the First Amendment means, or was designed to mean, a complete separation of church and state in America, or specifically a prohibition of the use of public funds in impartial support of religion, does violence to Jefferson's language in this bill and to his whole record. There is not a word in the bill that warrants the claim that Jefferson was opposed to impartial government aid to religion." O'Neill, "Nonpreferential Aid to Religion Is Not an Establishment of Religion," *Buffalo Law Review* 2 (1953): 248.

32. Cushing Strout, *The New Heavens and New Earth: Political Religion in America* (New York: Harper & Row, 1974), 97. See also *Gilfillan v. City of Philadelphia,* 637 F. 2d 924, 933 (3rd Cir. 1980) (acknowledging that Madison's views on church-state relations "may not have been shared by a majority of the drafters of the Constitution").

33. There is a body of literature that challenges the assumption that Madison was the principal author of the First Amendment. See Daniel L. Dreisbach, *Real Threat and Mere Shadow: Religious Liberty and the First Amendment* (Westchester, Ill.: Crossway Books, 1987), 266–67, nn. 33, 37. Also, Jefferson was in France at the time the First

Congress drafted the First Amendment; thus, his influence on the actual wording of the amendment was at most indirect.

34. John Courtney Murray strongly criticized the Court's assumption that the First Amendment reflected church-state thought in Virginia. Murray noted that "the First Amendment met sharp and serious objection in the Virginia senate [during the ratification process], on grounds of its inadequacy in comparison with the Virginia statute [for religious freedom], with the result that ratification was held up for nearly two years. Against this historical fact his [Justice Black's] central argument shatters; for it is derived from a supposed continuity in purpose and identity in meaning between the Virginia statute (the Madisonian idea) and the First Amendment." Murray concluded "that Virginia's hostile reception of the First Amendment destroys Justice Black's central contention that the Amendment in design, letter, and spirit is a faithful rendition of the radical Virginian ideas, which therefore become the canon for its interpretation." Murray, "Law or Prepossessions?" 27, 43.

35. Levy, *Establishment Clause*, 60.

36. Bradley, *Church-State Relationships in America*, 12.

37. Justice Rutledge briefly noted the debates in the First Congress. See *Everson*, 330 U.S. at 42–43 n. 34. At the conclusion of his extensive review of Virginia history, Justice Rutledge summarily noted: "In view of this history no further proof is needed that the Amendment forbids any appropriation, large or small, from public funds to aid or support any and all religious exercises. But if more were called for, the debates in the First Congress and this Court's consistent expressions, whenever it has touched on the matter directly, supply it." *Everson v. Board of Education*, 330 U.S. at 41 (Rutledge J., dissenting). One critic has responded: "What makes this passage so incredible is that neither Justice Rutledge's dissenting opinion nor its footnotes—either vaguely or precisely—indicate which debates in the First Congress prove that the First Amendment" promoted a strict separation between church and state. Robert L. Cord, *Separation of Church and State: Historical Fact and Current Fiction* (New York: Lambeth Press, 1982), 128.

38. On rare occasions the Supreme Court has made passing reference to the recorded debates in the First Congress. See, e.g., *McGowan v. Maryland*, 366 U.S. 420, 440–42 (1961). Ironically, the Court's most thorough review of the debates in the First Congress was offered in dissent by Justice Rehnquist in a devastating refutation of the Court's version of history. *Wallace v. Jaffree*, 472 U.S. 38, 91–114 (1985) (Rehnquist, J., dissenting). More recently, Justice David Souter countered Rehnquist and offered a brief analysis of the debates in the First Congress consistent with the *Everson* opinions. *Lee v. Weisman*, 505 U.S. 577, 612–16 (1992) (Souter, J., concurring). In a decision rendered the same term as *Everson*, Justice Felix Frankfurter counseled that "an amendment to the Constitution should be read in a 'sense most obvious to the common understanding at the time of its adoption'." *Adamson v. California*, 332 U.S. 46, 63 (1947) (Frankfurter, J., concurring), citing *Eisner v. Macomber*, 252 U.S. 189, 220 (1920) (Holmes, J., dissenting). See also the letter from Thomas Jefferson to William Johnson, 12 June 1823, in *The Complete Jefferson*, ed. Saul K. Padover (New York: Duell, Sloan & Pearce, 1943), 322 ("On every question of construction, carry ourselves

back to the time when the constitution was adopted, recollect the spirit manifested in the debates, and instead of trying what meaning may be squeezed out of the text, or invented against it, conform to the probable one in which it was passed.").

39. Some critics argue that Jefferson's "wall," which was offered as a figurative description of the First Amendment, had less to do with the separation between church and all civil government than with the separation between the federal and state governments. Jefferson used the wall to explain why he, as president, had refused to issue religious proclamations in the tradition of his predecessors. The constitutional question addressed in the Danbury letter was whether the First Amendment restricted only the Congress in matters respecting an establishment of religion, or whether its prohibitions extended to the coequal branches of the federal government, thereby denying the executive branch the prerogative to issue religious proclamations. Since the powers of the executive are derivative of the creative powers of the legislature, Jefferson concluded that he, as president, could not assume powers denied Congress. The text of the letter suggests, and Jefferson's actions as president confirm, that he concluded that the *federal* chief executive was as restrained in making religious proclamations as he believed the United States Congress to be pursuant to the First Amendment (and the Tenth Amendment principles of federalism and strictly delegated powers only). In summary, an examination of the Danbury letter and the context in which it was written indicates that it was not primarily a general pronouncement on the prudential relationship between church and state; rather, it was, more specifically, a statement delineating the legitimate jurisdictions of the federal and state governments on matters pertaining to religion. For a thorough examination of this argument, see Dreisbach, "'Sowing Useful Truths and Principles.'"

40. *McCollum v. Board of Education*, 333 U.S. at 247 (Reed, J., dissenting).

41. *Engel v. Vitale*, 370 U.S. 421, 445–446 (1962) (Stewart, J., dissenting).

42. *McCollum v. Board of Education*, 333 U.S. at 238 (Jackson, J., concurring). But see *Committee for Public Education and Religious Liberty v. Nyquist*, 413 U.S. 756, 761 (1973) (Justice Lewis F. Powell Jr. disputing that Jefferson's metaphoric wall has become as winding as his famous serpentine walls). See also Justice Jackson's admission in *Zorach*: "The wall which the Court was professing to erect between Church and State has become even more warped and twisted than I expected." *Zorach v. Clauson*, 343 U.S. 306, 325 (1952) (Jackson, J., dissenting).

43. *Wallace v. Jaffree*, 472 U.S. at 92, 106–7 (Rehnquist, J., dissenting). For a scathing critique of Rehnquist's use of history in *Jaffree*, see Leo Pfeffer, "The Establishment Clause: An Absolutist's Defense," *Notre Dame Journal of Law, Ethics and Public Policy* 4 (1990): 720–29. See also Derek Davis, *Original Intent: Chief Justice Rehnquist and the Course of American Church/State Relations* (Buffalo, N.Y.: Prometheus Books, 1991), 94–97.

44. *Berkey v. Third Avenue Railroad Co.*, 244 N.Y. 84, 94, 155 N.E. 58, 61 (1926). For further discussion on judicial uses of the metaphor, see Robert M. Healey, "Thomas Jefferson's 'Wall': Absolute or Serpentine?" *Journal of Church and State* 30 (1988): 441–62; Comment, "Jefferson and the Church-State Wall: A Historical Examination of the Man and the Metaphor," *Brigham Young University Law Review* 1978 (1978): 645–50.

45. Corwin, "Court as School Board," 14.

46. Corwin, "Court as School Board," 19.

47. This debate has generated an enormous body of scholarship. The following works are generally critical of the Court's incorporation of the nonestablishment provision: Chester James Antieau, "Religious Liberty under the Fourteenth Amendment," *Notre Dame Lawyer* 22 (1947): 271–309; Dreisbach, *Real Threat and Mere Shadow*, 77–82, 89–96; Charles Fairman, "Does the Fourteenth Amendment Incorporate the Bill of Rights?: The Original Understanding," *Stanford Law Review* 2 (1949): 5–139; Kurt T. Lash, "The Second Adoption of the Establishment Clause: The Rise of the Nonestablishment Principle," *Arizona State Law Journal* 27 (1995): 1085–154; William K. Lietzau, "Rediscovering the Establishment Clause: Federalism and the Rollback of Incorporation," *DePaul Law Review* 39 (1990): 1191–234; Francis William O'Brien, "The States and 'No Establishment': Proposed Amendments to the Constitution since 1798," *Washburn Law Journal* 4 (1965): 183–210; "Rethinking the Incorporation of the Establishment Clause: A Federalist View," *Harvard Law Review* 105 (1992): 1700–1719; Joseph M. Snee, "Religious Disestablishment and the Fourteenth Amendment," *Washington University Law Quarterly* 1954 (1954): 371–407.

48. Howe, *Garden and Wilderness,* 168.

49. Robert L. Cord, "Understanding the First Amendment," *National Review* 22 January 1982, 28.

50. Howe, *Garden and Wilderness,* 4.

51. Cord, *Separation of Church and State,* 19.

52. *Wallace v. Jaffree,* 472 U.S. at 92 (Rehnquist, J., dissenting).

53. Cord, *Separation of Church and State,* 82.

54. The case was reported on the front pages of the *New York Times* and the *Washington Post.* See Lewis Wood, "High Court Backs State Right to Run Parochial Buses," *New York Times,* 11 February 1947,1, 31; Dillard Stokes, "Religious, Political Issues Split High Court," *Washington Post,* 11 February 1947, 1, 7. It was also the subject of numerous case commentaries in legal journals. See, e,g,, commentaries in *Boston University Law Review* 27 (1947): 281–85; *Columbia Law Review* 49 (1949): 836–45, 968–92; *Cornell Law Quarterly* 33 (1947): 122–29; *Dickinson Law Review* 51 (1947): 276–77; *George Washington Law Review* 15 (1947): 361–64; *Harvard Law Review* 60 (1947): 793–800; *Iowa Law Review* 32 (1947): 769–74; *Jurist* 7 (1947): 259–80; *Kentucky Law Journal* 36 (1948): 324–31, 37 (1949): 220–39; *Louisiana Law Review* 8 (1947): 136–41; *Law Guild Review* 8 (1948): 387–99; *Michigan Law Review* 45 (1947): 1001-21; *Minnesota Law Review* 31 (1947): 739–42, 33 (1949): 494–516; *Missouri Law Review* 12 (1947): 465–68; *Nebraska Law Review* 27 (1948): 468–71; *New York University Law Quarterly Review* 22 (1947): 331–34; *North Carolina Law Review* 25 (1947): 330–34; *Notre Dame Lawyer* 22 (1947): 400-411; *Oregon Law Review* 27 (1948): 150–56; *St. John's Law Review* 21 (1947): 176–84; *Southern California Law Review* 21 (1947): 61–76; *University of Pennsylvania Law Review* 96 (1947): 230–41; *Virginia Law Review* 33 (1947): 349–51.

55. James M. O'Neill, *Religion and Education under the Constitution* (New York: Harper & Brothers, 1949), xi.

56. O'Neill, *Religion and Education,* 4.

57. O'Neill, *Religion and Education,* 56 (emphasis in original).

58. See Corwin, "Court as School Board," 3–22; Charles Fahy, "Religion, Education, and the Supreme Court," *Law and Contemporary Problems* 14 (1949): 73–91; Alexander Meiklejohn, "Educational Cooperation between Church and State," *Law and Contemporary Problems* 14 (1949): 61–72; John Courtney Murray, "Law or Prepossessions?" *Law and Contemporary Problems* 14 (1949): 23–43 ("The constitutional law written in the *Everson* and *McCollum* cases is obviously not what is called learned law. . . . [T]he whole Court must know that, as a piece of history, its argument in the *Everson* case is one which a considerable body of scholarship finds itself, in Justice Black's words, 'unable to accept.' . . . The tricks they play on the dead are astonishing.").

59. Edward S. Corwin, *A Constitution of Powers in a Secular State* (Charlottesville, Va.: Michie, 1951), 116 (emphasis in original).

60. For additional works of the period critical of the use of history in the *Everson* and *McCollum* opinions, see Virgil C. Blum, *Freedom of Choice in Education* (New York: Macmillan, 1958); Francis William O'Brien, *Justice Reed and the First Amendment: The Religion Clauses* (Washington, D.C.: Georgetown University Press, 1958); F. Ernest Johnson, "Church, School, and Supreme Court," *Religion in Life* 17 (1948): 483–93; Wilber G. Katz, "Freedom of Religion and State Neutrality," *University of Chicago Law Review* 20 (1953): 426–40; Joseph F. Costanzo, "Federal Aid to Education and Religious Liberty," *University of Detroit Law Journal* 36 (1958): 1–46; Costanzo, "Thomas Jefferson, Religious Education, and Public Law," *Journal of Public Law* 8 (1959): 81–108. Many of Professor Costanzo's articles were compiled in *This Nation under God: Church, State, and Schools in America* (New York: Herder & Herder, 1964).

61. R. Freeman Butts, *The American Tradition in Religion and Education* (Boston: Beacon Press, 1950), 10 (emphasis in original).

62. Conrad Henry Moehlman, *The Wall of Separation between Church and State* (Boston: Beacon Press, 1951), v.

63. Moehlman, *Wall of Separation,* xiii.

64. Moehlman, *Wall of Separation,* 210 n. 29.

65. Godfrey von Hofe, foreword to *The Separation of Religion and Government,* by Frank Swancara (New York: Truth Seeker, 1950), iii.

66. Swancara, *Separation of Religion and Government,* 89.

67. One scholar observed: "Pfeffer, a distinguished constitutional lawyer and historian, has produced a massive and influential body of work in support of the Supreme Court's arguments and reasoning as first set out in the *Everson* case. Pfeffer is sensitive to the historical context, although only insofar as it supports his argument. But for him and others, the bottom line is that history proves that the ideal of complete separation attributed to Thomas Jefferson accurately represented the intent of the Framers, was embodied in the First Amendment and, having been properly interpreted by the Court, remains our benchmark today." Clark, "Church-State Relations," 152–53. See also Dreisbach, *Real Threat and Mere Shadow,* 295–96 n. 89.

68. Samuel Krislov opined that "[n]o one comes to mind . . . to rival Pfeffer's intel-

lectual dominance over so vital an area of constitutional law [i.e., church-state law] for so extensive a period in this combination of pleading and intellectualizing." Krislov, "Alternatives to Separation of Church and State in Countries outside the United States," in *Religion and the State: Essays in Honor of Leo Pfeffer,* ed. James E. Wood Jr. (Waco, Texas: Baylor University Press, 1985), 421. See generally Leo Pfeffer, "An Autobiographical Sketch," in *Religion and the State,* 487–533. For an examination of Pfeffer's remarkable career as a church-state litigator, see Frank Sorauf, *The Wall of Separation: The Constitutional Politics of Church and State* (Princeton: Princeton University Press, 1976); Gregg Ivers, *To Build a Wall: American Jews and the Separation of Church and State* (Charlottesville: University Press of Virginia, 1995).

69. T. Raber Taylor, "Equal Protection of Religion: Today's Public School Problem," *ABA Journal* 38 (April 1952): 277–80, 335–42; Conrad Henry Moehlman, "The Wall of Separation: The Law and the Facts," *ABA Journal* 38 (April 1952): 281–84, 343–48.

70. Leo Pfeffer, "No Law Respecting an Establishment of Religion," *Buffalo Law Review* 2 (1953): 225–41, 267–72; James M. O'Neill, "Nonpreferential Aid to Religion Is Not an Establishment of Religion," *Buffalo Law Review* 2 (1953): 242–66, 272–78. Pfeffer ardently defended the Court and controverted the "O'Neill school" in a comprehensive review of O'Neill's thesis in Pfeffer, "Church and State: Something Less than Separation," *University of Chicago Law Review* 19 (1951): 1–29.

71. *McCollum v. Board of Education,* 333 U.S. at 217, 216 (opinion of Frankfurter, J.).

72. For a brief discussion of the antireligious—specifically anti-Catholic—sentiment that arguably fueled the Court's separationist stance and that of other ardent separationists, including Leo Pfeffer and the leading separationist organization, Protestants and Other Americans United for the Separation of Church and State (now known as Americans United for the Separation of Church and State), see James Hitchcock, "The Supreme Court and Religion: Historical Overview and Future Prognosis," *Saint Louis University Law Journal* 24 (1980): 193–201. See generally David G. Singer, "One Nation Completely under God?: The American Jewish Congress and the Catholic Church in the United States, 1945–1977," *Journal of Church and State* 26 (1984): 473–90.

For other works of the period generally supportive of the Court's position in *Everson* and *McCollum,* see Joseph L. Blau, ed., *Cornerstones of Religious Freedom in America* (Boston: Beacon Press, 1949; rev. ed., Harper Torchbooks, 1964) (church-state readings); Joseph Martin Dawson, *Separate Church and State Now* (New York: Richard R. Smith, 1948); Dawson, *America's Way in Church, State, and Society* (New York: Macmillan, 1953); V. T. Thayer, *The Attack upon the American Secular School* (Boston: Beacon Press, 1951); Milton R. Konvitz, "Separation of Church and State: The First Freedom," *Law and Contemporary Problems* 14 (1949): 44–60.

73. *Engel v. Vitale,* 370 U.S. 421 (1962); *Abington Township School District v. Schempp* and *Murray v. Curlett,* 374 U.S. 203 (1963).

74. For additional works of the period critical of the Court's version of history, see Chester James Antieau, Phillip Mark Carroll, and Thomas Carroll Burke, *Religion*

under the State Constitutions (Brooklyn, N.Y.: Central Book Co., 1965); Robert M. Healey, *Jefferson on Religion in Public Education* (New Haven, Conn.: Yale University Press, 1962); Richard E. Morgan, *The Supreme Court and Religion* (New York: Free Press, 1972); Robert M. Hutchins, "The Future of the Wall," in *The Wall between Church and State,* ed. Dallin H. Oaks (Chicago: University of Chicago Press, 1963), 17–25; Clifton B. Kruse, "The Historical Meaning and Judicial Construction of the Establishment of Religion Clause of the First Amendment," *Washburn Law Journal* 2, no. 1 (1962): 65–141; "First Amendment Religion Clauses: Historical Metamorphosis," *Northwestern University Law Review* 61 (1966): 760–76.

75. Howe, *Garden and Wilderness,* 9.

76. See generally Tom Gerety, "Legal Gardening: Mark DeWolfe Howe on Church and State: A Retrospective Essay," *Stanford Law Review* 38 (1986): 595–614; Arthur Sutherland, "Historians, Lawyers, and 'Establishment of Religion,'" in *Religion and the Public Order,* no. 5, ed. Donald A. Giannella (Ithaca, N.Y.: Cornell University Press, 1969), 27–50.

77. *Abington Township School District v. Schempp* 237, 241 (Brennan, J., concurring).

78. *Marsh v. Chambers,* 463 U.S. 783 (1983).

79. *.Lemon v.Kurtzman,* 602, 612–13 (1971).

80. See also *Lynch v. Donnelly,* 668, 673 (1984). For comment on the Court's adoption of an historical "test," see *County of Allegheny v. American Civil Liberties Union, Greater Pittsburgh Chapter,* 492 U.S. 573, 657, 670 (1989) (Kennedy, J., concurring in part and dissenting in part); *Lee v. Weisman,* 577, 631–32 (1992) (Scalia, J., dissenting).

81. James McClellan, "The Making and the Unmaking of the Establishment Clause," in *A Blueprint for Judicial Reform,* ed. Patrick B. McGuigan and Randall R. Rader (Washington, D.C.: Free Congress Research and Education Foundation, 1981), 295–325. See also James McClellan, "Hand's Writing on the Wall of Separation: The Significance of *Jaffree* in Future Cases on Religious Establishment," in *How Does the Constitution Protect Religious Freedom?* ed. Robert A. Goldwin and Art Kaufman (Washington, D.C.: American Enterprise Institute for Public Policy Research, 1987), 43–68.

82. Letter from the office of Senator Daniel P. Moynihan to Robert L. Cord, 7 July 1980.

83. William F. Buckley, foreword to *Separation of Church and State,* by Robert L. Cord, ix–x. Buckley further opined that "Professor Robert L. Cord, a recognized Constitutional scholar, . . . shatters the secularist anachronism, then pulverizes the fragments, demolishing beyond recovery the thesis of Professor Leo Pfeffer, adopted by pretty much the last few Supreme Court majorities, that the Framers of the Constitution meant not only to avoid a religious establishment, but virtually to establish unadulterated secularism as our operative national creed." (ix–x).

84. Levy, *Establishment Clause,* 221.

85. *Jaffree v. Board of School Commissioners of Mobile County,* 554 F. Supp. 1104 (S.D. Ala. 1983).

86. *Wallace v. Jaffree,* 472 U.S. at 91 (Rehnquist, J., dissenting).

87. For additional works critical of the history according to the *Everson* Court, see John S. Baker Jr., "The Establishment Clause as Intended: No Preference among Sects and Pluralism in a Large Commercial Republic," in *The Bill of Rights: Original Meaning and Current Understanding,* ed. Eugene W. Hickok Jr. (Charlottesville: University Press of Virginia, 1991), 41–53; Gerard V. Bradley, "Imagining the Past and Remembering the Future: The Supreme Court's History of the Establishment Clause," *Connecticut Law Review* 18 (1986): 827–43; "Constitutional Fiction: An Analysis of the Supreme Court's Interpretation of the Religion Clauses," *Louisiana Law Review* 47 (1986): 169–98; Robert L. Cord, "Church-State Separation: Restoring the 'No Preference' Doctrine of the First Amendment," *Harvard Journal of Law and Public Policy* 9 (1986): 129–72; Robert L. Cord, "Founding Intentions and the Establishment Clause: Harmonizing Accommodation and Separation," *Harvard Journal of Law and Public Policy* 10 (1987): 47–52; Robert L. Cord, "Interpreting the Establishment Clause of the First Amendment: A 'Non-Absolute Separationist' Approach," *Notre Dame Journal of Law, Ethics and Public Policy* 4 (1990): 731–47; Robert L. Cord, "Original Intent Jurisprudence and Madison's 'Detached Memoranda,'" *Benchmark* 3, nos. 1 & 2 (1987): 79–85; Norman DeJong, "Separation of Church and State: Historical Reality or Judicial Myth?" *Fides et Historia* 18, no. 1 (January 1986): 25–37; Daniel L. Dreisbach, "A New Perspective on Jefferson's Views on Church-State Relations: The Virginia Statute for Establishing Religious Freedom in Its Legislative Context," *American Journal of Legal History* 35 (1991): 172–204; Daniel L. Dreisbach, "Thomas Jefferson and Bills Number 82–86 of the Revision of the Laws of Virginia, 1776–1786: New Light on the Jeffersonian Model of Church-State Relations," *North Carolina Law Review* 69 (1990): 159–211; Peter J. Ferrara, *Religion and the Constitution: A Reinterpretation* (Washington, D.C.: Free Congress Research and Education Foundation, 1983); John Remington Graham, "A Restatement of the Intended Meaning of the Establishment Clause in Relation to Education and Religion," *Brigham Young University Law Review* 1981 (1981): 333–59; "Jefferson and the Church-State Wall: A Historical Examination of the Man and the Metaphor," *Brigham Young University Law Review* 1978 (1978): 645–74; Joseph M. Lynch, "Madison's Religion Proposals Judicially Confounded: A Study in the Constitutional Law of Conscience," *Seton Hall Law Review* 20 (1990): 418–77; Rodney K. Smith, "Getting Off on the Wrong Foot and Back on Again: A Reexamination of the History of the Framing of the Religion Clauses of the First Amendment and a Critique of the *Reynolds* and *Everson* Decisions," *Wake Forest Law Review* 20 (1984): 569–43; Jack R. Van Der Slik, "Respecting an Establishment of Religion in America," *Christian Scholar's Review* 13 (1984): 217–35; Jonathan K. Van Patten, "Standing in Need of Prayer: The Supreme Court on James Madison and Religious Liberty," *Benchmark* 3, nos. 1 & 2 (1987): 59–69.

For an insightful debate on the historical evidence, see Robert L. Cord and Howard Ball, "The Separation of Church and State: A Debate," *Utah Law Review* 1987 (1987): 895–925. For another useful exchange, see R. Freeman Butts, "A History and Civics Lesson for All of Us," and Robert L. Cord, "Church-State Separation and the Public Schools: A Re-Evaluation," in the May 1987 issue of *Educational Leadership,* reprinted in *Taking Sides: Clashing Views on Controversial Educational Issues,* ed. James

William Noll, 5th ed. (Guilford, Conn.: Dushkin Publishing, 1989), 64–80.

88. *Lee v. Weisman*, 505 U.S. at 612 (Souter, J., concurring).

89. For other important works on the historical understanding of church-state relations in America, see Arlin M. Adams and Charles J. Emmerich, *A Nation Dedicated to Religious Liberty: The Constitutional Heritage of the Religion Clauses* (Philadelphia: University of Pennsylvania Press, 1990); Robert S. Alley, ed., *James Madison on Religious Liberty* (Buffalo, N.Y.: Prometheus Books, 1985); Thomas J. Curry, *The First Freedoms: Church and State in America to the Passage of the First Amendment* (New York: Oxford University Press, 1986); Donald L. Drakeman, *Church-State Constitutional Issues: Making Sense of the Establishment Clause* (1991); Donald L. Drakeman, "Religion and the Republic: James Madison and the First Amendment," *Journal of Church and State* 25 (1983): 427–45; Edwin S. Gaustad, *Faith of Our Fathers: Religion and the New Nation* (San Francisco: Harper & Row, 1987); Gary D. Glenn, "Forgotten Purposes of the First Amendment Religion Clauses," *Review of Politics* 49 (1987): 340–67; Frank Guliuzza III, "The Practical Perils of an Original Intent–Based Judicial Philosophy: Originalism and the Church-State Test Case," *Drake Law Review* 42 (1993): 343–83; Douglas Laycock, "'Noncoercive' Support for Religion: Another False Claim about the Establishment Clause," *Valparaiso University Law Review* 26 (1991): 37–69; David Little, "Thomas Jefferson's Religious Views and Their Influence on the Supreme Court's Interpretation of the First Amendment," *Catholic University Law Review* 26 (1976): 57–72; Richard P. McBrien, *Caesar's Coin: Religion and Politics in America* (New York: Macmillan, 1987); Michael W. McConnell, "Coercion: The Lost Element of Establishment," *William and Mary Law Review* 27 (1986): 933–41; Michael W. McConnell, "The Origins and Historical Understanding of Free Exercise of Religion," *Harvard Law Review* 103 (1990): 1409–517; A. James Reichley, *Religion in American Public Life* (Washington, D.C.: Brookings Institution, 1985); Marvin K. Singleton, "Colonial Virginia as First Amendment Matrix: Henry, Madison, and Assessment Establishment," *Journal of Church and State* 8 (1966): 344–64; Theodore Sky, "The Establishment Clause, the Congress, and the Schools: An Historical Perspective," *Virginia Law Review* 52 (1966): 1395–466; Anson Phelps Stokes, *Church and State in the United States*, 3 vols. (New York: Harper & Brothers, 1950); Paul J. Weber, "James Madison and Religious Equality: The Perfect Separation," *Review of Politics* 44 (1982): 163–86.

90. *New York Trust Co. v. Eisner,* 256 U.S. 345, 349 (1921). Although Justice Holmes was not addressing a religion clause controversy when he wrote this, several justices of the Supreme Court have noted that Holmes's aphorism is particularly relevant to this area of the law. See, e.g., *Committee for Public Education and Religious Liberty v. Nyquist,* 413 U.S. 756, 777 n. 33 (1973) ("Our Establishment Clause precedents have recognized the special relevance in this area of Mr. Justice Holmes' comment that 'a page of history is worth a volume of logic.'"); *Walz v. New York Tax Commission,* 397 U.S. 664, 675–76 (1970). See also *Kovacs v. Cooper,* 336 U.S. 77, 95 (1949) (Frankfurter, J., concurring) ("In law also, doctrine is illuminated by history."). See generally Haig Bosmajian, "Is a Page of History Worth a Volume of Logic?" *Journal of Church and State* 38 (1996): 397–408.

91. Cord and Ball, "Separation of Church and State: A Debate," 901.

92. Clark, "Church-State Relations," 154.

93. Tribe, *American Contitutional Law,* 1163.

94. The "law office historian," imbued with the adversary ethic, selectively recounts facts, emphasizing data that support the recorder's own prepossessions and minimizing significant facts that complicate or conflict with that bias. Philip B. Kurland described "law office history" as so-called history "written the way brief writers write briefs, by picking and choosing statements and events favorable to the client's cause." Kurland, "The Origins of the Religion Clauses of the Constitution," *William and Mary Law Review* 27 (1986): 842.

95. Sutherland, "Historians, Lawyers," 27.

96. Jonathan K. Van Patten, "In the End Is the Beginning: An Inquiry into the Meaning of the Religion Clauses," *Saint Louis University Law Journal* 27 (1983): 6.

97. Sutherland, "Historians, Lawyers," 29.

98. Perry, "Justice Black," 71.

99. Clark, "Church-State Relations," 151.

100. Clark, "Church-State Relations," 151.

101. Sutherland, "Historians, Lawyers," 29.

102. Van Patten, "In the End," 6 ("A resort to history forces one to consult and reflect upon authorities independent of oneself. Omission of the historical materials pushes the analysis in a more personal or subjective direction.").

103. In *McCollum,* Justice Jackson candidly described his "duty" in judging between the constitutionally permissible secular and impermissible sectarian aspects of public education: "It is idle to pretend that this task is one for which we can find in the Constitution one word to help us as judges to decide. . . . Nor can we find guidance in any other legal source. It is a matter on which we can find no law but our own prepossessions." *McCollum v. Board of Education,* 333 U.S. at 237–38 (Jackson, J., concurring). Cord said of Jackson's surprising admission: "Indeed most justices on the Court have followed their 'own prepossessions' in interpreting the Establishment Clause, but not because of the paucity of 'legal sources,' as Justice Jackson declared. They have ignored the historical legal sources, with the exception of a few select documents, so that they can continue to decide Establishment Clause cases in harmony with the *Everson* decision and the many cases which follow it." Cord, *Separation of Church and State,* 223. See also John Courtney Murray, "Law or Prepossessions?" *Law and Contemporary Problems* 14 (1949): 23–43.

104. Howe, *Garden and Wilderness,* 4.

105. Tribe, *American Constitutional Law,* 1164.

106. Howe, *Garden and Wilderness,* 5. See also Corwin, *A Constitution of Powers in a Secular State,* 116 ("Undoubtedly the Court has the right to make history, as it has often done in the past; but it has no right to *make it up.*") (emphasis in original).

107. *Wallace v. Jaffree,* 472 U.S. at 99 (Rehnquist, J., dissenting). See also *Graves v. New York ex rel. O'Keefe,* 306 U.S. 466, 491–92 (1939) (Frankfurter, J., concurring) ("the ultimate touchstone of constitutionality is the Constitution itself and not what we have said about it.").

3

The New Common School: The Evangelical Response to *Everson*

Hubert Morken

Resistance to the "wall of separation" language and doctrine is strong among Evangelicals, who see the phrase being used to exclude religion and religious people from public affairs and public schools. This, they say, is a direct threat to the free exercise of religion protected by law. Evangelicals also see this secularization process shredding the fabric of decency so necessary for society to function. How do they respond? In legal and education-policy arenas, Evangelicals are working to change current structures, public and private, to satisfy their concerns and to meet common needs. The theories, strategies, and tactics of this religious community, in response to *Everson* and to its consequences for schools, are the subject of this chapter.[1]

Constructing the Common School

The common school system in America, otherwise known as public education, was established with the active participation of Evangelicals. With their religious faith grounded in the Bible and in its authority as they understood it, these people, predominantly Baptists and Methodists, helped to craft a system that eventually made education available to all children at public expense. Dominating American religion in the nineteenth century and, as one scholar notes, "democratizing" it, they also played a major role in democratizing education, in the process inserting popular religion into primary and secondary schools.[2]

To preserve order in the classroom and a positive environment for the religious faith of their largely Protestant student populations, public schools before World War II recognized God through public prayer, Scripture reading, and some treatment of Christian perspectives and contributions in American history. Yet to protect children from a state-imposed religion, something anathema

59

to Evangelicals, these schools as a rule limited their religious instruction to the basics shared by most children in the community. Some schools had more religion than others, and some leaned more toward one denominational view; nevertheless, schools taught only the rudiments of religion and were not meant to take the place of home or church, the primary locations for spiritual instruction.[3]

Those who helped create public education did not, in principle, want to impose Protestant doctrine on schools. Horace Mann (1796–1859), for example, the originator and booster of the common-school vision in Massachusetts, was a Unitarian not personally supportive of *sola scriptura*, the Virgin Birth, or the Trinity, all Protestant essentials. Nor did Mann want these orthodox doctrines taught in schools. The gospel should not be preached, he thought, but a reverence for God and the Bible, and some knowledge of both would suffice. Education reformers knew that a totally secularized education, with no recognition of God and his laws governing the universe, was inconceivable to pious parents, without whose support public education could not work. An elementary biblical theism, or civil religion, eventually was accepted, if not preferred, by the Protestant community and educators, perhaps largely because of their shared aversion to state-imposed religion. Schools perceived by Catholics and others as "Protestant" were something quite different. That schools largely produced by, and even for, Protestants were not meant to be Protestant in their teaching and orientation is a distinction easily missed then and now. Americans ranging from Unitarians to Evangelicals had succeeded in creating what might be termed a Judeo-Christian education, more about creation and everyday living than confessional in nature.[4]

To help bridge the gap between church and school, conservative Protestants created parachurch organizations that especially targeted students. By 1947, the year of the *Everson v. Board of Education* decision, Billy Graham and a cluster of young Evangelicals had started Youth for Christ (YFC), an international organization dedicated to reaching high-school-aged young people with the gospel. Schools taught something about Christianity but not enough to secure the personal faith of the young. Students were a harvest field of potential believers, not a parish. To reach this generation of the young, YFC clubs were started by Evangelicals who did not consider public schools that allowed and even encouraged prayer "Christian." The mission of YFC was to help Christian students to be "light and salt" within the schools, providing precisely what they lacked: explicit and comprehensive religious teaching and nurture.[5]

Evangelicals, past and present, clearly hold one core conviction on government and education: parents, and not the state or the church, have the exclusive duty and right to determine the education that children receive. For most who hold this view, the government may require schooling and use taxes to pay for it, but only parents, whatever their religion, may decide where their children are to go to school and, ultimately, how they are to be educated. Parents, the creators of children, are to nurture and teach them, providing them with other teachers when that is desirable. Putting parents on local public school boards was intended to permit them to supervise the education process to make sure it agreed with their wishes and not simply the designs of education professionals. Evangelicals also do not cede control of their children's education to the church. A church might have a school, but parents, not pastors, are to decide where their children are best educated. Most Evangelicals in the growing nation chose to put their children in public, not church, schools.[6]

The Supreme Court affirmed this right of parents "to direct the upbringing and education of children under their control," recognizing parental responsibility for education as a liberty on a par with freedom of religion or the right to marry, protected under both the common law and the Constitution. Since parents had the final responsibility for educating their children in a manner pleasing to God and good for the children, *then Evangelicals believed that the school their children attended should be supportive of what was taught at home.* While public schools were not to impose a set of sectarian doctrines, or even Evangelical beliefs, on children, they were not to undermine what was taught by parents. Schools should be generally sympathetic to the religious understanding of the community; and since schools, too, were under God's authority, they should acknowledge him.[7]

This form of pluralism, neutral in most matters of religious conviction and stressing common beliefs, such as reverence for God, received constitutional protection before *Everson.* Each community decided for itself how to include religion in its common school program (occasionally experiencing sharp conflicts between groups), accommodating the diverse opinions of particular communities as local and state officials and voters saw fit, operating in submission to state constitutions. The federal Constitution, which did not apply the First Amendment religion clauses to the states, allowed the public to adapt and modify the handling of religion in schools, permitting a variety of approaches in the country. Even tax support for parochial schools was not ruled out by this approach, because federalism gave state and local officials room to decide how taxes would be spent and how much religion would be appropriate in public schools. By allowing for local adjustments, religion and education before *Everson* rarely became national issues, as they were in Europe. A combination of federalism and respect for the rights of parents to oversee the education of their children made room for religion in public schools.[8]

Three groups of citizens were not part of the common school system in most communities: African Americans, who were excluded by segregation and placed in their own schools, Native Americans, who were largely educated on reservations; and those who chose to attend the Catholic parochial schools. Racial and ethnic prejudices kept whites apart from blacks and indigenous tribes; and parents who helped maintain a local school system for whites often viewed Irish Catholics and parochial schools as threats to the unity of the community, especially if church schools sought a tax subsidy. Thus, in the America of 1947, private schools were allowed, African Americans went to separate schools, Native Americans learned on reservations, and a basic theistic revelation was generally permitted, if not encouraged, in public schools.[9]

Dismantling the Common School

The common school is no more, its fate effectively sealed by *Everson* after the Supreme Court chose to apply the Constitution's establishment clause to the states. A precise and simple traditional definition of establishment—forbidding special governmental ties to one denomination—would have helped to restrain the Court's later decisions, but once the federalism wall was breached and local decisions on how to include religion in schools could be challenged by a national standard of law, the temptation was irresistible for some to use that standard to suppress the acknowledgment of God by public schools or to marginalize parochial schools. *Everson* is the great divide because it federalized religion and education practices; in effect, it invited officials and citizens to question and move against religion in public schools and to oppose tax support for religious schools. Common schools and the Constitution made room for state-supported religion; *Everson* in principle forbade it.[10]

Evangelicals, unlike leaders of the Catholic Church and Jewish organizations, were slow to understand the broader possible implications of *Everson*. The initial decision allowed public funding of transportation for parochial students, something many Evangelicals opposed. To Evangelicals, the decision's rhetoric seemed simply to maintain a wall of separation and to have little impact on public schools. They were wrong on both counts. Only when school-sponsored prayer and Bible reading were forbidden in subsequent cases and social chaos mounted in some schools did the alarm bells begin to sound in local communities. Even then, Evangelicals initially appeared divided and uncertain in their judgment of the Supreme Court and in their education strategy. What, then, has changed for conservative Protestants in fifty years as a result of *Everson?*[11]

Here appearances are deceptive. As *Everson* seemed at first to change nothing, claiming to support historic constitutional interpretation, so Evangelicals, who stand for parental authority in education, acknowledgment of God in the classroom, and separation of church and state, appear not to have changed either, continuing for the most part to send their children to public schools. This apparent continuity is false. Public schools were once shared in relative harmony, and some acrimony, with other citizens; after *Everson*, they became secular schools or government schools, almost foreign territory for Evangelicals and students of other faiths. One group of authors consoles parents by writing, "Daniel excelled in his public schools. There's hope for your child, too!" When public schools are compared to Babylon, they must seem an alien and even hostile environment, difficult to survive without a struggle, and not a natural place for learning. Evangelicals, like Presbyterian minister Rev. D. James Kennedy of Coral Ridge Ministries, blame *Everson* for this alienation.[12]

Realistically, public schools depend on more than tax dollars to keep their doors open: they need the affections and loyalties of families in communities that invest heavily in schools. Evangelicals once freely and gladly entrusted their children to the care of a public school teacher, without much deliberation or examination of options. This decision is now frequently the subject of intense discussion by young parents not happy with available choices. There is a rising tide of disaffection with government-controlled education, even when most parents have not voted with their feet to leave. Today in the Evangelical community, secularism in schools is rejected; schools are blamed for social disorder; Supreme Court education decisions are denounced; free exercise of religion in schools is defended; home schooling is increasing dramatically; Christian schools are growing in number and size; pressure is mounting for school choice; candidates are running in school board elections; debate on education standards is intense; school policies are scrutinized closely; education reform is a first priority; and state-controlled education is challenged.[13]

Not all the blame for this ferment can be laid at the feet of *Everson*. Evangelicals, like many other citizens, resist the cultural disintegration, pedagogical fashions, and education bureaucracies that shape instruction. What is most revealing, however, is the belief of many Evangelicals that problems in education and in the homes and streets of America are linked to, and can be explained by, the removal of state-approved religion from schools. If schools are considered the source of crime rather than its remedy, they lose their legitimacy.

Linking the Absence of Religion in Education to Crime

Dr. Carl F. H. Henry, the leading Evangelical theologian and editor of *Christianity Today,* in a speech delivered in Washington, D.C., in 1957, ten years after *Everson*, blamed the rise in crime partly on the misunderstood and misapplied "doctrine" of the separation of church and state. The Bible and its teachings, so relevant to everything of value in the culture, had been driven underground in public schools, gone "subterranean" he said, because even the mention of the Creator as the "living God" was now considered sectarian and a violation of the separation doctrine. How could the Declaration of Independence now be taught or understood? he wondered. Angry at seeing revealed religion marginalized, ignored in teaching the young, he quoted from *The Development of Modern Education* (1952) by Frederick Eby, a professor from the University of Texas:[14]

> Never have sex perversions; unscrupulous disregard of the evil effect of liquor, narcotics and tobacco upon children; divorce; rape; murder; political chicanery; debauchery; gambling; corrupt athletics; and contempt for law and order been so rampant and unblushing as they are today. The revolting sexual perversion extending from multiple divorce to criminal assault upon women and little girls, frequently ending with brutal murder of the victim; the increase of sexual relations of high school students; the heartless killings of youth of high IQ out of sheer moral idiocy; all such behavior testifies to the deterioration of public and private morality and sanity. . . . One conclusion is certain: the strong claims of a century ago that a system of public schools would do away with crime now looks absurd. . . . Not only has public education failed to eliminate crime but it is in some measure responsible for the increase of these various evils.[15]

This was no surprise, Henry fumed, with the teaching of the Bible "increasingly banned from our public schools." He held up the specter that the United States would be like the Soviet Union if Christians let the public schools be secularized in the name of separation, contrary to the wishes of the public. Public schools should teach the Bible, he argued, not "enlist students in this or that church or denomination or religion." Henry presented multiple reasons to give God and revealed religion a central place in the curriculum. Considering the issue unresolved, Henry argued in 1973 in a five-part series in *Christianity Today* for at least voluntary recognition of God and a major effort to study religion, the Bible, and Christian perspectives in the public school classroom.[16]

What Henry defended was fast fading away. His was a last hurrah for the system that Horace Mann had worked so hard to construct a century earlier. Public schools, in the American tradition, had been vested with the task of helping to civilize students, with the expectation that crime rates would fall. If children were properly instructed, Mann and succeeding generations of educators believed, safe streets were assured. Quoting from the Scriptures, "Train up a child in the way he should go, and when he is old he will not depart from it," Mann assured his readers that public schools empowered to teach the principles of right living from the Bible were bound to succeed in lifting up the whole culture and civilization. The Bible was an essential part of the curriculum that Mann recommended for Massachusetts, and he was proud to report that under his leadership and influence it could be used in every school district in the state.[17]

Among the last defenders of Horace Mann's program are Evangelicals. David Barton, a prolific Evangelical author and activist, essentially has applied the Mann agenda of cultural transformation, perhaps without realizing it, to critique the post-*Everson* court decisions removing state-approved prayer from the schools. Armed with statistics showing how rapidly SAT scores dropped and premarital sexual activity, suicide, divorce, and violence increased after the New York Regents' prayer was disallowed (*Engel v. Vitale,* 1962), Barton argues that this proves a connection between prayer and student behavior. Mann made no such claim for prayer, for literacy, or for any part of his program. He did, however, argue vehemently that if students were exposed over time to his whole education process, which included the study of the Bible, all such problems would decline. The point of this comparison is that both Mann and Barton see education as a unity that, when comprehensively applied, will work. Remove all state-approved religion, and education collapses, Barton and Henry argue, and it is hard to see how Mann would disagree.[18]

These three agree—the Unitarian educator-visionary, Mann; the theologian and social conscience of contemporary Evangelicals, Henry; and an extraordinary grassroots activist, Barton—that public schools have great power for good or evil, influencing the minds and character of millions of young, impressionable people. Fully aware of this power, Evangelicals seek *refuge, influence, and alternatives*, confident that schools no longer founded on prayer and knowledge of the Bible are in trouble. State endorsement of religion in principle has been removed by the Supreme Court; according to Henry and Barton, crime and chaos follow.

Evangelicals, many of whom hold these views, have concluded that if schools are left in secular hands with a secular agenda, they will collapse and society will implode. Meanwhile an education strategy is being adopted to cope in the present and to prepare for a better future: First, secure free exercise of religion in public schools. Second, exert influence in schools and on school boards. Third, protect the autonomy of home schools and private schools. Fourth, provide resources for an alternative to public schools. Fifth, make room for combinations of public, private, and home schools.

The apparent goal of these five elements of an emerging Evangelical strategy, stated by its defenders, is to break old molds to deliver the best education at a reasonable cost to all children. This strategy assumes the death of the old common school and the arrival of new, flexible alternatives. In the interim, securing free exercise of religion and a quality education are two distinct but related objectives for Evangelicals. There is a logical sense to the sequence; ensuring liberty inside and outside public schools is essentially a defensive move, guaranteeing breathing room before controversial and difficult issues like funding are tackled. *Everson* is becoming, with some sorrow and no little regret, an accepted fact. What eventually will replace the common school is only just beginning to appear.[19]

Securing Free Exercise of Religion in Public Schools

With civil religion excluded from schools—a much resisted process that is taking decades to complete—and after congressional failure in the early 1980s to pass school prayer legislation, Evangelicals turned to the protection of their individual rights in public education as their first concern. Persecution of Evangelicals who simply expressed their Christian faith as individuals gave rise to religious First Amendment organizations, something that would not have happened without *Everson*.[20]

One true story will suffice to illustrate what Evangelicals faced, at least in more progressive suburban communities. Outside Philadelphia at a winter concert of the high school choir, the honored senior soloist elected to sing "O Holy Night" as her tribute to her Lord's birth. She was forbidden. Her somewhat secular physician-father, not nearly so religious as his daughter, threatened a lawsuit if she were not allowed to sing the song of her choice. Town meetings followed. Rules had to be drawn up to permit the singing of a Christmas carol picked by a student.[21]

Faced with such resistance, Evangelicals sought to secure what little religion remained in the schools under the free exercise of religion and free speech clauses of the Constitution. This action comports well with their basic belief that any establishment of religion, no matter how it is justified, circumscribed, and limited, will always be problematic, because it is within government's discretionary power. One administration may favor religion, the next may oppose it. What government gives, it can take away or change, as *Everson* demonstrates. Freedoms of religion and speech were another matter, considered by Americans beyond the reach of political authority. Seeing freedom of religion and speech as their permanent refuge, Evangelicals soon pressed hard for student rights to sing, pray, and read the Bible at school.[22]

In 1975, the Christian Legal Society (CLS), a professional association for attorneys founded by Evangelicals, resolved to establish a legal arm, the Center for Law and Religious Freedom, to take on carefully selected religious freedom cases, defending pastors and especially religious rights in public schools. The favored First Amendment strategy for CLS in the 1980s was to search for broad areas of agreement to reduce conflict and to remove reasons for litigation. For example, CLS was heavily involved in the design and implementation of the Equal Access Act (EAA) passed by Congress in 1984 and signed into law by President Reagan. This act allowed for voluntary student religious meetings on public school campuses during school hours in carefully restricted circumstances. Preferring this option to any form of mandatory school prayer, CLS invested one million dollars in an education campaign effort to win the cooperation of public school administrators to make room for student religious clubs. CLS, along with other Christian organizations, worked with the American Civil Liberties Union (ACLU) and the Jewish community to create implementation guidelines.[23]

The National Legal Foundation (NLF), a public-interest law firm founded by Pat Robertson in 1985, selected cases that held promise for establishing precedent at the appellate level. One such case, *Board of Education v. Mergens* (1990), tested the Equal Access Act. The NLF wanted a clean case, unencumbered by extraneous issues or complicating facts, to resolve the issue of equal access by religious clubs to public high school campuses. Not a supporter of the EAA, Robert Skolrood, the executive director of NLF, would have preferred a case that rested simply on the First Amendment free exercise clause. The EAA limited free exercise to a "limited open forum" that in Skolrood's opinion could permit public school administrators to impose undue restrictions on voluntary religious or political activity on their campuses. This introduced the potential for arbitrary treatment of religious liberty by government. Even though the case was won in the Supreme Court by a vote of 8-1, Skolrood considered the EAA, which the CLS had worked so hard to pass, more a liability than an asset in the struggle to preserve religious liberty.[24]

In the case of *Robert E. Lee v. Daniel Weisman* (1992), Robert Skolrood's amicus brief made a historical case for allowing prayer as a benediction at public school commencements. As long as prayer is not required in a regular classroom context and as long as the school in no way coerces students to pray or to believe in prayer, a benediction should be viewed simply as an acceptable way to give solemnity to a public occasion, Skolrood said. Prayer is religious, he argued, but a benediction does not in any way constitute an establishment of religion. The "history and ubiquity" of benedictions in American public life, including public education, lends strong support to uphold this tradition. Skolrood's special interest in this argument, which the Supreme Court rejected by a one-vote margin, was to preserve, in the name of free exercise of religion, at least a remnant of the historic foundations of American common schools.[25]

Lee v. Weisman was also an occasion for Evangelicals to ask the Supreme Court to reconsider its definition, created by *Everson* and later cases, of "establishment" of religion. In his amicus brief, filed on behalf of Concerned

Women for America and Free Speech Advocates, Thomas Patrick Monaghan (now at the American Center for Law and Justice), suggested a different test, proposed by Justice Anthony Kennedy, barring the "coercion" of religious conduct or belief or the giving of "direct" financial benefits to religion. In Monaghan's view, prayer at a graduation forced no one to pray, and vouchers benefiting parents who send their children to private schools, including parochial ones, would be acceptable, partly because the schools had a secular purpose. Monaghan, himself a Catholic, knew that Evangelicals generally rejected *Everson*'s proscription against "aiding all religions" that led the Court to limit commencement prayers and held up the use of vouchers. As John W. Whitehead, founder of the Rutherford Institute, reasoned, making room for some religion in school, even publicly expressed personal faith, inevitably requires the government's positive assistance. But until the Supreme Court reversed itself or Congress acted (which Congress tried and failed to do in 1996 largely because Evangelicals divided, backing two different legislation alternatives [see chapter 9]), Whitehead was concerned to protect the personal religious liberties of public school teachers and students, who are free under the First Amendment, he contended, to engage fully in the "market place of ideas."[26]

Exerting Influence in Schools and on School Boards

Evangelicals' efforts to join together to exert influence within public education after *Everson* go back at least to 1953, when the Christian Educators Association International (CEAI) was formed by Benjamin S. Weiss, a retired Los Angeles public school teacher and administrator with close ties to young leaders like Billy Graham. A relatively small organization, with a dues-paying membership today of six thousand education professionals and a magazine, CEAI seeks to encourage an Evangelical presence within public education.[27]

Forrest L. Turpen, the executive director of CEAI, considers the "wall of separation" rhetoric a real problem, because it gives the false impression that all religion has been excluded by the Court. Parents and school administrators need to be informed that students are still able to express their faith at school, he says, and teachers may include information about Christian contributions to American history in their classes. Evangelicals like Turpen are not uncomfortable with their minority status in the schools. They have no desire to impose their beliefs on anyone nor to see the government do so; they simply want unbiased and equal treatment. When it comes to civil religion, with perhaps some reservations, they have basically accommodated their thinking to *Everson*.[28]

Other Evangelicals, like Mel and Norma Gabler of Longview, Texas, engage in textbook wars. Textbooks that treat Christians badly or, more commonly, omit any reference to them; promote behavior offensive to parents; establish secularism or some other religion; promote skepticism; or are poorly written and inadequately documented are subject to their critical review. Accused of being censors, the Gablers have persisted for decades, giving their opinions in public hearings set up by law in Texas for that purpose.[29]

School board elections have been contentious arenas for Evangelicals in recent years, gaining notoriety especially after their success in San Diego in 1990. Whether the issue is the academic curriculum, sex education, teacher qualifications, school discipline, charter schools, or funding, one can find religiously motivated parents, including Evangelicals, active in local, state, and even national education politics.[30]

Helping parents deal with education issues is now a significant enterprise among Evangelicals. The Family Research Council, for example, puts out *Moms and Dads School Survival Guide*, which discusses a wide range of issues and options in public and private education. Parents increasingly have both the motivation and the resources to look closely at their choices and, if they desire, to lobby governments. This is not a passive portion of the electorate. In Pennsylvania, for example, the Pennsylvania Family Institute (PFI), affiliated with Dr. James Dobson and Focus on the Family, publishes *Pennsylvania Families and Schools*, a monthly education newsletter. Mr. Tom Shaheen of PFI reports that almost 90 percent of his communications with supporters in Pennsylvania relate to education.[31]

Recently, Evangelical leader Kay Coles James, leaving her position as secretary of health and human resources for the Commonwealth of Virginia, agreed to accept Governor George Allen's invitation to serve on the state board of education, and she became Regent University's Dean of the Robertson School of Government. Regent University, itself an Evangelical graduate school, plans to establish an institute of educational policy to target public education needs. Leaders like James are not content with the status quo, but they are not ready to write off public education. Sharing the same concerns, the Family Foundation, a Virginia-based advocacy group, published the 125-page *Virginia Education Report Card* assessing the strengths and weaknesses of school districts in the state, giving every indication that efforts to influence public education are increasing among Evangelicals.[32]

Today parents who place their children in public schools often do so after considering other options. The one-size-fits-all days are no more. Parents may choose to home school or to send their children to a private school. The federal government estimated that enrollment in private elementary and secondary schools in 1995 was 5.7 million students, about 11 percent of the total student population, in over twenty-five thousand schools, more than twenty thousand of them church related. Making sure that state law protects the authority of parents to choose the school for their child is the third step in Evangelical education strategy.[33]

Protecting the Autonomy of Home Schools and Private Schools

One group of religious-liberty litigators, the Home School Legal Defense Association (HSLDA), focuses exclusively on the rights of families that choose to educate their children at home. Founded in 1983 by attorneys Michael P. Farris and J. Michael Smith and now representing over fifty thousand families, HSLDA developed a complete package of legal services to meet the needs of home educators. Motivated by conservative Christian beliefs that give parents the duty to teach their children, HSLDA commonly finds itself working with, rather than against, the ACLU. Explaining why HSLDA and ACLU positions are compatible though motivated by contrary presuppositions, Michael Farris wrote in a 1990 article entitled "Conservatives Declare War on Religious Freedom":[34]

> Economic conservatives are utterly utilitarian. Religious freedom produces too much diversity and too much potential for chaos, and, as we all know, chaos is bad for profitable retailing. The ACLU is our friend on most free exercise issues. George Will and Justices Scalia and Rehnquist are our opponents. How is this possible? The ACLU believes that self is God. They always favor the individual against the government. So, in a battle for the exercise of religion, the liberals are our friends and the conservatives are our enemies.[35]

Farris said that he differed with the ACLU on most law-and-order controversies, wanting to preserve "the moral absolutes of God's law" because "murder in the form of abortion, and adultery in the form of pornography, cannot be countenanced." However, he agreed in many respects with the ACLU's approach to criminal rights. Defending sixty-six pastors in Kentucky and Nebraska in 1983 awakened Farris to the role law plays in restraining public officials. Of course, the constant pressure of public school officials against home schoolers goes a long way toward explaining this sensitivity of the HSLDA leadership. Caught in something of a political dilemma, the HSLDA saw Republicans influenced by conservative big-business interests and Democrats owned by the public school bureaucracy, neither supportive of home-school liberty. Farris saw only Justice Sandra Day O'Connor as a clear and positive voice on the Supreme Court.[36]

In state legislatures, HSLDA works to get protective home-school laws passed, claiming that thirty-five states already have such statutes and the remaining fifteen permit it under other laws or regulations. Farris cultivates an optimistic vision of the future for this movement. His conviction that public schools do not work leaves him convinced that home schoolers will be a growing segment of the population for years to come. Claiming that as many as one million children are already being home schooled, he anticipates the day when public education will no longer maintain its dominant position in American education. If home schoolers choose home school as their parents did, he predicts a long-term shift in education demographics. "After being a persecuted minority of home schoolers, we will hopefully remember the tolerance we have desired, if and when we ever become a majority. Civil tolerance of all faiths and forms of education should be the goal of a truly educated person."[37]

Another attorney who has been in the forefront of protecting home school and private school rights is William Bentley Ball, of Harrisburg, Pennsylvania, partner in the firm Ball, Skelly, Murren & Connel. Well known for his advocacy before the Supreme Court in cases such as *Wisconsin v. Yoder* (1972) and *Lemon v. Kurtzman* (1971), Ball is also a legislative strategist who has worked with Catholics and Evangelicals to forge effective legislation ensuring the independence of schools by preventing illegitimate state interference.[38]

Ball has no quarrel with the state when it reasonably enforces fire and health rules in parochial schools, nor is he concerned when reading, writing, and arithmetic are required. The state has a genuine interest in requiring education and in ensuring that minimum standards are met. What is not acceptable, in his view, is government control of who can be a teacher or how a course can be taught and order maintained in the classroom. To place Pennsylvania law on the side of parochial-school autonomy, and with the help of local Evangelical and Catholic leadership, Ball obtained the passage of legislation prohibiting state board of education supervision of church schools:

> It is the policy of the Commonwealth to preserve the primary right and policy of the parent or parents, or person or persons *in loco parentis* to a child, to choose the education or training for such child. Nothing contained in this act shall empower the Commonwealth, any of its officers, agencies or subdivisions to approve the course content, faculty, staff or disciplinary requirements of any religious school referred to in this section without the consent of said school.[39]

Having worked to secure independence in the law for both home schoolers and private religious schools, attorney Ball was prepared to labor once again for public funds for parents who send their children to church schools. There was no point, he said, in getting funding if private schools were run indirectly by the state through government regulatory bodies. As truly independent schools, they could produce a quality product worthy of public financial support. With a governor supportive of school vouchers and additional help anticipated in the legislature, William Ball was optimistic that in 1997 Pennsylvania could make progress in this direction. Securing some form of tax relief or vouchers for parents is the fourth element in Evangelical strategy.[40]

Providing Resources for an Alternative to Public Schools

Two radically different critiques of the funding of American education, written by Evangelical scholars, reject public schools as they have historically existed in America. James Skillen, founder of the Association for Public Justice, sees the common school at its best as an abandonment of Christian education and potentially a betrayal of parents' most elementary obligations. He looks for inspiration to a European model of confessional pluralism in schools, long practiced in Holland and France. These systems allow for tax subsidies for schools maintained by church denominations. In Skillen's view, all schools are public schools, and creative ways to encourage different groups and communities to invest in education alternatives will benefit the entire nation.[41]

The Skillen model rejects a state monopoly of education, even while funding schools by tax revenues. Each child of the same age or grade in school should receive, he argues, the same amount of state money for education, to be given to the school of his or her choice. Under this plan, special provision would be made for the extra costs for children with disabilities, but essentially there would be equal funding for all children in all schools. Skillen would do away with public education as we have known it, expanding the definition of "public" to include all "directly or indirectly" tax-funded schools, including those established by churches.[42]

It is clear that there is more than one lesson to learn from European examples. In France, where a significant number of schools have traditionally been Catholic, there has been substantial pressure against continuing these schools either because they are too much like government-run schools and therefore, critics say, they do not deserve to exist, or because they are so different that they threaten national unity. As author Charles L. Glenn points out, funding separate systems does not do away with political conflict. Indeed, confessionally based education, whether or not it is mediated by parental choice, may increase conflict, turning education into a perpetual political issue.[43]

Another Evangelical opinion that also rejects the American common school goes in the opposite direction from Skillen. In this view, articulated by constitutional law scholar and 1996 national vice-presidential candidate for the Tax Payers Party Herbert W. Titus, all public education (with some exceptions, e.g., the military service academies) is a violation both of elementary principles of education and of constitutional law because, he is convinced, the state has no authority to teach. Titus would entirely privatize the funding and management of schools, abolishing public education. [44]

In recent years, Titus points out, the government has rejected state aid to parochial schools, never doubting the right of government to run its own schools. In law, he says, the principle cuts both ways. Public education began as religious education supported by the state, and it is still religious, but its religion is secularism. The problem, Titus argues, is not the content of course instruction but the presence of government, which by its very nature limits the ability of people to think freely without fear of coercion. Education, from this perspective, is a field where reason and conscience alone rule; the state's jurisdiction is limited to where it has authority to apply force. As James Madison opposed tax contributions of any kind to support religion, Titus would cut off tax support for education on the grounds that at issue is the right of people to think freely.[45]

However, I argue that common schools under parental supervision, locally funded and controlled, should not be equated with a centralized school system run by educators who operate independently of the community. Titus is right to warn against education dictated by government, but he is wrong to claim that tax funding creates such a system. Parents who started and maintained tax-supported common schools in America considered *themselves,* as local citizens, the government of the community, not some outside power. Evangelicals agreed with public schools, not just because they supported popular democracy—which they did—but because they saw this as an opportunity to work with other parents in the community to give their children the best possible start in life. Public schools in America were once community schools, not the agents of a remote power called the State, as they are today.

Many states are looking for ways to fund alternative schools. Evangelicals disagree on mechanisms for funding, some preferring tax credits to avoid potentially dangerous government regulation, and others favoring tuition vouchers. The more radical education reformers want to go further and essentially do away with government schools by letting market mechanisms drive them out of existence or by abolishing them outright. Whichever funding alternative Evangelicals select or governments adopt, substantial reform sooner or later must deal with the issue of money, for teachers must be paid. Linking teachers to students in a variety of ways is the fifth element in Evangelical education strategy.

Making Room for Combinations of Public, Private, and Home Schools

The future of American education may lie less in the minds of jurists, legislators, theorists, administrators, and activists proliferating across the landscape-and more in the influence of mothers. Mrs. Deborah Bell of Palmyra, Pennsylvania, mother of four children, has a master's degree in English, home schools her children, and has written *The Ultimate Guide to Home Schooling* (1997).[46]

Recently, Bell faced a problem. How were her twin sons going to play for Penn State if they did not get to play high school football? In Pennsylvania, local school districts may at their discretion allow home schoolers to participate in varsity sports. Initially the board opposed her request, raising several objections. Bell dealt with each of the objections, eventually winning the board over. Soon one son was the starting quarterback, the other playing in the line. Necessity remains the mother of invention, and Mrs. Bell wouldn't take no for an answer. She had a right and a reason for her sons to be included in community sports. If the board had said no, she said, she would have come back in a month.

Rejecting isolation for her family, yet prizing her opportunity to be her children's teacher, Bell is pleased that in Pennsylvania she is allowed to enroll her home-schooled children in two public school classes if she so desires. One night a week, Bell gives English lectures to local home schoolers, who gather for enrichment by qualified professionals. When Bell was asked in a recent interview if she wanted public funds for home schooling, she replied that she was not sure, she had not really thought about it. The question intrigued her, but as a person fully occupied teaching four growing children, she was a realist, determined to succeed in her immediate responsibilities, not inclined to speculate beyond the horizon, but ready if called upon to move mountains today.

Clearly there is a blurring of public, private, and home schools, a melding of resources for each child. Getting the law to facilitate creative exploration of education alternatives will be the wave of the future, if parents have their way. Evangelicals teach that parents must decide how education is to be done. In the America once led by Evangelicals, common schools were the preferred answer, with racial segregation, Indian reservations, and room for private options. Today's Evangelicals are losing confidence in educators and in the laws that regulate schools. Meanwhile, new technologies are already making an impact, which suggests that if the common school of the past were to reappear, it would not look at all like the little red schoolhouse. In this context of breathtaking new possibilities, breaking the inertia that prevents creative change is the role Evangelicals have begun to assume out of necessity after

Everson. Not surprisingly, what is emerging is an approach that makes room for parental choice for all Americans, a new definition of the common school.

Constructing the New Common School

It was not the intention of the Supreme Court to end public education as we know it. The law of unintended consequences surely applies in this instance. First, prior to *Everson*, Evangelicals and Catholics disagreed on education: Catholics wanted tax support for their schools, and Protestants opposed it. *Everson* helped heal this division. Second, by excluding revealed religion, *Everson* may have contributed to chaos inside the classroom, as Evangelical supporters of the common school have argued; but it may have done something positive as well in forcing new thinking about schools and their relation to parents, churches, and the community. The result, certainly not intended by *Everson,* is the occasion to revisit at a much deeper level the issues of religion, government, and public life. Few today outside the education establishment want to see the dead hand of government monopoly ruling schools. For America to be freely educated and mature, community schools must emerge that are as fully owned by parents as the common schools ever were.

The theoretical contribution of Evangelicals to education in America is their understanding of parental responsibility, denying the government and the church the central place in education. From this perspective, the debate engendered by *Everson* that focuses so heavily on religion misses the point entirely, and parental authority is undermined by it. Religion should not be the issue, nor government support for religion. Power is not the issue either— not the dominance of Protestants nor the loss of that dominance. Constitutional scholars will continue to debate the merits of First Amendment interpretations for a long time to come; and social historians will track the rise, fall, and resurgence of Evangelical influence in schools. But neither group of scholars yet comprehends what Evangelicals have been saying and doing to permit parents, whatever their religion, to oversee the design and running of schools. To them, other issues are secondary.

If parents are in charge, in principle, then church-state issues need to be removed from this discussion. The greatest disaster resulting from *Everson* is that it made religion the center of attention and civil government too important, to the detriment of family authority. The best remedy for this dispute, according to Evangelicals, is the recovery of the pre-*Everson* sense that communities of parents ought to be allowed to make their own arrangements. Parental authority is real and ought to be respected, whether Evangelical parents are a majority or a minority, whether there is one tax-supported community school or a dozen alternative schools from which to select. Neither policy nor law should limit parents too much, in this view; otherwise families will be tempted to abandon their educational burdens, with catastrophic consequences for all. Everson *built a wall of separation between parents and schools.*

Contemporary Evangelicals, like Catholics before them, have the economic and political resources to work for choice in education, and increasing problems in government-run schools have given them the incentive to use those resources. Some parents elect to push for reform in public education, while others explore private options. In setting up and evaluating these different schooling arrangements, defined and protected by law, the hard-and-fast distinctions between public, private, and home schools are breaking down. Educators of all stripes will look for ways to work together, although some prefer not to cooperate or try to dominate, limiting schooling alternatives in their communities.

The practical lesson of *Everson* certainly is that schools cannot be run without the support of parents. Most Evangelicals sooner or later say that for them, school must include prayer, the Bible, and public support, at least in the form of tax relief. If public prayer is excluded, some Evangelical leaders and many of their followers have said, that school will die, consumed in disorder. *Everson* has given us the opportunity to test that hypothesis, in the context of hope for a better educational future. Meanwhile, Evangelicals must decide on a common legislative strategy if they are to make more progress on the issue of religious expression in public schools, something they were not able to do in the 104th Congress.

In conclusion, by separating state-supported religion from public education, the Supreme Court has encouraged the establishment of the new common school, open to all interested families, defined by the talents and choices of the children, parents, educators, and churches that create them. Giving some form of tax relief or funding to these schools, already heavily supported by Evangelicals and Catholics, is an issue that will reach the Supreme Court, because *Everson* turned religion in education into a federal issue. Evangelicals have always said education is under parental jurisdiction, not essentially a state or church matter. Using this reasoning, long accepted in American law, perhaps Evangelicals will once again help lead the way to a new understanding of community schools—that is, local schools, supported by parents, that permit prayer and government to work together for the common good. Prior to *Everson*, federalism made such schools possible. After *Everson*, it will take a vigorous reaffirmation of parental rights, already recognized in principle by the Supreme Court, to open the school doors wide once more.

Notes

1. For a recent Evangelical warning against the direction taken by the Supreme Court, see Charles W. Colson, "Kingdoms in Conflict," *First Things,* no. 67 (November 1996): 34–38. For an example of how the Supreme Court rejected the use of *Everson* by a school district attempting to justify its prohibition of religious speech and activity by students, see Alexander D. Hill and Chi-Dooh Li, "Religious Speech in Public Schools: A Case Study in Contradictions," *Journal of Church and State* 37, no. 3 (Summer 1995): 623–40.

2. Methodists and Baptists eventually numbered two-thirds of Protestant pastors and church members. See Nathan O. Hatch, *The Democratization of American Christianity* (New Haven and London: Yale University Press, 1989), 3–5; Lawrence A. Cremin, *American Education: The National Experience, 1783–1876* (New York: Harper & Row, 1980), 50–73.

3. Charles Leslie Glenn Jr., *The Myth of the Common School* (Amherst: University of Massachusetts Press, 1988), 115–78; Cremin, *American Education,* 148–85; Frederick Eby, *The Development of Modern Education* (Englewood Cliffs, N.J.: Prentice Hall, 1952), 546–81; Frank C. Nelson, *Public Schools: An Evangelical Appraisal* (Old Tappan, N.J.: Fleming H. Revell, 1987), 31–64.

4. Lawrence A. Cremin, ed., *The Republic and the School: Horace Mann on the Education of Free Men* (New York: Teachers College, Columbia University, 1957), 12–13; Joel Spring, *The American School. 1642–1990* (New York: Longman, 1990), 73–114; Glenn, *Myth,* 146–78; Cremin, *American Education,* 133–42; For a philosophic defense of civil religion, see Jean-Jacques Rousseau, *The Creed of the Priest of Savoy* (New York: Frederick Ungar, 1956).

5. *Everson v. Board of Education,* 330 U.S. 1 (1947). William Martin, *A Prophet with Honor: The Billy Graham Story* (New York: William Morrow, 1991), 89–105; Joel A. Carpenter, ed., *The Youth for Christ Movement and Its Pioneers* (New York and London: Garland, 1988), 111–14. My father, Rev. David Morken, a founder of YFC, was responsible in the 1940s for establishing it in China and Japan (unpublished memoirs); my uncle, Rev. Hubert Mitchell, also a founder, planted YFC in India at the same time.

6. Cremin, *American Education,* 139–40. For a contemporary example of parental authority, see the parental rights amendment to the Colorado state constitution, defeated in the 1996 election. The amendment would have added to a list of inalienable rights in article 2, section 3, the words "and of parents to direct and control the upbringing, education, values, and discipline of their children." Coalition for Parental Responsibility, Denver, Colo.

7. *Pierce v. Society of Sisters,* 268 U.S. 510, 534 (1925); *Meyer v. State of Nebraska,* 262 U.S. 390 (1923).

8. *Everson v. Board of Education*; Cremin, *American Education,* 208–17, 371–413; Edward J. Larson, "The 'Blaine Amendment' in State Constitutions," in *The School-Choice Controversy: What Is Constitutional?* ed. James W. Skillen (Grand Rapids, Mich.: Baker Books, 1993), 35–50.

9. Cremin, *American Education,* 37–38, 166–70, 218–45, 384–85; Spring, *American School,* 104–10.

10. *Everson* included the following statement: "The establishment of religion clause of the First Amendment means at least this: Neither a state nor the Federal Government can set up a church. Neither can pass laws which aid one religion, aid all religions, or prefer one religion over another." *Everson v. Board of Education,* 15; Hill and Li, "Religious Speech."

11. The author's experience in public schools is illustrative. My father, a missionary evangelist, sent me to a missionary school in Shanghai in 1949 and later in Tokyo. When we returned to California in 1953, he put my brothers and me into a private Christian day school. The atmosphere was negative and repressive, and we begged our parents, after only one day, to take us out. They then enrolled us in a public school that had a positive and wholesome atmosphere more like our missionary schools in Asia. I sent my own four children to public elementary and junior high schools and then to the Stony Brook School, an Evangelical college preparatory school in New York. I now have grandchildren in public schools. In contrast to my family experience, orthodox Presbyterians sounded the alarm on public schools much earlier. See John W. Robbins, ed., *Education, Christianity, and the State: Essays by J. Gresham Machen* (Jefferson, Md.: Trinity Foundation, 1987); for Jewish responses, see Gregg Ivers, *To Build a Wall: American Jews and the Separation of Church and State* (Charlottesville: University Press of Virginia, 1995), 17–33, 66–83. See also Stephen Bates, *Battleground: One Mother's Crusade, the Religious Right, and the Struggle for Control of Our Classrooms* (New York: Poseidon Press, 1993).

12. D. James Kennedy, *Defending the First Amendment* (Fort Lauderdale, Fla.: Coral Ridge Ministries, 1993), 11–12; Steven W. Fitschen and Herbert W. Titus, *God Save This Honorable Court* (Fort Lauderdale, Fla.: Coral Ridge Ministries, 1994), 1–10; Arnold Burron, John Eidsmoe, and Dean Turner, *Classrooms in Crisis: Parents Rights and the Public School* (Denver, Colo.: Accent Books, 1986), 8.

13. H. Wayne House, ed., *Schooling Choices: An Examination of Private, Public, and Home Education* (Portland, Ore.: Multnomah Press, 1988).

14. Carl F. H. Henry, "Christian Responsibility in Education," *Christianity Today* 1, no. 17 (27 May 1957): 11–14.

15. Eby, *Development,* 679–80.

16. Henry, "Christian Responsibility," 13–14; Carl F. H. Henry, "Religion in the Schools," parts 1–5. *Christianity Today* 17, no. 24 (14 September 1973); 18, no. 1 (12 October 1973); 18, no. 3 (9 November 1973); 18, no. 5 (7 December 1973); 18, no. 7 (4 January 1974); 18, no. 9 (1 February 1974).

17. Horace Mann, "Twelfth Annual Report," quoting Prov. 22:6, in Cremin, *Republic,* 100–112.

18. *Engel v. Vitale,* 370 U.S. 421 (1962); David Barton, *America: To Pray or Not to Pray?* (Aledo, Texas: WallBuilder Press, 1988); *What Happened in Education?* (Aledo, Texas: Specialty Research Associates, 1990); *Original Intent: The Courts, the Constitution, and Religion* (Aledo, Texas: WallBuilder Press, 1996).

19. I am indebted to William Bentley Ball for stimulating my thinking on the

sequence of steps in an effective strategy. Clearly, history does not always follow logic.

20.   Allen D. Hertzke, *Representing God in Washington: The Role of Religious Lobbies in the American Polity* (Knoxville: University of Tennessee Press, 1988), 161–98; Hubert Morken, "The Evangelical Legal Response to the ACLU: Religion, Politics, and the First Amendment" (paper presented at the annual meeting of the American Political Science Association [APSA], Chicago, September 1992); Eric A. DeGroff, "Prayer in Public Schools: A Legal and Legislative Update" (materials prepared for conference "Restoring Civic Virtue," Virginia Beach, Va., Regent University School of Law, 1996), tab 6, 1–20.

21.   A true story recounted to the author with vivid local color by Dr. and Mrs. Joseph H. Winston, Moorestown, N.J., fall 1996. The Winstons know the family involved.

22.   Daniel Dreisbach points out that free speech rather than free exercise of religion became a preferred basis for argument by Evangelical litigators; interview by author, fall, 1996; Hubert Morken, "Public Secondary Education: Equal Access and the Clash over Student Religious Expression" (paper presented at the annual meeting of the APSA, Atlanta, September 1989).

23.   Lesa Holda, "The Christian Legal Society" (unpublished paper, Regent University, 1992) 25; ACLU, "The Establishment Clause and Public Schools," *ACLU Legal Bulletin,* 1992; Morken, "Public Secondary Education," 11–16; and Morken, "Evangelical Legal Response," 4–11.

24.   *Board of Education of Westside Community Schools v. Mergens By and Through Mergens,* 496 U.S. 226 (1990); Robert Fuggi, "The National Legal Foundation," unpublished paper, Regent University, 1992; Morken, "The Evangelical," 20–24.

25.   Brief Amicus Curiae of the National Legal Foundation in support of Petitioner, *Lee v. Weisman,* 505 U.S. 577 (1992), 47.

26.   In the 104th Congress, some Evangelicals wanted legislation to permit prayer in schools and others were committed to ensuring equal access and equal treatment. For a study of the resulting conflicts that prevented the passage of legislation, see Jacquelene McKee, "Crafting a Republican Strategy for Religious Freedom: Congressman Henry Hyde and the 104th Congress" (M.A. thesis, Regent University, 1996); Brief Amici Curiae of Concerned Women for America and Free Speech Advocates, *Robert E. Lee v. Daniel Weisman;* John W. Whitehead, *The Rights of Religious Persons in Public Education* (Wheaton, Ill.: Crossway Books, 1994), 49–64, 258, 273 n. 2; Nelson, *Public Schools,* 161–95.

27.   Benjamin S. Weiss, the founder of Christian Educators Association International, was a family friend of the author; Ruth Strand, "The Life of Benjamin Weiss" (unpublished paper, Christian Educators Association International, 1969).

28.   Forrest L. Turpen, interview by author, Virginia Beach, Va., fall 1996; pamphlet of Christian Educators Association.

29.   Mel Gabler and Norma Gabler, *What Are They Teaching Our Children?* (Wheaton, Ill.: Victor Books, 1987).

30.   Robert Holland, *Not with My Child You Don't* (Richmond, Va.: Chesapeake Capitol Services, 1995); Hubert Morken, "The San Diego Model: Religious-Identity

Concealment as Political Strategy" (paper presented at the annual meeting of the APSA, Washington, D.C., September 1993).

31. Family Research Council, *Moms and Dads School Survival Guide* (Washington, D.C.: Family Research Council, 1996); Pennsylvania Family Institute, *Pennsylvania Families and Schools* 1, nos. 1–9 (1996); Thomas Shaheen, interviews by author, Virginia Beach, Va., and Harrisburg, Pa., fall 1996; Joseph Guarino, of Virginia Citizens for Excellence in Education, interview by author, Virginia Beach, Va., fall 1996.

32. Robert Booth Fowler and Allen D. Hertzke, *Religion and Politics in America: Faith, Culture, and Strategic Choices* (Boulder, Colo.: Westview Press, 1995), 136, 172; Jeanne Allen, *The School Reform Handbook: How to Improve Your Schools* (Washington, D.C.: Center for Education Reform, 1995); Cheri Pierson Yecke, *Virginia Education Report Card* (Fairfax, Va.: Family Foundation, 1996).

33. Department of Education, *Mini-Digest of Education Statistics* (Washington, D.C.: Government Printing Office, 1995), Enrollment: Table 2, available at http://www.ed.gov/NCES/pubs/MiniDig95/enroll.html#02; Internet; accessed 5 December 1996; U.S. Bureau of the Census, *Statistical Abstract of the United States, 1995,* (Washington, D.C., 1995), table 233; John W. Whitehead, *Home Education: Rights and Reasons* (Wheaton, Ill.: Crossway Books, 1993).

34. Morken, "Evangelical Legal Response," 15–19.

35. Michael P. Farris, "Conservatives Declare War on Religious Freedom," *Home School Report*, Spring 1990, 4–5.

36. Morken, "Evangelical Legal Response," 15–16.

37. Home School Legal Defense Association (HSLDA), "Summary of Home School Laws in the Fifty States," reprinted from *Home Schooling in the United States: A Legal Analysis*, by Christopher J. Klicka (HSLDA, 1996); HSLDA fact sheet; Michael Farris, "The Politics of Home School Population," *Home School Report*, Spring 1988, 16; Morken, "Evangelical Legal Response," 19.

38. *Wisconsin v. Yoder*, 406 U.S. 205 (1972); *Lemon v. Kurtzman*, 411 U.S. 192 (1973); William Bentley Ball, *Mere Creatures of the State?* (Notre Dame, Ind.: Crisis Books, 1994); William Bentley Ball, *In Search of National Morality: Manifesto for Evangelicals and Catholics* (San Francisco: Ignatius Press; Grand Rapids, Mich.: Baker Book House, 1992).

39. Commonwealth of Pennsylvania, Public School Code of 1949, P.S. 13-1327(b)(2)75.

40. William Bentley Ball, interview by author, Harrisburg, Pa., fall 1996. For a compilation of Pennsylvania education reforms, see Charles E. Greenwalt II, ed., *Educational Innovation: An Agenda to Frame the Future* (Lanham, Md.: University Press of America, 1994).

41. Skillen, *School-Choice Controversy*, 35–50.

42. Rockne M. McCarthy, James W. Skillen, and William A. Harper, *Disestablishment a Second Time: Genuine Pluralism for American Schools* (Grand Rapids, Mich.: Christian University Press, 1982); Rockne M. McCarthy, et al., *Society, State, and Schools: A Case for Structural and Confessional Pluralism* (Grand Rapids, Mich.: William B. Eerdmans, 1981).

43. Glenn, *Myth*, 264–78.

44. Hubert Morken, "Herbert W. Titus and Philip E. Johnson, the Children of Liberalism: Religious Conversion, Law, and Politics" (paper presented at the annual meeting of the APSA, Washington, D.C., September 1991), 41–45.

45. Herbert W. Titus, "God, Evolution, Legal Education, and Law," unpublished manuscript, 1980.

46. Deborah Bell, interview by author, Harrisburg, Pa., fall 1996; Deborah Bell, *The Ultimate Guide to Home Schooling* (Dallas: Word Publishing, 1997).

4

Catholic Jurisprudence on Education

Jo Renée Formicola

Some scholars have asserted that Catholics have been "victimized" by the de facto Protestant educational infrastructure in America.[1] A result of Protestant leadership in the establishment of the public school system in the nineteenth century, this abuse, they argue, was clearly visible in federal attempts to placate nativists and other anti-Catholics who feared the "papists" after the Civil War. Indeed, President Ulysses Grant did call for a constitutional amendment in 1875 to deny financial assistance to any school that advanced "sectarian, pagan or atheistical dogmas."[2] And, taking up his appeal, the House of Representatives passed the Blaine amendment, a bill designed to deny federal funding for religious schools on both the national and state levels. Although final enactment failed by only two votes in the Senate, unofficially and by "gentlemen's agreement," the use of public monies for parochial education was a dead issue by the turn of the century.

Seemingly without executive or legislative allies, then, the Catholics responded historically to a lack of accommodation for their religious/educational interests by turning to the judiciary. Such a strategy seemed worthwhile, too, when the Supreme Court, in *Pierce v. Society of Sisters* (1923), upheld the right of parents to educate their children in parochial schools.[3] Thus began the development of the burgeoning Catholic school system in America within the Protestant, secular one—a school system that today boasts over 8,000 elementary and secondary schools, as well as 227 institutions of higher learning.[4]

With its first legal victory in *Pierce*, the Catholic Church, acting primarily as a friend of the court, began to challenge governmental actions that it considered hostile, adversarial, or biased with regard to its religious/educational interests.As a result, a tapestry of Catholic educational jurisprudence has emerged steadily over the last fifty years. Based on theology, pragmatism, precedent, and assertiveness, this complicated fabric has been woven with various threads, all designed to foster a closer relationship between the United

States government and the Catholic educational system.

A closer look at Catholic jurisprudence on education, then, reveals how these principles have been used to advance Church religious interests. Citing a variety of amicus briefs filed by the National Catholic Welfare Conference and its successor organization, the National Conference of Catholic Bishops, as well as the National Catholic Education Association, this chapter will articulate the elements of a maturing and coherent Catholic jurisprudence on education. Evidenced in *Everson v. Board of Education, Lemon v. Kurtzman, Zobrest v. Catalina Foothills Board of Education*, and *Board of Education v. Grumet*, these cases span five decades and a variety of issues on religion and education.[5] Thus, they demonstrate how the Church has used the legal process to advance both its pastoral and its civic responsibilities. This chapter will also maintain, however, that greater separation, rather than a closer accommodation, is the most appropriate means by which the Church can accomplish its salvific goal.

The Threads of *Everson*

Substantively, *Everson* dealt with the right of the State of New Jersey to enforce a statute that allowed local municipalities to reimburse parents for the cost of transporting their children to Catholic schools. Arguments made by Arch Everson, the executive director of the New Jersey Taxpayers Association, represented a separationist point of view and were based on the contention that the establishment clause of the First Amendment had been violated. He claimed, first, that tax monies had been expended for a private purpose and, second, that the use of the power of the state to tax for the support of church schools was a violation of both the First and the Fourteenth Amendments. Everson's legal allies included the American Civil Liberties Union, the Seventh-Day Adventists, the Southern Baptist Convention, the Northern Baptist Convention, the National Baptist Convention, the American Jewish Congress, the New York Bar Association, and the National Liberal League, all of whom filed amicus briefs in the case.

The State of New Jersey defended its action by maintaining that it was within its right to provide transportation as a "child benefit" and that, in so doing, it neither established a religion nor violated the due process clause of the Fourteenth Amendment. It was bolstered in this view by the amicus brief of the State of Massachusetts, which reflected a similar view: that the appropriation of tax monies to pay for the transportation of students to parochial schools served a public purpose and that to deny aid such aid would "upend a system that had legally been in place for fourteen years."[6] Massachusetts argued, therefore, that transportation aid should be considered as a matter of the protection and health of children.[7] The State of New York concurred.[8]

The Catholic Church, strongly represented in Massachusetts and New York, served as the main supporter of the State of New Jersey. Although Catholicism was the largest religious denomination in the United States after World War II, Catholics still found themselves outside the social and political mainstream and depended on their church-run schools to maintain their ethnic identities, to teach their religious beliefs, and to provide a sense of community. Therefore, when the Supreme Court announced that it was going to hear the case of *Everson v. Board of Education* in 1947, the decision was immediately viewed with alarm by influential members of the Catholic hierarchy, particularly Francis Cardinal Spellman of New York and Samuel Cardinal Stritch of Chicago.[9] Perceiving the Court's action as an attempt to compromise the viability of the American Catholic educational system, Spellman and Stritch used their positions within the Church to bolster the State of New Jersey. They directed the legal counsel for the National Catholic Welfare Conference, the organization that spoke for the Church, together with John Courtney Murray, the eminent Jesuit moral theologian and scholar, to write an amicus brief on behalf of the National Council of Catholic Men and the National Council of Catholic Women. It was expected that the brief would articulate arguments to protect Catholic educational interests, and, at the same time, clarify the public-purpose nature of parochial education in America.[10]

In filing its own amicus brief, the Church dealt with two issues; the broad matter of church-state relations, and the specific question of busing. With regard to the former, John Courtney Murray, a moral theologian and primary author of the brief, articulated the major Catholic *theological* principles of church and state: that the general purpose of all such relations was to maintain the freedom of the Church to teach, rule, and sanctify its adherents; and that government, therefore, was expected to guarantee the independence of the Church to fulfill its divine mission.[11]

According to the logic of Murray et al., then, religious education fell into the sphere of church responsibility, an obligation that the state should not hinder, but to which it should accommodate. As a consequence, the Catholics claimed that Church members, acting as parents, had the primary right to educate their children in schools of their own choosing, particularly in those schools that would inculcate their personal spiritual values. They contended that the state's role in education was, therefore, a secondary or derivative right, one that, in effect, disallowed any state control of religious education. In short, the Catholics held that public authority could not enter the pluralistic world of organized believers.[12]

With regard to the specific issue of transporting Catholic students to parochial schools, Murray et al. further argued that an "area of interdependence"[13] existed between church and state, an overlap embodied in the education of the nations' citizenry. This argument was recognized by the Supreme Court in *Cochran v. Louisiana* as valid.[14] The Catholics contended that the *Cochran* case legitimized the lending or supplying of textbooks to students in both private and parochial schools on the basis of child benefit.

However, they carried their argument much further. The Catholics extrapolated that *Cochran* established the precedent on which they could also claim that the Jeffersonian metaphor of the wall of separation was "displaced" in matters of education.[15] They argued that the initial ruling against the use of public funds for the transportation of students to parochial schools was a "distortion" of the original intent of the First Amendment,[16] that state aid for religious education served a public purpose, that it did not undermine tax law, and that it did not breach the wall of separation between church and state.

Based on the arguments of the litigants and the major amici in *Everson*, the decision of the Court came as a disappointment to the separationists and the accommodationists alike. Arch Everson and his supporters were particularly dismayed by the fact that the Court validated child benefit theory and ruled that the State of New Jersey had the right to expend public monies to transport students to parochial schools. And the Catholics were most concerned because the Court now set a crucial precedent by too narrowly circumscribing the definition of the establishment of religion.

Indeed, *Everson* was, and remains, a landmark case, not simply because it allowed public funding for the transportation of parochial school students, but because the justices interpreted the original intent of the First Amendment to mean that no government intrusion into the free exercise of religion was allowed and that the same principle should be applied to the establishment clause of the First Amendment as well. Thus *Everson* set the precedent that neither the state nor the federal government can (a) set up a Church; (b) pass laws that aid religion, whether all religions or one religion over another; (c) take part in influencing individuals to participate in, or remain away from, Church; (d) enforce a religious belief or disbelief; (e) punish individuals for religious belief or disbelief or for church attendance or nonattendance; (f) levy taxes to support religious activities or institutions; (g) participate in the affairs of religious organizations; or (h) allow religious organizations to be involved in the business of the state or federal government.[17] John Courtney Murray summed it up best for the Catholics when he lamented, "We have won on busing, but lost on the First Amendment."[18]

No sooner had the judicial dust cleared from the *Everson* case than *McCollum v. Board of Education* began to wend its way through the appeals process.[19] At issue was the constitutionality of an act of the Champaign, Illinois, Board of Education that permitted religious teachers to use public school facilities for religious instruction. Again, the National Catholic Welfare Conference considered filing an amicus brief and consulted its church-state expert, John Courtney Murray. Still smarting from *Everson*, he advised that "no piecemeal, merely legal argument" could win the case.[20]

Eventually, however, Murray vigorously attacked the Court's narrow interpretation of the First Amendment clause in both *Everson* and *McCollum*. As editor of two major Catholic publications, *Theological Studies* and *America*, Murray used his considerable influence within the Church to criticize the Court.[21] On other occasions, he decried the decision in *Everson,* once even boldly calling it "a piece of bad history, muddy political theory, and bad judicial thinking."[22] He called the justices' interpretation of the First Amendment "rigid, ruthless and sweeping" and warned that the Supreme Court had created a "religion of democracy."[23] Thus, substantially rejecting *Everson*'s holding, the Catholics waited and hoped for a better legal opportunity to gain a government accommodation for their religious and educational interests in the future.

The Threads of *Lemon*

In 1970, the National Catholic Education Association, in conjunction with several other denominational groups, finally saw an opening to press for their religious/educational views again by petitioning the Supreme Court as amicus curiae in the case of *Lemon v. Kurtzman*. Revolving around the constitutionality of state statutes in both Pennsylvania and Rhode Island allowing the states to support the salaries of instructors who taught secular subjects in church-related schools, the case brought Catholic involvement in the hope of persuading the Court to allow salary assistance for secondary school teachers.

The amicus brief contained four arguments, two of which were endemic to the merits of the case, and two of which continued the broader theological arguments made in *Everson*. With regard to salaries, the Catholics maintained that the denial of financial assistance to their teachers would provoke more than a religious-education problem; indeed, they argued that it would create a public crisis. The Catholics asserted that the parochial schools had been providing quality secular education for a large segment of the population, a job that the state would have to perform if the Catholic schools could no longer afford to do it. They believed that the state would have to pay to educate Catholic students because the financial change would increase the monetary burdens on parochial schools and in turn require an increase in tuition and a limit on the availablity of parochial education to the Church's primary constitutents, the children of the lower and middle classes.Without some state assistance for the salaries of teachers in parochial schools, the Catholics argued, the state would have to provide, *at an even greater cost*, education for most of the children in church-related schools, thus swelling the populations of the state schools and compromising their continued viablity.[24] At the same time, amicus argued that the very existence of religious schools supported the free exchange of ideas in the academic marketplace. To jeopardize the financial basis of church-related schools, then, according to the Catholics, was to endanger the "dynamism of [the] marketplace of truth."[25] Synthesizing the opinions of the Supreme Court justices in *Pierce v. Society of Sisters* and *Board of Education v. Allen*,[26] the Catholics argued that the Pennsylvania statute was an important means to foster openness, originality, innovation, and experimentation in all its schools, both public and private.

The other two arguments, however, were extensions of the theological claims made in *Everson*. One maintained that the law of Pennsylvania was an effective coordination of parental and states' rights in the secular education of children, and the other asserted that the statute met accepted tests for the separation of church and state. The underlying principles addressed in this case, then, were broad: the matters of free exercise and, the most "determinative"[27] of all, the establishment issue. Thus, as an amicus, the Catholics were looking for a judicial reinterpretation of the narrow understanding of the establishment clause as set out in *Everson*.

Arguing from original intent, the Catholics contended that the framers of the First Amendment defined establishment as the "sponsorship, financial support and active involvement of the sovereign in religious activity,"[28] as Madison had maintained in his "Memorial and Remonstrance," rather than on the subsequent type of child benefit assistance allotted by the state for educational purposes alone. They argued that with regard to subsidizing the salaries of teachers who taught secular subjects in parochial schools, however, a different situation existed. Amicus contended that in this case, constitutional law and nonreligious education operated harmoniously and coordinated both parental and state rights in the secular education of school children.[29] Most important, they asserted that free exercise meant that the Court should uphold the constitutional right of each parent to send his or her child to a secularly qualified or religiously related school. To do less, the Catholics asserted, would be to forfeit a believer's constitutional right to participate in the general benefits of the state.

With regard to the interpretation of the establishment clause, however, the education issue in *Lemon* became the means by which the Catholics would again challenge, and the Court would further define, the meaning of "religious establishment." Amicus addressed its seminal church-state concerns: the need to maintain the freedom of the Church to carry out its religious responsibility to teach, rule, and sanctify its adherents, and the right of its members to choose those schools that would best fulfill the sacred and secular needs of their children. Clearly, the Catholics wanted to obtain these ends through an accommodation between church and state. They sought an alteration in the Pennsylvania and Rhode Island state financial systems, a reorientation that would allow those states to reimburse teachers of secular subjects in parochial schools.

The Supreme Court, however, did not accept the Catholics' rationale. Admitting that it could "only dimly perceive the lines of demarcation in this extraordinarily sensitive area of constitutional law" and that the "language of the Religion Clauses of the Amendment is at best opaque,"[30] the justices ruled on the merits and declared that salary support for teachers in parochial schools constituted a violation of the principle of separation of church and state. Further, they decided more broadly on the issue of establishment and created a three-pronged test by which to judge whether the government was, in effect, unduly involved with religious institutions. All statutes were required to have a secular legislative purpose; their primary effect was to neither advance nor inhibit religion; and they were not to foster an excessive government entanglement with religion.

Therefore, the Court ruled that, given the Church's dual responsibility to teach religious values as well as educational information to students in Pennsylvania's parochial schools, the state's support for teachers in those schools had created an entangling alliance between church and state. The Catholics, again, in the view of the Court had been unable to prove that "States and parents are entitled to something better than an 'all or nothing choice.'"[31]

The Threads of *Zobrest*

In 1993, the United States Catholic Conference again acted as amicus curiae in support of a suit brought by two petitioners, Andrea and Larry Zobrest. In this case, their deaf son, Jim, had been denied a sign-language interpreter because he attended a parochial school. The Catalina Foothills Board of Education argued that to pay for such a service was a violation of the principle of separation of church and state and that such expenditures would authorize an insidious relationship, or even worse, a "symbolic union,"[32] between religion and government.

The Catholics, in the conference's amicus brief, countered with two opposing claims: first, that a state-paid interpreter was not an establishment of religion; and second, that the denial of such a benefit to a student in a parochial school in effect constituted discrimination. The Zobrests, it was argued, had been denied equal protection of the law solely because of their religious beliefs, a hostile act that had been rejected historically by the Supreme Court.[33]

In this case, the Supreme Court held for the Zobrests, ruling narrowly that the payment of an interpreter for a deaf student was a child benefit. One of three significant church-state cases heard during the 1992–93 term that reflected an accommodationist point of view,[34] *Zobrest* seemed to open a judicial window allowing Catholic jurisprudence on education to ventilate the Supeme Court approach to First Amendment issues.

The arguments put forward by the Catholics in *Zobrest* were significant because they were, in effect, different and manifested a shift in traditional Church jurisprudence on education. Still concerned with the Church's basic need to maintain its autonomy to teach, rule, and sanctify its adherents, as well as the right of parents to choose the appropriate education for their children, the Church moved its theological stance more toward the center of the judicial continuum in *Zobrest*. Slightly altering its historical demand for accommodation to an acceptance of a "benevolent neutrality," the Church seemed to be more willing to accept the post-*Everson* judicial and political realities.

With regard to the merits of the case, the Catholics also utilized a defense that was more pragmatic and integrative than they had previously advanced in other amicus briefs and litigation. Stressing individual, rather than institutional, concerns, amicus argued for welfare programs that would provide, among other things, an interpreter as a medium for educational information for a disabled person. Such a standard, the Church claimed, precluded an establishment of religion and instead should be viewed as serving a "public benefit."[35]

While the types of arguments made in *Everson* were still considered valid and reflected the most theological and theoretical of the religious education cases up to that time, the original school bus case laid the groundwork for the Catholics to delineate between the purpose of church-state relations and the dynamic interplay of government, religion, and education. Building on the theological principles of both religious autonomy and parental rights, the Catholics consistently argued that religious education was a part of the right to free exercise of religion and a parental choice that served a public as well as a religious purpose. Thus, arguments on the merits consistently flowed from these standards, justifying child benefit theory and other notions of public benefits.

With *Zobrest*, however, the Catholics began to take a more realistic judicial stance. Basing their arguments on the right of the disabled to receive aid as a result of benefits assured by the Americans with Disablilities Act, they gave theological and other legal considerations less emphasis. Framing their arguments on more than just the religious clauses of the First Amendment, the Catholics integrated the rights of free speech and free assembly in *Zobrest*.

And, at the same time, they also stressed the application of the equal protection clause of the Fourteenth Amendment to the issue of religious liberty.

Thus began a conscious attempt on the part of the Catholic Church to enlarge the concept of freedom of religion and to use it to challenge the Supreme Court on the rules and tests that characterized its decision making in the past. This can further be seen in the recent case of *Board of Education v. Grumet.*

The Threads of *Grumet*

In 1977, the Satmar Hasidim, a large minority in the city of Monroe, New York, were incorporated, forming an independent village known as Kiryas Joel. Operating privately funded religious schools, the Hasidim chose to educate their children in the mores of their strict Jewish sect by themselves. This included speaking Yiddish, gender separation, distinctive garb, and other rigorous religious rituals. Their handicapped children, however, had to attend a school at a "neutral site," that is, at an annex to a Hasidic school, in order to qualify for public funding. After nearly a decade of such arrangements, the Supreme Court in 1985 held public expenditures unconstitutional, the result of its rulings in *Aguilar v. Felton* and *Grand Rapids v. Ball.*[36]

In response, the Hasidic residents sought relief by petitioning the New York legislature to pass a statute that would create and fund a separate school district within Kiryas Joel to serve the needs of their disabled children. Complying with this request, the government of New York enacted Chapter 748 of the Laws of 1989, in the hope of solving the unique problem of protecting the Hasidic children from the secular influences of the outside society.

Very soon thereafter, Louis Grumet, executive director of the New York School Board Association, brought suit against the Board of Education of Kiryas Joel. Contending that Chapter 748 was a violation of the principle of separation of church and state, he claimed that the law was an example of a religious gerrymander; that it supported a religious exclusion; and that the State of New York, in the process, had become an active sponsor in the establishment of religion.

As the case approached the Supreme Court, it attracted a significant number of amici.[37] The Catholics, among the concerned parties, viewed the case with extreme interest and decided to file an amicus brief. Based on their continuing theological concern for the general protection of the autonomy of the Catholic Church as provided by the First Amendment, the hierarchy also intended now to monitor the "proper development"[38] of Supreme Court jurisprudence in that area.

The Catholic views expounded in *Grumet* reflected both their theological tradition, and a newly found, innovative, and aggressive legal approach to the case. Essentially, the Catholics blamed the Hasidic dilemma on a "lack of [judicial] clarity"[39] brought about by the Supreme Court's often ambiguous decisions on religious liberty and education decisions. Returning to their two original principles of church and state, as expounded in *Everson* and later education cases, the Catholics supported the Hasidic claims that it was the obligation of the state to protect the autonomy of religious institutions to teach, rule, and sanctify their followers and that it was the right of parents, as believers, to choose the kind of education that would best serve the needs of their children. The Catholics maintained in their amicus brief in *Grumet* that both canons should be implemented by a "permissible," "legitimate," and "necessary" accommodation between church and state.[40]

The board of education on behalf of the Hasidim argued for a zone of accommodation, defending its actions by maintaining that the state had met the conditions of the *Lemon* test: first, that its action served a secular legislative purpose by providing bilingual, bicultural education within a secular learning environment; second, that it neither advanced nor hindered religion by providing state benefits neutrally to any child qualifying as disabled; and, third, that it avoided the possibility of excessive entanglement through the creation of an objective monitoring process. Grumet, however, turned the arguments around, claiming that the primary effect of the establishment of a special Hasidic school district *of itself* advanced religion and would, as a result, also cause state officials to become excessively entangled with matters of religion.

The Catholics presented a different line of argumentation for judicial consideration. In a more aggressive legal strategy, they attacked the inconsistency of the Supreme Court's establishment clause jurisprudence and opposed its "reflexive application" of the *Lemon* test to every church-state case.[41] They further called on the Court to "reconsider and abandon" both *Aguilar* and *Grand Rapids*, attacking those precedents as "twin blind guides" that only added to the "jurisprudential confusion" on the First Amendment.[42] Citing the high cost and low quality of the required alternative delivery methods, plus the bewildering accounting systems, amicus argued that *Aguilar* and *Grand Rapids* magnified "the disadvantages already inflicted on the class of children most in need of remedial attention" and "added another layer of disruption" to their lives.[43] The need for accommodation, the Catholics contended, was due to the detrimental effects perpetuated by the Supreme Court and its decisions based on "unsubstantiated hypotheticals," rather than on the legitimate needs of religious institutions.[44]

Then, in a second assault, the Catholics argued for the creation of a "suspect classification," that is, for an allowable preferential treatment for the handicapped, subject to strict scrutiny. Arguing the merits now, they asserted that the classification should be based not on religion but on the legitimate need of the state to advance a compelling interest: the instruction of disabled children.

The Supreme Court disagreed, ruling 6-3 that the establishment of a separate school system based on denominational lines, for whatever compelling state interest, created a legislatively drawn religious classification. The justices, however, left room for compromise: Justice Sandra Day O'Connor maintained in her concurring opinion that the district might be within a permissible zone of accommodation in the future, if it were to be created through legislation applicable to any municipality. Within a week, new legislation was, indeed, enacted, and Louis Grumet again brought suit against the State of New York.

The most interesting fallout of the case, from the Catholic point of view, however, was that the Supreme Court announced in January 1997 that it would reopen the debate on *Aguilar*—an unprecedented action. Taking up the argument of the Catholics in *Grumet*, the Clinton administration and the State of New York appealed to the Court to reconsider its ruling in *Aguilar.* As a result, Catholics now potentially found themselves in a position to provide remedial education to their students directly, an action that would help low-achieving students among its twenty-two thousand students in New York State alone.[45]

The Tapestry Comes into Focus

Catholic jurisprudence on education in America ever the past fifty years has produced a coherent tapestry, not a haphazard crazy quilt. The picture is woven with many threads, all of which serve to highlight the central theme, that is, the *theological* or *pastoral* independence, responsibilities, interests, and concerns of the Church. Thus, the first component of Catholic jurisprudence is to maintain, and increase where possible, the freedom of the Church to teach, rule, and sanctify its adherents. The status of the Catholic relationship to the American government has always been the crucial consideration in the Church's judicial challenges; therefore, the underlying legal arguments have always emphasized religious freedom over the protection of religious establishment, even in religious education cases.

The maintenance of Church freedom through litigation, then, has been the challenge of Catholic jurisprudence, particularly in light of the American constitutional principle of separation of church and state.[46] In Europe and other parts of the world where the Catholic Church has been able to maintain a privileged status as a result of concordats or other political arrangements, traditional judicial arguments have been based mainly on theology and natural law, and have been buttressed by political support. But, while some scholars have contended that natural law is the "official legal philosophy of the Catholic Church,"[47] the same cannot be said of American Catholic jurisprudence.

Instead, the use of innovative approaches characterizes the second component of Catholic jurisprudence: the fact that greater emphasis is now being placed on arguments from legal precedent rather than from religious dogma. During the 1990s, particularly, judicial rationales based on an integration of the rights of free speech, free assembly, and equal protection have enlarged the Catholic view of the First Amendment. Since *Everson* and *Lemon*, the Church has gradually moved away from supporting the rules and tests advanced by their precedents as it had in the past. This new unified approach has been developing since *Zobrest* and can be seen even more clearly in *Lee v. Weisman*.[48] At issue was the right of the Providence, Rhode Island, school board to allow voluntary prayer at a graduation ceremony. Acting as a friend of the court in this case, the Catholics approached the issue not simply from an establishment perspective, but also as a free speech issue.[49] Contending that religious liberty had to be viewed in the context of prior restraint and censorship, amicus also tied religious liberty to the other aspects of the First Amendment. Unfortunately, the Supreme Court ruled narrowly in the case, denying voluntary prayer but maintaining that its holding was based, not on the question of free speech, but on the question of what constitutes a voluntary event. Nevertheless, had the matter been decided more broadly, one could speculate that the Church's arguments would have been adopted or at least supported by the Court.

Third, Catholic jurisprudence has become more pragmatic and centralized. Indeed, the current solicitor general of the Office of Legal Counsel of the United States Catholic Conference (USCC), which serves the National Conference of Catholic Bishops—that is, the institutional agency of the Church, maintains that today cases are argued in light of calculated judicial policy rather than on simple Church doctrine.[50] This means, then, that the "times, technology, ecumenism, and the need for consensus building" are becoming major factors in the way that the institutional Catholic Church now approaches First Amendment cases.[51] Since *Everson* and the arguments within the Catholic inner circle of hierarchy, lawyers, and church-state specialists over the very involvement of the Church in the case, Catholics have institutionalized their efforts in legal affairs within a major office at the United States Catholic Conference (USCC). Serving the National Conference of Catholic Bishops, the pastoral and policy-making arm of the Church in the United States, the Office of Legal Counsel monitors First Amendment cases on the state level through each of the fifty Catholic Conference offices that operate in each state. The Office of Legal Counsel of the USCC assists state conferences where needed and eventually decides whether or not to file amicus briefs in particular cases. These decisions are based on merit and interest, as well as on the amount of time, financial resources, and expertise that the legal counsel has to make a difference. The counsel takes on approximately from one to six major cases a year, cases in which the USCC acts alone or in partnership with other religious organizations on matters of common interest. In short, the institutional Catholic Church in America today, headed by its politically savvy bishops, functions like any other interest group, targeting cases and causes that will advance its own special concerns.

Fourth, Catholic jurisprudence today also reflects a more assertive call for government accommodation, protection, and the inclusion of religious values in American education. In *Everson*, the Catholics originally tried to show that education was a matter of joint concern for both the Church and the state, thus constituting an area in which both institutions should cooperate. As a result, the Catholics hoped to create a climate for accommodation, that is, a closer relationship between the Church and the U.S. government that would make it possible for the Church to carry out its pastoral or teaching responsibilites in a climate of "benevolent neutrality." Expecting moral and financial support from the federal government for child benefits, the Catholics refused to accept the very clear lines drawn by the Court between that accommodation and what it meant by the establishment of religion. They continued to try to advance their notion of accommodation in a series of education cases involving release time and school prayer during the 1950s and 1960s, culminating in *Lemon*. Seeking remuneration for teachers who provided secular instruction in secondary-level parochial schools in that case, the Catholics persisted in their demand for accommodation, even into the 1990s. In *Zobrest,* the calls for greater accommodation were couched in terms of aid to the disabled, which, it was argued, was a dual obligation of the Church and the state. This argument was approved by the Court, and, strengthened by this turn of events, the Catholics advanced their most assertive claim for accommodation thus far in *Grumet*. Calling for the reversal of both *Aguilar* and *Grand Rapids,* they have openly opposed the requirement to provide remedial education at neutral sites. Significantly, the Court has agreed with the Catholic amicus argument and is going to reconsider these cases in its 1997 term.

Thus, the amicus briefs examined in the selected cases in this chapter reveal a continued commitment by the Church to maintain and advance its freedom for pastoral as well as civic reasons. They also make it possible to articulate the legal philosophy by which the Catholic Church intends to accomplish such an accommodation; that is, through a pragmatic, unified, and assertive jurisprudence designed to promote the specific Catholic educational agenda. But in light of other recent Supreme Court decisions, the question persists: is such a jurisprudence an appropriate or effective means to accomplish the Church's salvific responsibilities?

A Tapestry in Need of Reweaving

While the pursuit of a Catholic jurisprudence based on theology, pragmatism, precedent, and assertiveness has served as a valid means to advance Catholic religious and educational interests in the past, the economic and political context of these issues must now serve to impel the Church to question the effectiveness of a continued legal strategy also predicated on the need for a state accommodation to religious education in the United States. Clearly, the prediction of the Seventh-Day Adventists, which served as a warning in their amicus brief in the *Everson* case, still rings true today: religious involvement with the government "will lead inevitably to some form of state control of such religious schools."[52]

Indeed, a balance sheet of Supreme Court decisions on matters of church and state since *Everson* reveals that the judiciary has consistently rejected an accommodationist interpretation of the First Amendment. Rarely even attempting to define an acceptable "zone of accommodation" to religion, the Court has nonetheless allowed some ambiguities to exist and some exceptions to occur, as in the cases of *Zobrest* and *Grumet*. However, barring these notable aberrations, the Court has consistently advanced an educational jurisprudence based on a clear and tightly circumscribed separation between church and state. It has done this situationally during the past half century and has developed a corpus of law reflecting the need to protect religious liberty as it is embodied in the dynamic tension between the free exercise and establishment clauses of the First Amendment. Balancing religious rights with public needs and sacred practices with constitutional norms, the Court has consistently reinterpreted and redefined church-state relations, in turn deciding the merits of specific religious-education issues.

It has done this by creating judicial vehicles to challenge the unrestricted right of religious exercise, the most serious precedent having been established in *Sherbert v. Verner.* In 1963 the Court ruled that a "substantial burden" could be placed on religion for a "compelling" state interest, thus justifying the future reversal of many traditional religious practices at church-related educational institutions. These have included, but not been limited to, the eradication of discrimination against women, blacks, and homosexuals.[53]

The last example is most pertinent here, as it involves the religious, educational, and constitutional dilemma of a Catholic institution of higher learning, Georgetown University. The quandary was posed when a group of gay and lesbian students sought recognition and funding for their social organization, the

Gay People of Georgetown University (GPGU), in 1979. The matter escalated into a First and Fourteenth Amendment crisis when the university denied GPGU's petition, claiming that to recognize the group would give it legitimacy, be a violation of Catholic theological orthodoxy, and an "inappropriate endorsement for a Catholic university."[54] The students, on the other hand, argued that their civil rights had been violated and brought suit before the local court of the District of Columbia, and eventually the court of appeals.

During a decade-long legal battle,[55] the university also had to endure several significant financial assaults, a result of the fact that Georgetown was not in compliance with the human rights law of the District of Columbia. The university, as a consequence, had been denied the legal certification necessary to sell between $85 million and $200 million worth of bonds for a new student center and the restoration of other university buildings. When the court of appeals ultimately ruled in favor of the local government ten years later, it justified its decision on the fact that the state had a compelling interest to eliminate the university's biased treatment of gays and lesbians. The court maintained that the eradication of discrimination took precedence over the right of the university to implement its religious principles on campus. Further, it required that Georgetown University recognize GPGU and provide it with funding. At the same time, however, the court allowed the university to print a disclaimer on the publications of GPGU asserting that the organization did not represent the views of Georgetown University. Rather than take a chance that an unfavorable ruling would enjoin every Catholic university in the United States, Georgetown decided not to appeal the ruling to the Supreme Court. It agreed to all the terms of the summary judgment of the court and had to absorb the financial losses it had incurred.

Later, Georgetown University attempted to retaliate by challenging the ratification of the budget of the District of Columbia, an act that required the approval of the District of Columbia Committee of the House of Representatives. Even with some powerful congressional allies, however, Georgetown University lost its game of political hardball. Because the local and federal governments could control the university's right to sell bonds, provide federal assistance to students, and fund faculty projects and research, Georgetown and other church-related institutions of higher learning had, and continue to have, few legal options in clashes between religious values and public policy.

Further, this particular case also highlights the fact that if religious values cannot be protected from state intrusion where public funding serves as the lever to force religious compliance to state interests, greater accommodation could seriously jeopardize the ability of the Catholic Church to maintain its freedom and accomplish its salvific mission. Since the Georgetown case, most Catholic colleges have been wrestling with the best way to incorporate the muticultural diversity and ecumenism that they espoused so eagerly in the post-Vatican II years. The proliferation of gay rights groups and the call for pro-choice clubs, coupled with the controversies over AIDS awareness, sex education, and the availability of birth control, have created significant moral quandaries on Catholic campuses across America. Indeed, many universities have become increasingly concerned about the loss of their religious identity and have been challenged by the current pope, John Paul II, in his encyclical *Ex Corde Ecclessiae*, to return to their traditional missions and convictions.

The continued striving of the Catholic Church in America for a legal accommodation with regard to university education and life, then, could serve as a harbinger of potential problems for the Church's secondary and elementary schools as well. Indeed, an accommodationist judicial philosophy necessarily compromises the very principle of religious autonomy that the Church seeks to preserve.

If the Church is to maintain the commitment to its traditional mission, then it will have to make some hard choices: either reject federal funding totally or be willing to accept more inclusive notions of religious freedom and state involvement. The former is virtually impossible, given the reliance of Catholic institutions of higher learning and their students on government loans, assistance, and grants. The latter is at least plausible, if problematic.

The current economic and political realities of religion, education, and the law require the leadership of the Catholic Church in America to seize opportunities for growth and educational reforms that are already in the process of occurring. Voucher systems and tuition tax credits are already in place in Wisconsin and Minnesota, are being tested in New Jersey, and are under discussion in Vermont. New York has already unveiled a voluntary alliance with private and parochial schools, about 85 percent of which are Catholic schools, to help educationally troubled students. At the same time, Catholic elementary and secondary institutions will have to review and renew their mission to the inner city. In short, these changes will have to serve as a replacement for an accommodationist Catholic jurisprudence and help to redefine the legal notion as it has evolved. Indeed, the challenge to the Church today is to *accommodate creatively and flexibly to the state while remaining separate from it*, because only then will it be able to begin to find more effective legal ways to implement its religious responsibilities and education interests as it approaches the potentially changing law of the millennium.

Notes

1. Douglas Laycock, "A Survey of Religious Liberty in the United States," *Ohio State Law Journal* 47, no. 2 (November 1986): 418. This includes, particularly, the required reading of Bible passages from the King James version.

2. Anson Phelps Stokes, *Church and State in the United States* (New York: Harper, 1950), 2: 68.

3. *Pierce v. Society of Sisters*, 268 U.S. 510 (1925).

4. Felician Foy, ed., *The Catholic Almanac* (Huntington, Ind.: Our Sunday Visitor Publishing Division, 1995), 532.

5. *Everson v. Board of Education,* 330 U.S. 1 (1947); *Lemon v. Kurtzman,* 403 U.S. 602 (1971); *Zobrest v. Catalina Foothills Board of Education,* 125 U.S. (1993); *Board of Education v. Grumet,* 114 S. Ct. 2481 (1994).

6. See the amicus brief of the State of Massachusetts in *Landmark Briefs and Arguments of the Supreme Court of the United States: Constitutional Law,* ed. Philip B. Kurland and Gerhard Casper (Washington, D.C.: University Press of America, 1975), 889.

7. Amicus brief of the State of Massachusetts, 899.

8. Amicus brief of the State of New York, in *Landmark Briefs,* ed. Kurland and Casper, 982.

9. George E. Reed, former member of the National Catholic Welfare Conference Legal Department, interview by author, 23 June 1992.

10. The brief was written within two weeks by a team that consisted of James N. Vaughn, Jeremiah P. Lyons, George E. Flood, Eugene J. Butler, and George E. Reed. John Courtney Murray purportedly wrote most of part 5, which dealt with the philosophy of the First Amendment. Responding to the suggestions of Monsignor McManus, the general secretary of the National Catholic Welfare Conference (NCWC), Murray et al. were to emphasize the "reasonableness" and "importance" of religious liberty to American church-state relations. Reed interview. See also the letter of Monsignor William McManus to Monsignor Howard Carroll, 10 October 1946, NCWC Education Files, Archives of the Catholic University of America.

11. For a fuller explanation of these views, see John Courtney Murray, *We Hold These Truths* (New York: Sheed & Ward, 1960).

12. Amicus brief of the National Council of Catholic Men and the National Council of Catholic Women, 948. (Hereafter referred to as Catholic brief.)

13. Catholic brief, 965.

14. *Cochran v. Louisiana State Board of Education,* 281 U.S. 370 (1930)

15. Catholic brief, 96l.

16. Catholic brief, 961.

17. Majority decision in *Everson v. Board of Education,* 15–16.

18. A conversation between John Courtney Murray, S.J., and Monsignor William McManus of the National Catholic Welfare Council, reported by Father Joseph Komanchak in his unpublished manuscript on Murray's role in *Everson v. Board of Education,* 14.

19. *McCollum v. Board of Education,* 333 U.S. 203 (1948)

20. See the text of "Murray on the Arguments in the *McCollum* Case," from the Parson Papers in the Woodstock College Archives, 8. Generously provided by Father Joseph Komanchak of the Religious Education Department of the Catholic University of America.

21. Murray's influence within the Church infrastructure ascended during the 1950s into the 1960s with his Catholic interpretation of church-state relations, and particularly with the publication of *We Hold These Truths* (New York: Sheed & Ward, 1960). Although he was quieted at one point by the Vatican, he became the chief exponent of religious liberty and freedom of conscience at the General Council (1962–65) and even served as a consultant to President John F. Kennedy.

Murray was not alone in the Catholic condemnation of *Everson* and *McCollum*. Many Catholic intellectuals felt the same way. For example, Father Joseph Brady, a leading academic of the day, wrote a book on the two cases and entitled it *Confusion Twice Confounded*, a title he felt was appropriate because the Supreme Court had been both a "victim" of, and a "great contributor" to, the public confusion concerning the "place of religion in Amercian public and constitutional life." See Joseph Brady, *Confusion Twice Confounded* (New Jersey: Seton Hall University Press, 1955), 1.

22. John Courtney Murray, "Education for Professional Responsibility," a speech delivered sometime in April or May 1948, 9. Transcribed as "Murray's Wilmington Speech on *Everson* and *McCollum*." Generously provided by Father Joseph Komanchak of the Religious Education Department of the Catholic University of America.

23. "Murray's Wilmington Speech," 12.

24. See the amicus brief of the National Catholic Education Association (NCEA) provided by the United States Catholic Conference, 11–17, for the entire argument. Interestingly, since *Everson* and the continued growth of Catholic schools, amicus now threatened the existence of the state's schools, reversing the positions of nearly twenty-five years earlier!

25. Amicus brief of the NCEA in *Lemon v. Kurtzman*, 10.

26. *Pierce v. Society of Sisters*, 510; *Board of Education v. Allen*, 392 U.S. (1968).

27. Amicus brief of the NCEA in *Lemon v. Kurtzman*, 6.

28. Amicus brief of the NCEA in *Lemon v. Kurtzman*, 31.

29. Amicus brief of the NCEA in *Lemon v. Kurtzman*, 8.

30. The majority opinion of the Court in *Zobrest v. Catalina Foothills Board of Education*.

31. Amicus brief of the NCEA in *Lemon v. Kurtzman*, 9.

32. The argument was advanced in the Ninth Circuit. See 963 F. 2d at 1194.

33. See, e.g., *Zorach v. Clauson*, 343 U.S. 306 (1952); and *Wallace v. Jaffree*, 472 U.S. 38 (1985).

34. See the accommodationist opinions in *Lamb's Chapel v. Center Moriches*, 124 U.S. 352 (1992), and *Church of the Lukumi Babalu Aye, Inc. v. Hialeah*, S.Ct. 2217 (1993).

35. See amicus brief of the National Conference of Catholic Bishops in *Zobrest v. Catalina Foothills Board of Education,* provided by the United States Catholic Conference, 2.

36. *Aguilar v. Felton,* 473 U.S. 402 (1985); *Grand Rapids v. Ball,* 473 U.S. 373 (1985).

37. See a detailed explanation of all the positions of the amici in Jo Renée Formi-

cola, "*Everson* Revisited: 'This is Not . . . Just a Little Case Over Bus Fares,'" *Polity* 28, no. 1 (Fall 1995).

38. See amicus brief of the United States Catholic Conference (USCC) for the National Conference of Catholic Bishops, for *Board of Education v. Grumet*, as provided by the USCC, 1.

39. Amicus brief of USCC in *Board of Education v. Grumet*, 4.

40. Amicus brief of USCC in *Board of Education v. Grumet*, 4.

41. Amicus brief of USCC in *Board of Education v. Grumet*, 11.

42. Amicus brief of USCC in *Board of Education v. Grumet*, 11.

43. Amicus brief of USCC in *Board of Education v. Grumet*, 25.

44. Amicus brief of USCC in *Board of Education v. Grumet*, 28.

45. Linda Greenhouse, "Court to Consider Reversing Decision on Parochial Aid," *New York Times*, 18 January 1997, sec. A, p. 1.

46. Such behavior appears to be the approach of choice for religious groups today, particularly the religious right. See, e.g., John Moore, "The Lord's Litigators," *National Journal* 26, no. 27 (2 July 1994):1560–65.

47. Stig Stromholm, *A Short History of Legal Thinking in the West* (Stockholm: Norstedts, 1985), 268.

48. *Lee v. Weisman*, 112 S. Ct. 2649 (1992).

49. A copy of the brief is available through the United States Catholic Conference.

50. Philip Harris, solicitor general of the United States Catholic Conference, interview by author, 18 June 1993.

51. Harris interview.

52. Amicus brief of the Seventh-Day Adventists in *Landmark Briefs,* ed. Kurland and Casper, 904–5.

53. *Sherbert v. Verner,* 374 U.S. 398 (1963); on women, see *McLeod v. Providence Christian School,* 408 NW 2nd 146, Michigan Appellate Court 1987; on blacks, see *U.S. v. Bob Jones University,* 461 U.S. 574 (1983); and on homosexuals, see *Gay Rights Coalition of Georgetown University Law Center v. Georgetown University,* Superior Court for the District of Columbia; Civil Action no. 5863-80.

54. Father Timothy Healy, then president of Georgetown University, letter to alumni, 28 March 1988, 1–2.

55. For a recounting of the specifics, see Jo Renée Formicola, "The Gays, Georgetown, and the Government," chap. 12 in *Church Polity and American Politics,* ed. Mary Segers (New York: Garland, 1990).

5

Everson and Its Progeny: Separation and Nondiscrimination in Tension

Angela C. Carmella

Everson v. Board of Education[1] has always been considered a "strict separationist" decision.[2] Each of its opinions, the majority and both dissents, gives meaning to the Jeffersonian metaphor of a "high wall of separation between church and state," and together, they reveal a Court in fundamental agreement that the primary value embodied in the establishment clause from its very origins is this separation of religion from government. In the decades following *Everson*, its separationist interpretation often required the *exclusion* of religion from public schools, public property, and publicly funded programs. The inclusion of religion in public institutions and programs was occasionally justified as a permissible accommodation of religion;[3] but the Supreme Court never clearly articulated a doctrine of accommodation, and it continues to be understood among many legal academics as an unprincipled and unpredictable deviation from separation.[4]

Since the 1981 case of *Widmar v. Vincent*,[5] however, the Supreme Court has, in a number of cases, explicitly employed doctrines other than that of accommodation (often, but not always, under the free speech clause) to achieve this inclusion. While the separationist interpretation continues to be used, the Court in a long line of cases from *Widmar* to the 1995 decision in *Rosenberger v. University of Virginia*[6] has ignored the wall of separation and chosen instead to use concepts of equality, parity, generality, neutrality, and evenhandedness to place religious expression and activity on equal footing with comparable secular expression and activity. When framed as an issue of equal treatment or equal access, religious expression and activities can (and sometimes must) be included in, rather than excluded from, public schools, public spaces, and publicly funded programs. These cases have resulted in a new emphasis on the value of nondiscrimination in the distribution of, and access to, public benefits, resources and facilities.[7]

Thus, the Supreme Court's current establishment clause jurisprudence contains absolutely contradictory modes of reasoning, one focusing on separation, which demands the exclusion of religion from public "goods," and the other focusing on nondiscrimination, which permits or requires its inclusion. But these nondiscrimination and equal access concepts are not new to establishment clause jurisprudence; nor were they introduced into the jurisprudence through *Widmar*. In fact, they are present, and held in contradictory tension, in *Everson* itself. On the facts of *Everson*, parochial school students were included in a government program of bus fare reimbursements precisely because their exclusion would be discriminatory. The opinion's holding was rooted in a notion that all children must be treated the same, regardless of where they go to school. Under the historical discussion in *Everson*'s dicta, however, it seemed that the choice of parochial school should matter because religion is distinctly ineligible for government aid. Thus, parochial school students should be excluded from any publicly funded program. This inherent contradiction within Everson has set the jurisprudential development of the establishment clause along two very different trajectories.

The recently proposed amendment to the Constitution known as the Religious Equality Amendment is a mechanism for requiring the nondiscrimination interpretation in specific categories of cases, particularly in the context of education. The amendment would ensure that religious expression and conduct are treated like their secular counterparts in public institutions and in the distribution of public benefits. Proponents of the amendment reassure Congress that the change will not threaten most separationist holdings. The greatest change would be in making parochial schools eligible for generally available aid, including voucher programs, and in making public schools more amenable to student religious expression.[8]

This chapter questions the wisdom of any effort to amend the Constitution in this way. No doubt the Supreme Court's work in this area grows more confused by the year. But the contradictory tendencies of exclusion and inclusion, from *Everson* forward, are caused not only by the sloppy manner in which *Everson* was crafted but also and primarily by the multifaceted nature of religion and its complex relationship to government. The tensions cannot be eliminated because the paradigms of separation and nondiscrimination emphasize different truths about religion. Separation emphasizes the first truth, which is that religion is like no other human activity. With horizons beyond the temporal law, it claims a "higher authority," a prior authority, that supersedes any government. This total claim on a person gives it a special place and power in the lives of religious adherents. Nondiscrimination, on the other hand, emphasizes the second truth, which is that religion is like many other things; it shares properties with other human activities. Since religion is lived within the temporal world, it involves speech and association, the education of children, the delivery of social services and health care, the collection and investment of money, and the building of institutions. The real task of rethinking the Court's jurisprudence begins with subordinating the principles of separation and nondiscrimination to the primary goal of the establishment clause and free exercise clause: religious liberty.

Early Establishment Clause Interpretations

In the mid-1940s, the Ewing Township Board of Education reimbursed parents for costs incurred while sending their children to school on public buses. This was done pursuant to legislation in New Jersey that authorized school districts to make rules concerning transportation of children to school. Because the program included the reimbursement of fares paid by parents sending their children to Catholic schools,[9] it was challenged as an establishment of religion on the grounds that tax revenues were being used to support and maintain parochial schools.

In *Everson v. Board of Education,* the Court found the program constitutional.[10] Most significantly, the Court reasoned that a distinction needed to be drawn between laws designed to support religious institutions and laws that provided funds for the welfare of the general public. The former were undoubtedly unconstitutional under the establishment clause. The latter, however, when religion-blind on their face and in the way they are administered, were permissible. While the government cannot contribute tax monies to support a religious institution, government also cannot

> hamper its citizens in the free exercise of their own religion. Consequently, it cannot exclude individual Catholics, Lutherans, Mohammedans, Baptists, Jews, Methodists, Nonbelievers, Presbyterians, or the members of any other faith, *because of their faith, or lack of it,* from receiving the benefits of public welfare legislation. . . . [We must not] prohibit New Jersey from extending its general state law benefits to all its citizens without regard to their religious belief.[11]

The Court reasoned that because the program of bus fare reimbursements was a general program, denial of the reimbursement for parochial parents while it was provided to other parents would show hostility toward religious believers for choosing to send their children to religious schools.[12] The First Amendment "requires the state to be neutral in its relations with groups of religious believers and non-believers; it does not require the state to be their adversary."[13] Therefore, rather than exclude the parents of parochial school children from the program to ensure that no aid would go to religious schools, the Court included these parents to ensure that government was not their "adversary."[14]

Thus, the nondiscrimination or equal access reasoning was born in the initial interpretation of the establishment clause out of concern for the "free exercise" of citizens. The connection between nonestablishment and free exercise is not at all unusual, for both concepts emerge from the same commitment to religious liberty. Because civil penalties and prohibitions on religious exercise typically fell to those who did not belong to the established churches in colonial America, Jefferson and Madison believed firmly that disestablishment, in the Virginia context, required the removal of such deprivations. They believed that maintaining "denominational neutrality"[15] by forbidding the state to privilege any religion also promoted the free exercise of religion. As the quoted language from *Everson* suggests, nondiscrimination in the government's distribution of public goods, especially in a burgeoning welfare state, best achieved the goal of "no privilege, no burden" on account of religion.

But the majority opinion ventured beyond the nondiscrimination reasoning to a historical exegesis of Jefferson's "wall of separation" metaphor. In a tectonic shift within the opinion, suddenly the goal of "no privilege, no burden" for one's beliefs was deemed best achieved when religious practice was entirely disconnected from any government activity. Justice Black concluded that the establishment clause

> means at least this: Neither a state nor the Federal Government . . . can pass laws which aid one religion, aid all religions, or prefer one religion over another. . . . No tax in any amount, large or small, can be levied to support any religious activities or institutions, whatever they may be called, or whatever form they may adopt to teach or practice religion. . . . In the words of Jefferson, the clause against establishment of religion by law was intended to erect a 'wall of separation between church and State.'[16]

What emerges from this discussion of the metaphor of the high wall of separation was "utterly discordant"[17] with the nondiscrimination mechanism employed by the Court to reach its decision. A wall that separates church and state must exclude religion from benefit programs, especially in a large welfare state, to ensure that no tax revenues in any amount, large or small, flow to a church. A nondiscrimination analysis, on the other hand, functions to include religion, as a privately chosen activity, in any general benefit program, thus ensuring that all religious persons and groups are treated the same as nonreligious ones. While the Court seemed to place "general public benefits programs" outside the reach of this separationist analysis by drawing a distinction between such programs and the direct support of religious institutions, it never squarely faced the contradiction. The Court simply asserted at the opinion's conclusion that "[t]he First Amendment has erected a wall between church and state. That wall must be kept high and impregnable. We could not approve the slightest breach. New Jersey has not breached it here."[18]

The inconsistency was not lost on the dissenters, who further articulated a separationist reading of the historical materials. They criticized Justice Black's opinion for failing to apply the separationist interpretation to the facts before it, for surely if the founders intended that there be a high wall between "church and state," tax revenues could never flow across the wall to support any aspect of Catholic education. And bus fare reimbursements certainly did.[19] The nondiscrimination analysis appeared to deviate from a different, "correct" interpretation driven by the opinion's rigid separationist dicta. In fact, dissenters were concerned that the nondiscrimination analysis could not be contained. Justice Rutledge wrote,

No more unjust or discriminatory in fact is it to deny attendants at religious schools the cost of their transportation than it is to deny them tuitions, sustenance for their teachers, or any other educational expense which others receive at public cost.[20]

The dissenters highlighted the difficulty in deciding which analysis to apply and the radically different implications of each.

Underlying the contradiction within *Everson* is the definitional problem of religion. Religion either has secular counterparts or is thoroughly distinct from other types of human activity. It is either treated on a par with those secular counterparts or placed in a sphere wholly separated from government. It is either included within a category of comparable activities or excluded from any such category.[21] By emphasizing the concept of parity between religious and secular, which is necessary to a nondiscrimination analysis, the Court downplayed the distinctive nature of religion. The Court asserted that the township "does no more than provide a general program to help parents get their children, regardless of their religion, safely and expeditiously to and from accredited schools."[22] But the dissenters railed at how the Court "overlooks" the unique nature and role of religion and the way in which the Constitution differentiates "between religion and almost every other subject matter of legislation."[23]

It is, of course, true that religion is both like nothing else and like many other things. Religious schools provide a good illustration of this multifaceted nature of religion. They provide religious education and religious environments that secular schools, public and private, do not. They exist only because of a faith community and its faith commitment. But they also provide education in secular subjects, as do secular schools. They are involved in the nationwide enterprise of educating young people, perhaps the single most important public task of each generation. Thus the religious schools are both distinct from and similar to nonreligious schools. The legal determination each court and legislator makes is whether and when religious education, and the private choice for it, must be treated as a distinct, sacred endeavor that the state must not profane with its touch; and whether and when it must be treated as the provision of a public service that the state can regulate and fund like any other private provider. The *Everson* majority chose the latter perspective; the dissenters chose the former.

The two cases to follow *Everson* each spin out this tension between "no-aid" separation and "equal aid" nondiscrimination, between unique religion and religion-like-other-things. *McCollum v. Board of Education*[24] held that in-class religious instruction within the public school building, provided by outside clergy, was unconstitutional. The separationist analysis, building on the history developed in *Everson*, was fully and quite literally articulated here. Because government-sponsored activities occurred within the walls of the public school building, religious instruction had to be excluded, walled out—that is, placed on the other side of the wall of separation. The Court wrote, "Here not only are the State's tax-supported public school buildings used for the dissemination of religious doctrines. The State also affords sectarian groups an invaluable aid in that it helps to provide pupils for their religious classes through use of the State's compulsory public school machinery. This is not separation of Church and State."[25]

Four years later the Court retreated from a strict prohibition of "release time" programs. The arrangement challenged and found constitutional in *Zorach v. Clauson*[26] permitted students to leave school early to attend religious instruction at the church or synagogue of their choice. Students who did not do so attended a study hall period. Here the Court distinguished the facts from those of *McCollum*: no public school classrooms were used and no funds expended. While conceding that the separation of church and state "must be complete and unequivocal,"[27] the Court explained that the implications of a rigid separation "in every and all respects" would mean "the state and religion would be aliens to each other—hostile, suspicious, and even unfriendly."[28] It is not necessary for "government [to] show a callous indifference to religious groups."[29]

The analysis used in the opinion is often referred to as "accommodationist," meaning a nonneutral privileging of religion inconsistent with a separationist reading of the establishment clause. But reading *Zorach* and *McCollum* together, it becomes clear that their conceptual underpinnings were rooted in nondiscrimination principles much like that in *Everson*'s holding: there should be rough parity between religion and its secular counterparts. The Court in *Zorach* acknowledged the importance of religion in the lives of Americans and recognized that both secular and religious instruction needed to be part of the lives of schoolchildren whose parents were raising them in some faith. For parents who had chosen to send their children to religious schools, both types of instruction were already offered. For parents whose children were in public schools, however, only secular education was offered; the release-time programs were a way of making religious education available. The Court noted that government obviously could not coerce attendance, or undertake or finance or house the religious instruction, "[b]ut it can close its doors or suspend its operations as to those who want to repair to their religious sanctuary for worship or instruction."[30] In other words, the public schools could provide a "slot" in the week's curriculum. Just as *Everson* permitted a program of free bus rides to both public and parochial school children, the upshot of *McCollum* and *Zorach* together was that both secular and religious instruction were available to both public and parochial school children. By ensuring the availability of religious instruction of one's choice regardless of the school one attended, government protected religious liberty in a nondiscriminatory way—that is, it neither privileged nor burdened anyone "because of their faith or lack of it."[31]

The Two Trajectories of Everson

Lemon *and Strict Separation*

In the early 1960s strict separation became entrenched as the appropriate establishment clause paradigm. Decisions that required the exclusion of devotional religious practices like Bible reading and prayer from public school classrooms began to articulate simplified standards for compliance with the clause.[32] A law must have a secular purpose and a primary effect that neither advances nor inhibits religion. A third element—the prohibition of excessive entanglement of church and state—was announced in a 1970 decision that upheld property tax exemptions for religious institutions in order to avoid the entanglement in church affairs that would result from state oversight and foreclosures on religious property.[33]

These three standards—secularity of purpose, neutrality of effect, and autonomy of operation—were brought together in 1971 in *Lemon v. Kurtzman*.[34] The application of the "*Lemon* test" to a challenged law resulted, for the most part, in excluding religion from public revenues, schools, and spaces. Whenever public benefits flowed directly to a religious organization, separation became the operative analysis. The benefit was constitutional if it first went to an individual and was therefore considered only "indirectly" given to the organization, or if it flowed only to secular aspects of the organization's work. But if the organization was "pervasively sectarian," it was nearly impossible to segregate its religious activities from its secular ones. In case after case throughout the 1970s and into the 1980s, various types of aid to parochial schools that were deemed "pervasively sectarian" were struck down as being in violation of the *Lemon* test. Because most forms of aid to these schools were deemed to have the automatic nonneutral effect of advancing religion, a cure was impossible. Any government monitoring to ensure that religion was not advanced constituted impermissible entanglement.[35] *Lemon* came to be understood as the mechanism for maintaining the "high and impregnable" wall of separation. In what was perhaps the *Lemon* test's most rigid application, *Aguilar v. Felton* held that public school teachers could not enter parochial school buildings to provide remedial education to children entitled to these services by federal statute.[36] Outside the context of parochial schools, the Court also employed a separationist understanding of the proper relationship between religion and government. Case after case invoking *Lemon* required the exclusion of religious texts, speech, and symbols from public school, public space, and public funds.[37]

Widmar, Mueller *and Nondiscrimination*

For many decades the separationist analysis was ascendant, the accommodation theory was offered as its awkward alternative, and *Everson's* nondiscrimination holding was marginalized.[38] But the ascendancy of the separationist paradigm as articulated through applications of the *Lemon* test began to wane by the mid-1980s. Most commentators noted this at the time, but they tended to focus on the Court's equivocation in applying *Lemon* in several cases.[39] Far more significant was the retrieval of *Everson's* nondiscrimination holding, which began in the early 1980s with *Widmar v. Vincent.*[40] Now the nondiscrimination paradigm provides a different lens through which to view many establishment clause issues.

In the 1981 *Widmar* decision, college students at a state university had been denied access to facilities for their Bible study meetings. The state's argument was that use of university buildings for religious worship or teaching would breach the wall of separation. The Court disagreed, holding that the state could not deny this Bible study group access to the school's facilities. Because the school had made its facilities generally available for over one hundred student activities, it had created an open forum. Under the free speech clause, government cannot exclude speech from an open forum based on the content of that speech, and therefore religious speech could not be excluded from a forum in which all types of speech were welcomed.[41] The Court now found that an equal access policy was compatible with its establishment clause jurisprudence.

Compatibility is an interesting way of describing this jurisprudential development. The state's argument was no more than an honest application of the separationist analysis that had been employed repeatedly by the Court: to permit religion's access within the walls of the state university was to advance it, violating *Lemon*'s second prong, and thus to establish religion. Even where other types of speech were permitted, religious speech was different. It was religious! And the establishment clause mandated that it be treated differently, that it must be "discriminated" against, that it must be excluded.[42] But the Court chose to emphasize the different goal of equality and expressed a nondiscriminatory alternative: include religious activity on the same basis as comparable secular activities. Plainly stated, *Widmar* revisited the contradictions inherent in *Everson* and chose to follow the holding of that case. In *Everson*, the Court treated the parochial school student like the public school student; in *Widmar*, it treated religious speech like other forms of speech.

Widmar was obviously founded upon the well-settled open, or public, forum doctrine under the free speech clause. This enabled the Court to borrow a preexisting "equal access" structure to use as an alternative to the separationist reading of the establishment clause. But this structure was already present in *Everson*. In both cases the state was offering a public good—funds in one, facilities in the other—and the governing principle was nondiscrimination.[43]

Shortly after *Widmar* was decided, conservative religious groups petitioned Congress to enact the Equal Access Act, which was essentially an extension of *Widmar*'s holding to the high school context. This required any public high school receiving federal monies to give equal access to religious clubs on the same basis as any other noncurricular activity.[44] In the 1984 passage of the act, *Everson*'s nondiscrimination principle, specifically as it was articulated in *Widmar*, became embodied in federal legislation, at least with respect to high school extracurricular activities. Congress reasoned that to single out and exclude private religious expression and conduct would discriminate against religious people and groups on the basis of religion, which is clearly forbidden by the First Amendment. In 1990 a challenge to the constitutionality of the Equal Access Act failed. The Supreme Court in *Board of Education v. Mergens* held that where a high school creates a limited open forum under the statute and permits religious clubs on the same basis as other clubs, it does not violate the establishment clause.[45] In fact, excluding religious groups "would demonstrate . . . hostility toward religion."[46] Again the school district was simply applying the separationist interpretation of the establishment clause. How could it have known that the Court would view the situation through a completely different lens?

After *Widmar*, the nondiscrimination analysis continued to provide a competing paradigm to separation. *Lemon* ceased to be the sole analysis for establishment clause cases. In particular, cases concerning private religious access to public spaces and public property began to focus on the "limited public forum" or "public forum" analysis, in which private religious speech and symbols enjoy equal treatment with secular speech and symbols.[47] In the 1992 case of *Lamb's Chapel v. Center Moriches Union Free School District,* a public school that routinely rented its facilities to groups after school hours for social, civic, and recreational purposes had refused to rent to a church group showing a film about family and child-rearing issues.[48] The Court found that the school district had created a limited public forum. Because the district would permit the voicing of all views on family and child-rearing except religious ones within this forum, it therefore had discriminated on the basis of viewpoint in violation of the free speech clause. In another recent decision, *Capitol Square v. Pinette,* the Court held that the Ku Klux Klan had the right to erect a cross in a traditional public forum. This group's private religious expression had access to the open forum on the same basis as did any other group's expression.[49]

Even in these cases, however, where the equal access analysis is explicit, the tension between paradigms of nondiscrimination and separation still surfaces. One bloc of justices, namely, Scalia, Thomas, Kennedy, and Rehnquist, would avoid any establishment clause analysis, opting instead for absolute protection of religious expression on the same basis as other private expression in any limited or full public forum under free speech doctrines.[50] In *Lamb's Chapel,* however, Justice White applied the *Lemon* test to ensure that the religious expression in the limited public forum did not violate the establishment clause; and in *Pinette,* several justices concurred separately to assert that even a public forum can impermissibly advance or endorse religion. By subjecting the forum to the separation analysis, the Court has left open the possibility of excluding religious viewpoints and religious symbols even from otherwise generally accessible locations.

In addition to cases concerning religious access to public spaces and public property, which tend to invoke the open forum doctrines, a second line of cases more factually similar to *Everson* itself concerns equal access to generally available benefits.[51] The first case in this line came in 1983. In *Mueller v. Allen,* a tax deduction for certain educational expenses was made available to all parents in Minnesota.[52] Just as the *Everson* Court ignored the fact that the primary beneficiaries of the bus reimbursement program were Catholic school students, here the Court ignored the fact that the vast majority of those taking advantage of this tax deduction would be those sending children to private religious schools. Predictably, the *Mueller* dissenters followed *Lemon*'s separationist analysis and argued that this tax deduction constituted a subsidy for attending religious school and directly advanced religion. But the majority reached all the way back to *Everson*, citing it for having justified general benefits to all school children attending both public and private schools.[53] The Court wrote, "Just as in *Widmar v. Vincent,* where we concluded that the state's provision of a forum neutrally 'open to a broad class of nonreligious as well as religious speakers' does not 'confer any imprimatur of State approval,' so here: 'the provision of benefits to so broad a spectrum of groups is an important index of secular effect.'"[54] It is important to note that in several cases decided over the last decade in which laws were held unconstitutional because some public resource was available only to religious groups or activities, members of the Court have suggested that simply making a broader class of beneficiaries would "cure" the invalid statute.[55]

Next came the 1986 decision of *Witters v. Washington Department of Services for the Blind.*[56] This decision was based upon a similar notion of inclusion of religious choice in a program of general benefit. Washington State had denied a blind man the vocational rehabilitation assistance available to other blind students because he was planning to use the money for seminary study to become a pastor. The Court held that the establishment clause did not compel this result. The program made funds generally available, the money went to the student, and the placement of the funds was a private decision of that student. The Court found that state aid was not being given directly to a religious institution and that *Lemon*'s second prong was not violated.[57]

In 1993 *Zobrest v. Catalina Foothills School District* followed this "equal access" structure, holding that a deaf student is not barred from having an in-school sign language interpreter (to which he is entitled by a statute aiding all handicapped students) simply because he attends a Catholic school.[58] Citing *Mueller* and *Witters,* the Court wrote, "We have consistently held that government programs that neutrally provide benefits to a broad class of citizens defined without reference to religion are not readily subject to an Establishment Clause challenge just because sectarian institutions may also receive an attenuated financial benefit."[59] It must be noted that in order to invoke the nondiscrimination paradigm in each of these three cases, the Court had to characterize these "attenuated financial benefits" to religious organizations as the indirect result of individual choice. A direct benefit to a pervasively sectarian institution would have triggered the separation analysis.

Two years after *Zobrest,* the Court's decision in *Rosenberger v. University of Virginia* similarly resulted in the inclusion, as opposed to exclusion, of religion in a broad-based program at a state university.[60] A student activity fee charged by the school was used, in part, to reimburse the printing costs of a broad range of student publications, but the school refused to reimburse the costs for a Christian publication on the grounds that to do so would directly fund religion and constitute its establishment. The Court disagreed, holding instead that the refusal to fund constituted impermissible viewpoint discrimination under the free speech clause.[61] Quoting from *Everson*, the Court stated that when enforcing the establishment clause we must "be sure that we do not inadvertently prohibit [the government] from extending its general state law benefits to all its citizens without regard to their religious belief."[62] Moreover, any attempt to limit *Everson*'s nondiscrimination concept to speech in public facilities under *Widmar* would fail; the *Rosenberger* Court refused to draw a distinction between access to facilities (the *Widmar–Mergens–Lamb's Chapel* line of cases) and access to funds (the *Mueller-Witters-Zobrest* line of cases), finding that the student activity fund could be treated under the same principles as facilities because it was a "forum more in a metaphysical than in a spatial or geographical sense,"[63] but a forum nonetheless.

Mueller, Zobrest, and *Rosenberger* were 5-4 decisions, with strong separationist dissents that emphatically declared that the general availability of a program or benefit alone is not dispositive of its constitutionality. The *Zobrest* dissent reminded us that the Court in *Aguilar v. Felton* struck down a program that provided a general benefit to all poor children in need of remedial studies in order to keep public school teachers out of parochial school classrooms. The *Rosenberger* dissenters similarly reminded us that "evenhandedness," their term for nondiscriminatory equal access, is a necessary but never sufficient condition for upholding a general benefit and that factors other than breadth of recipients are always determinative of constitutionality. Equal treatment, for the *Rosenberger* dissent, is meant to be a "prerequisite to further enquiry into the constitutionality of a doubtful law. . . . It does not guarantee success under Establishment Clause scrutiny."[64] This "further enquiry" focuses on factors that define aid as direct or indirect, the recipient as an individual or a "pervasively sectarian" institution, and the funded activity as religious or secular.

It is true that there is no consensus on the Court that the generality and neutrality of a program are dispositive of its constitutionality. Most justices hold such programs to one test or another under the establishment clause: the program at issue is either compatible with the clause or not. Thus the Court is poised dead center between these two fundamentally different ways of relating religion and government. Justice O'Connor's concurrence in *Rosenberger* acknowledged that the two "bedrock principles" of nondiscrimination and "no aid" are in conflict. For the majority in that case, the reimbursement of the Christian publication costs simply ensured equal treatment of all "student journalistic efforts." For the dissent, it was the "direct funding of core religious activities by an arm of the State."[65] The definitional dilemma, inherent in *Everson*, remains. Is religion something that can be and should be treated like other, secular activities, or can it and should it be treated as something so unique, so sacred that it must be kept separate from government facilities and funds? Will a constitutional amendment help make that decision?

The Religious Equality Amendment

By the 1995 term the Court had substantially developed *Everson*'s nondiscrimination analysis, even if principles for its application were unclear. It had become a major competing paradigm to the separation analysis. In fact, Congress, too, had gotten into the act. In addition to the 1984 passage of the Equal Access Act, it recently passed reforms to welfare laws, including a provision making all social service activities undertaken by religious organizations eligible for public funding on a par with secular providers.[66] While it has always been the case that funding religiously based social service activities passed constitutional muster more readily than funding religious education,[67] this new federal statute, together with the Equal Access Act, places Congress at the forefront of encouraging the nondiscrimination paradigm when dealing with speech in public forums and with monies generally available on religion-blind criteria.

Moreover, an effort has recently begun in Congress to amend the Constitution to mandate the use of the nondiscrimination analysis wherever religion can be treated in parity with comparable secular expression or conduct. Known as the Religious Equality Amendment (REA), several versions have been proposed.[68] Representative Dick Armey's version has been taken most seriously by commentators and proponents and reads as follows:

> In order to secure the right of the people to acknowledge and serve God according to the dictates of conscience, neither the United States nor any State shall deny any person equal access to a benefit, or otherwise discriminate against any person, on account of religious belief, expression or exercise. This amendment does not authorize government to coerce or inhibit religious belief, expression, or exercise.[69]

Commentary has begun to appear,[70] and hearings have been held,[71] with proponents of the competing paradigms voicing their support or disapproval. For the most part, the REA appears to be aimed at overruling separationist decisions that prohibit various types of aid to parochial schools. In testimony before Congress, Professor Carl Esbeck explained:

> The Amendment prohibits discrimination on account of a school's or welfare provider's religious character. It makes no difference whether a school or

provider is pervasively sectarian or whether the nature of the direct aid is such that it can be diverted to a religious use. Most importantly, the courts no longer need to insure that government funds are used exclusively for secular, neutral, or nonideological purposes as opposed to religious matters. Religious-equality theory gets the judiciary entirely out of the business of such alchemy. All that is required is that the program have a public purpose.[72]

This interpretation would make it possible for states and municipalities to offer assistance to religious schools as part of aid given generally to private schools or generally to public and private education.[73] A voucher program available to parents for both religious and secular schools would be constitutional under the REA. The REA would also place private religious expression on a par with secular expression in the public school context. Thus, the reasoning behind the recent welfare reform measures, which permit funding of religious providers of social services on the same basis as secular providers, would be extended to religious schools; and the reasoning behind the Equal Access Act, which permits extracurricular religious clubs in public high schools, would be extended to lower grades. Furthermore, private religious expression in any public institution would be acceptable on the same basis as other forms of expression.

The interpretive problems posed by the competing paradigms of separation and nondiscrimination would not be completely resolved by the REA. Because these problems inhere in the nature of religion, the division of cases under the REA and the establishment clause would not be self-evident; they would still evoke arguments concerning the appropriate paradigm, as are evident in the 5-4 decisions in *Zobrest* and *Rosenberger.* In fact, the establishment clause would come to be equated with a separationist interpretation, just as the new amendment would embody the nondiscrimination interpretation. The tension between exclusion and inclusion would continue in the interpretations of two constitutional provisions, not just one. And even for cases clearly within its scope, the amendment will not necessarily succeed in placing the nondiscrimination analysis beyond the reach of some final review for "compatibility" with establishment clause tests.

But far above these practical considerations, the most significant concern raised by the REA is the fact that it attempts to answer the fundamental definitional question concerning the nature of religion: it decides that private religious expression and conduct are comparable to private secular expression and conduct. The drafters' choice is understandable. In the last fifty years, whenever the Court emphasized the uniqueness of religious practice, it excluded that practice from public resources under the establishment clause. To acknowledge the uniqueness of religion was automatically to invoke the separation paradigm. It is not surprising, then, that the drafters have done just what the Court has done when it wanted to circumvent the separationist analysis and give religion access to those public resources: view religion as an activity with secular counterparts.

But the reverse of the separationist "exclusion" of unique religion has been its specific protection under the free exercise clause. When religion's uniqueness has been denied, it has been reduced to nothing more than its secular counterpart, and its protection under the free exercise clause has suffered. This became apparent in 1990, when the Supreme Court held in *Employment Division v. Smith* that any facially neutral, generally applicable law was constitutional regardless of its impact on particular religious expression or practice.[74] This decision defined religion as nothing more than its secular counterparts. On its facts, a Native American using peyote for ritual purposes was treated the same as a person using it for recreational purposes. This dilution of protection was no doubt connected to the "equalizing" of religion in the establishment clause area. The parity sought under the nondiscrimination paradigm to afford equal access to benefits also brings with it equal treatment under burdensome laws.

Any effort to rethink the meaning of the establishment clause, and certainly any effort to control its interpretation by way of constitutional amendment, must begin with an acknowledgment of the multifaceted nature of religion—its uniqueness and its commonality. But in this connection it must be understood that religion enjoys constitutional protection only because of its unique place in human experience. Does that leave only a separation paradigm under the clause? No. For a coherent jurisprudence to develop, the uniqueness of religion must be disconnected from the separation paradigm: the "sacred" should not automatically trigger its separation from other human endeavors. Nor should religion's shared properties automatically trigger its equal treatment under a nondiscrimination paradigm. Instead, religious liberty must be retrieved as the primary goal of both the establishment and free exercise clauses because religion is *always* unique, *always* a phenomenon sui generis. Separation and nondiscrimination, as well as other concepts, such as accommodation, are merely means to that greater end. It is therefore necessary to focus primarily on protecting the integrity and vitality of religious expression and exercise, for only religious liberty, not separation or parity, is the goal of the religion clauses.

Notes

1. *Everson v. Board of Education,* 330 U.S. 1 (1947).

2. For purposes of this essay, "separation" refers to those situations where religion is treated as a unique activity and is specifically disabled with respect to (1) public funding, (2) access to public space, or (3) rights to expression; "accommodation" refers

to those situations where religion is specifically exempted or funded or given space or expression rights; "nondiscrimination" and "equal access" refer to those situations where religion is treated like other similarly situated activities and is eligible for funds, space, or expression rights on the same terms as those comparable activities.

3. See, for instance, *Board of Education v. Allen*, 392 U.S. 236 (1968); *Lynch v. Donnelly*, 465 U.S. 668 (1984); *Church of Jesus Christ of Latter-Day Saints v. Amos*, 483 U.S. 327 (1987).

4. The best attempt to articulate such a theory is Michael W. McConnell, "Accommodation of Religion," *Supreme Court Review* 1985 (1985): 1; and Michael W. McConnell, "Accommodation of Religion: An Update and a Response to the Critics," *George Washington Law Review* 60 (March 1992): 685.

5. *Widmar v. Vincent*, 454 U.S. 263 (1981).

6. *Rosenberger v. Rector and Visitors of University of Virginia*, 115 S. Ct. 2510 (1995).

7. This essay does not argue that every establishment clause issue fits into this nondiscrimination framework. The framework can be used only where it is arguable that some public good is generally available on religion-blind criteria.

Many other legal academics have noted the importance of these jurisprudential developments. See, e.g., Ira C. Lupu, "The Lingering Death of Separationism," *George Washington Law Review* 62 (January 1993): 230; Michael Stokes Paulsen, "Lemon Is Dead," *Case Western Reserve Law Review* 43 (Spring 1993): 795; Jay Alan Sekulow et al., "Religious Freedom and the First Self-Evident Truth: Equality as a Guiding Principle in Interpreting the Religion Clauses," *William & Mary Bill of Rights Journal* 4, no. 1 (Summer 1995): 351.

8. Steven T. McFarland, "The Necessity and Impact of the Proposed Religious Equality Amendment," *Brigham Young University Law Review* 1996: 627.

9. Private, for-profit schools were not included in the program.

10. *Everson v. Board of Education*.

11. *Everson v. Board of Education*, 16 (emphasis in original).

12. Because private, for-profit schools were not included in the program, it was not as "general" a benefit as it could have been—as the dissent points out. But the majority ignores this fact and treats the program as general aid to schoolchildren. The Court notes at 17 that the "general program" involves payment of "fares of pupils attending public *and other* schools" (my emphasis).

13. *Everson v. Board of Education*, 18.

14. *Everson v. Board of Education*, 16. The Court made it clear, however, that the state could provide transportation only to public school students.

15. *Larson v. Valente*, 456 U.S. 228 (1981)

16. *Everson v. Board of Education*, 15–16.

17. *Everson v. Board of Education*, 19 (Jackson dissenting).

18. *Everson v. Board of Education*, 18.

19. Justice Jackson (dissenting) wrote that the effect of the First Amendment "was to take every form of propagation of religion out of the realm of things which could directly or indirectly be made public business and thereby be supported in whole or in

part at taxpayers' expense." *Everson v. Board of Education,* 26. Justice Rutledge (dissenting) wrote that the "test" is that "money taken by taxation from one is not to be used or given to support another's religious training or belief, or indeed one's own." *Everson v. Board of Education,* 44.

20. *Everson v. Board of Education,* 58 (Rutledge dissenting).

21. Justice Rutledge, in dissent, wrote that the object of the First Amendment "was to create a complete and permanent separation of the spheres of religious activity and civil authority by comprehensively forbidding every form of public aid or support for religion." *Everson v. Board of Education,* 31–32.

22. *Everson v. Board of Education,* 18.

23. *Everson v. Board of Education,* 26 (Jackson dissenting).

24. *Illinois ex rel. McCollum v. Board of Education,* 333 U.S. 203 (1948).

25. *Illinois ex rel. McCollum v. Board of Education,* 212.

26. *Zorach v. Clauson,* 343 U.S. 306 (1952).

27. *Zorach v. Clauson,* 312.

28. *Zorach v. Clauson,* 312.

29. *Zorach v. Clauson,* 314.

30. *Zorach v. Clauson,* 314. The schools simply "accommodate their schedules to a program of outside religious instruction." *Zorach v. Clauson,* 315.

31. Of course the dissenters in *Zorach* thought of it differently. Justice Black wrote, "The First Amendment has lost much if the religious follower and the atheist are no longer to be judicially regarded as entitled to equal justice under law." *Zorach v. Clauson,* 320.

32. *Engel v. Vitale,* 370 U.S. 421 (1962); *Abington Township School District v. Schempp,* 374 U.S. 203 (1963).

33. *Walz v. Tax Commissioner,* 397 U.S. 664 (1970). On this analysis, the notion that tax-exempt status was a government "benefit" was subordinated to the entanglement concerns that arose from churches being taxed.

34. *Lemon v. Kurtzman,* 403 U.S. 602 (1971).

35. See, e.g., *Lemon v. Kurtzman,* 602; *Committee for Public Education v. Nyquist,* 413 U.S. 756 (1973); *Meek v. Pittenger,* 421 U.S. 349 (1975); *Grand Rapids v. Ball,* 473 U.S. 373 (1985). Note that in many of the cases, some aid is permitted (such as textbooks for secular subjects, which do not involve issues of teacher discretion on religious topics) while other aid is declared unconstitutional.

36. *Aguilar v. Felton,* 473 U.S. 402 (1985).

37. See, e.g., *Stone v. Graham,* 449 U.S. 39 (1980); *Wallace v. Jaffree,* 472 U.S. 38 (1985); *Edwards v. Aguillard,* 482 U.S. 578 (1987); *County of Allegheny v. ACLU of Pittsburgh,* 492 U.S. 573 (1989); *Texas Monthly v. Bullock,* 489 U.S. 1 (1989); *Lee v. Weisman,* 505 U.S. 577 (1992).

38. Note, for instance, that Justice Brennan's concurrence in *Walz v. Tax Commissioner* (holding tax exemption for churches constitutional) reasoned that it was constitutional on grounds that religious institutions should be treated like other tax-exempt nonprofits that give diversity and texture to civic life, and not on the majority's grounds that it avoided church-state entanglement.

39. *Marsh v. Chambers*, 463 U.S. 783 (1983); *Lynch v. Donnelly*, 668.

40. *Widmar v. Vincent*, 263.

41. An exclusion can be justified by a compelling state interest embodied in a regulation that is narrowly tailored to that end. The state had argued that the establishment clause's requirement of separation of church and state represented this compelling interest, but the Court disagreed.

42. Justice White's dissent in *Widmar* notes the problem of emphasizing religious speech as speech. In evaluating the majority's assumption that "religious worship *qua* speech is not different from any other variety of protected speech as a matter of constitutional principle," he wrote: "I believe that this proposition is plainly wrong. Were it right, the Religion Clauses would be emptied of any independent meaning in circumstances in which religious practice took the form of speech. . . . [Citations omitted.] If the majority were right that no distinction may be drawn between verbal acts of worship and other verbal acts . . . [many of our] cases would have to be reconsidered." *Widmar v. Vincent*, 284–85.

43. The Court would later make this connection explicit, asserting that there was no difference between the two. *Rosenberger v. Rector*, 2510.

44. *Equal Access Act*, 20 U.S. Code, vol. 20, sec. 4071 (1984). A school with a "limited open forum" cannot discriminate against student activities on the basis of "religious, political, philosophical, or other content of the speech." 20 U.S. Code, vol. 20, sec. 4071(a) (1984).

45. *Board of Education v. Mergens*, 496 U.S. 226 (1990). A plurality found that the act did not send a message of government endorsement of religion and therefore did not have the primary effect of advancing religion; the concurring opinion (whose votes made up the majority holding) wrote that the important factor was that no state coercion was involved.

46. *Board of Education v. Mergens*, 248.

47. Cases like *Lynch v. Donnelly* and *County of Allegheny v. ACLU of Pittsburgh* were understood to involve government speech and therefore not to be amenable to the open-forum analysis.

48. *Lamb's Chapel v. Center Moriches School District*, 508 U.S. 384 (1993).

49. *Capitol Square Review and Advisory Board v. Pinette*, 115 S. Ct. 2440 (1995).

50. *Lamb's Chapel v. Center Moriches School District* (concurring opinions of Kennedy and Scalia); *Capitol Square Review and Advisory Board v. Pinette* (opinion of Scalia).

51. Note that this line of cases, like *Everson* itself, finds that aid to "religion" through general programs is *permissible;* it does not, however, require the extension of benefits. Thus, it differs from open-forum analyses under the free speech clause that may require the inclusion of religious speech.

52. *Mueller v. Allen*, 463 U.S. 388 (1983).

53. *Mueller v. Allen*, 398.

54. *Mueller v. Allen*, 397.

55. In *Texas Monthly v. Bullock*, the Court held unconstitutional a sales-tax exemption for religious literature; Justice Blackmun suggested that a law that gave such an

exemption to all religious and philosophical literature relating to life-and-death issues and ultimate meaning would be constitutional. In *Board of Education of Kiryas Joel v. Grumet*, 512 U.S. 687 (1994), the Court held a law specifically creating a public school district within a Hasidic village unconstitutional; Justice O'Connor, in a separate concurring opinion, stated that a general law permitting the creation of separate public school districts applicable to all municipal villages would be constitutional.

56. *Witters v. Washington Department of Services for the Blind*, 474 U.S. 481 (1986).

57. *Witters v. Washington Department of Services for the Blind*, 487–88. Although the majority does not invoke *Mueller*, concurrences by Justices Powell and O'Connor emphasize the link between *Mueller* and this case: "State programs that are wholly neutral in offering educational assistance to a class defined without reference to religion do not violate the second part of the *Lemon v. Kurtzman* test, because any aid to religion results from the private choices of individual beneficiaries." *Witters v. Washington Department of Services for the Blind*, 490–91.

58. *Zobrest v. Catalina Foothills School District*, 509 U.S. 1 (1993). The Court found it significant that "a government-paid interpreter will be present in a sectarian school only as a result of the private decision of individual parents."

59. *Zobrest v. Catalina Foothills School District*, 8.

60. *Rosenberger v. Rector*, 2510.

61. Note, however, that if the university had directly reimbursed the publication (and not the printer) for printing costs, the Court would not have employed the nondiscrimination analysis.

62. *Rosenberger v. Rector*, 2521.

63. *Rosenberger v. Rector*, 2517.

64. *Rosenberger v. Rector*, 2541.

65. *Rosenberger v. Rector*, 2533.

66. *Personal Responsibility and Work Opportunity Reconciliation Act of 1996, U.S. Statutes at Large* 110 (1996): 2105, sec. 104. Sec. 104 is entitled "Services Provided by Charitable, Religious, or Private Organizations."

67. *Bowen v. Kendrick*, 487 U.S. 589 (1988).

68. H.J. Res. 127, 104th Cong., 1st sess. (1995) (Istook); H.J.Res. 184, 104th Cong., 2d Sess. (1996) (Armey); S.J. Res. 24, 104th Cong., 1st Sess. (1995) (Cochran); S.J. Res. 33, 104th Cong., 1st Sess. (1995) (Cochran); H.J. Res. 121, 104th Cong. 1st. Sess. and S.J. Res. 45, 104th Cong., 1st Sess. (1995) (Hyde-Hatch).

69. H.J. Res. 184, 104th Cong., 2d Sess. (1996).

70. Academic commentary includes Frederick Mark Gedicks, "Introduction: An Ambivalent View of the Religious Equality Amendment," *Brigham Young University Law Review* 1996: 561; Richard F. Duncan, "Public Schools and the Inevitability of Religious Inequality," *Brigham Young University Law Review* 1996: 569; John H. Garvey, "All Things Being Equal . . .," *Brigham Young University Law Review* 1996: 587; Sanford Levinson, "Constitutional Imperfection, Judicial Misinterpretation, and the Politics of Constitutional Amendment: Thoughts Generated by Some Current Proposals to Amend the Constitution," *Brigham Young University Law Review* 1996: 611; Steven

T. McFarland, "The Necessity and Impact of the Proposed Religious Equality Amendment," *Brigham Young University Law Review* 1996: 627; Rodney K. Smith, "Converting the Religious Equality Amendment into a Statute with a Little 'Conscience'," *Brigham Young University Law Review* 1996: 645.

71. Testimony at committee hearings has included House Committee on the Judiciary, *Hearings before the Subcommittee on the Constitution on Legislation to Further Protect Religious Freedom, Testimony of the American Jewish Committee,* 104th Cong., 2d sess., 23 July 1996; House Committee on the Judiciary, *Hearings before the Subcommittee on the Constitution on Legislation to Further Protect Religious Freedom, Testimony of Gregory S. Baylor,* 104th Cong., 2d sess., 23 July 1996; House Committee on the Judiciary, *Hearings before the Subcommittee on the Constitution on Legislation to Further Protect Religious Freedom, Testimony of William A. Donohue, Ph.D.,* 104th Cong., 2d sess., 23 July 1996; House Committee on the Judiciary, *Hearings before the Subcommittee on the Constitution on Legislation to Further Protect Religious Freedom, Testimony of Carl H. Esbeck,* 104th Cong., 2d sess., 23 July 1996; House Committee on the Judiciary, *Hearings before the Subcommittee on the Constitution on Legislation to Further Protect Religious Freedom, Testimony of Review. Elenora Giddings Ivory,* 104th Cong., 2d sess., 23 July 1996; House Committee on the Judiciary, *Hearings before the Subcommittee on the Constitution on Legislation to Further Protect Religious Freedom, Testimony of Forest Montgomery,* 104th Cong., 2d sess., 23 July 1996.

72. House Committee on the Judiciary, *Hearings before the Subcommittee on the Constitution on Legislation to Further Protect Religious Freedom, Testimony of Carl H. Esbeck,* 104th Cong., 2d sess., 23 July 1996.

73. Of course government always has the right to limit its support to public institutions; the REA only requires equal treatment for religious organizations when all similarly situated organizations (all private or all public and private) are to benefit from some general program. House Committee on the Judiciary, *Hearings before the Subcommittee on the Constitution on Legislation to Further Protect Religious Freedom, Testimony of Carl H. Esbeck,* 104th Cong., 2d sess., 23 July 1996.

74. *Employment Division, Department of Human Resources of Oregon v. Smith,* 494 U.S. 872 (1990).

6

The Wrong Road Taken

Stephen V. Monsma

> *Two roads diverged in a wood, and I—*
> *I took the one less traveled by,*
> *And that has made all the difference.*
> —Robert Frost, "The Road Not
> Taken"

Fifty years ago the Supreme Court faced the remnants of a de facto nineteenth-century Protestant establishment of religion. It was a socially, politically, and historically complex situation, one filled with tough theoretical issues. The Court faced several roads it could take. It is the contention of this chapter that in *Everson v. Board of Education* the Court chose the wrong road, with negative—even disastrous—results. *Everson* must rank as one of the worst decisions made by the Supreme Court—ranking with *Dred Scott* and *Plessy v. Ferguson*. It was bad law, rooted in not much more than the justices' own worldviews; it responded to a difficult, complex situation in the most simplistic of terms; and it has led to fifty years of muddled church-state law and the reduction of religious liberty in the United States.

At the outset it is important to see more exactly the situation that confronted the Supreme Court in 1947 and the path that it chose. The nineteenth century had been marked by an informal, de facto Protestant establishment. Historian Timothy Smith made this point in reference to the public school system as it emerged: "The school systems of cities both large and small were in fact instruments of an informal Protestant establishment. In a society weighted so heavily toward the Protestant side in wealth and numbers and traditions, little conscious effort was required to make them so."[1] Thus the nineteenth-century common schools were marked by readings from the Bible, moral lessons, and prayers. In addition, Christian references often suffused the statements of political leaders and acts of legislatures, funds were provided for a wide range of religious charities, laws promoting Sunday observances were common, and crusades against slavery and alcohol were steeped in Protestant Christianity.

But as the early decades of the twentieth century wore on, the forces of religious diversity and secularization gathered momentum. Catholics became a much larger presence in both numbers and political influence, the Jewish community emerged as a major force, and the Protestant churches were divided by fights over Biblical orthodoxy, with the modern, less literalistic forces winning control of most of the mainline denominations and seminaries. Meanwhile, the forces of secularization gained strength, especially among the more highly educated leadership groups in society.

As the United States emerged from World War II, the de facto Protestant establishment of the nineteenth century was largely a thing of the past, but various symbolic manifestations of it were still in evidence. This was especially true of the public schools, which were often marked by prayer, Bible readings, and the recognition and celebration of Christian holidays. Underneath this gloss, however, the public schools were largely secular in nature. It was in this context that the Catholic leadership put in place a renewed push for public funds for their increasingly expensive separate schools. Various other religious groups, such as Missouri Synod Lutherans, Dutch Reformed groups, some fundamentalist and evangelical Protestant groups, Orthodox Jews, Mormons, and Jehovah's Witnesses, struggled to live out their faith in the vaguely Protestant public schools or worked to establish their own schools.

The Road Taken

It was in this context that the Supreme Court in its 1947 *Everson* decision took the road of a renewed insistence on a strict separation between church and state that was to be marked by no government aid or support for religion. It is important to be clear on the extent to which Justice Hugo Black's majority opinion articulated a strict—even an absolute—separation of church and state. In words that continue to haunt church-state relations it declared:

> No tax in any amount, large or small, can be levied to support any religious activities or institutions, whatever they may be called, or whatever form they may adopt to teach or practice religion. Neither a state nor the Federal Government can, openly or secretly, participate in the affairs of any religious organizations or groups and vice versa. In the words of Jefferson, the clause against establishment of religion by law was intended to erect "a wall of separation between church and state." . . . That wall must be kept high and impregnable.[2]

Three things stand out in these words and in the vision of church-state relations they insist is the law of the land. First, they assert the no-aid-to-religion principle. They do so in absolute terms. "No tax in *any amount, large or small*" is permitted if it is intended to support *any* religious activity or *any* religious institution, of whatever nature. Second, the Supreme Court insisted that government may not take part in the affairs of "*any* religious organizations or groups," and—most astonishing—no religious organization or group may participate in the affairs of government. This latter position is asserted by the small "vice versa" at the end of the second sentence in the above quotation. The Court did not give any real guidance as to what it meant by this assertion, and there have been no attempts to enforce it legally, but it stands as a testimony to the radical doctrine of church-state separation the Court adopted as the law of the land in *Everson*. Third, the above quotation drives home and dramatizes the radical church-state separation doctrine articulated in the first two sentences of the quotation by adopting as a principle of constitutional interpretation Thomas Jefferson's "wall of separation" metaphor.

One can debate whether or not the interpretation of the First Amendment contained in the above quotation is good jurisprudence; however, no one can deny the absolute terms in which it was couched. It clearly and unambiguously interpreted the First Amendment as insisting upon a radical separation of church and state. That is the road that was taken.

Everson was a 5-4 decision, but the radical church-state separation position embraced by the majority was equally embraced by the minority of four. The 1947 Supreme Court was unanimous in arguing that the First Amendment created a near-absolute separation between church and state. The issue that divided the Court was whether Ewing Township, New Jersey, had violated the First Amendment by reimbursing not only the parents of public school children for transporting their children by bus to their schools, but also the parents of children attending Catholic schools. (There apparently were no other nonprofit, nonpublic schools in the school district, and thus the reimbursement scheme applied only to parents sending their children to public and Catholic schools.) The majority said no; the minority, yes. The dissenting opinion written by Justice Rutledge and joined by the other three dissenting justices echoed Black's extreme separationist ideology when it stated that the object of the First Amendment "was to create a complete and permanent separation of the spheres of religious activity and civil authority by comprehensively forbidding every form of public aid or support for religion."[3]

In this chapter I argue that in taking the road of radical church-state separation and no aid to religion, the Supreme Court took the wrong road, and that has made all the difference. The Court's answer to the remnants of a de facto Protestant establishment was to remove all religion from the public realm. It is my contention that in so doing it moved from one establishment, that of a generic Protestantism, to another establishment, that of a generic secular worldview. It did not move—as I believe it should have—from the informal establishment of a generic Protestantism to a true neutrality marked by a religious pluralism that welcomes and cooperates equally with persons and groups of all religious faiths and of none. In the next three sections of this chapter I consider three basic problems with the *Everson* decision, I then consider the religious freedom and public policy difficulties to which the decision has led, and in the last section of this chapter I suggest the outlines of an alternative, superior road that the Supreme Court could have taken.

A Decision Cut Loose from Historical Moorings

The first problem with the *Everson* decision is that it was not rooted in a careful analysis of original intent or sound historical reasoning. The Supreme Court claimed original intent as a basis for its decision, but fifty years later one is astounded by the simplistic reasoning and shallow historical analysis employed by Justice Black in his majority opinion. A jurisprudence of original intent is difficult, at best, because one is attempting, on the basis of incomplete, conflicting historical records, to decipher the intent of a body of persons who acted over two hundred years ago. This did not deter the Supreme Court majority in *Everson*. In seven pages Black purports to cut through all the historical complexities and see clearly the intent of the First Congress, which adopted the Bill of Rights. He is able to do so because he embraces the facile assumption that the First Amendment had the same purpose and intent as the Bill for Religious Liberty adopted three years earlier in Virginia. "This Court has previously recognized that the provisions of the First Amendment, in the drafting and adoption of which Madison and Jefferson played such leading roles, had the same objective and were intended to provide the same protection against governmental intrusion on religious liberty as the Virginia statute."[4] This is followed by a reference to three earlier Supreme Court decisions, none of which offers any more complete historical analysis aimed at supporting the claim that the First Amendment had the same intent as the Virginia Bill for Religious Liberty. In fact, the superficial nature of Black's analysis is revealed by the fact that he is dead wrong about Jefferson's playing a major role in the adoption of the First Amendment. Jefferson was not even a member of the First Congress but was thousands of miles away serving as the American ambassador in Paris. James Madison did play a major role in the adoption of the First Amendment, but to equate Madison's intent and Congress's action is unwarranted. Madison in fact proposed language for the First

Amendment that was quite different from what was finally adopted. The assertion that the First Amendment to the new federal Constitution had the same intent as a religious liberty amendment adopted by a state legislature totally ignores the fact that in 1789 the Bill of Rights was written to serve a quite different function (limiting the powers of the new, stronger federal government) than were state efforts to protect fundamental rights. A long list of reputable scholars and several Supreme Court justices have again and again raised fundamental questions about the assumptions underlying Black's original-intent reasoning.[5]

In his dissenting opinion Justice Wiley Rutledge gives a more thorough analysis of original intent than does Black in his majority opinion. But he also bases his analysis of original intent on the easy assumption that Virginia's earlier struggles over questions of religious liberty and James Madison's positions are determinative of the First Congress's intent. At one point Rutledge refers to Madison as being the First Amendment's author and at another point asserts the First Amendment was "the direct culmination" of the Virginia struggle for religious freedom.[6]

But I do not wish to spend too much time on the issue of original intent. There are far more serious problems with the *Everson* decision than its attempt to use original intent to support a strict separationist interpretation of the First Amendment. My chief reasons in bringing up original intent at all are that it demonstrates the superficial, almost offhand approach the Court took to a highly significant, extremely complex issue and that it has meant that the decision was not well moored in history. Each decision of the Supreme Court— and especially major, precedent-setting and precedent-shattering decisions such as *Everson*—answers some points of law but raises others and leaves many unanswered. If a decision is clearly rooted in careful historical analysis, that analysis can help provide answers to those unanswered questions. But when—as here—the historical analysis is extremely weak, the new principles of law being articulated are not given greater focus or precision by historical analysis within which they are rooted. The seven pages of historical analysis offered by the Court majority provide almost no guidance in terms of the decision's meaning and interpretation.

A Decision Rooted in a Sectarian View of Religion

To understand the nature and weaknesses of the *Everson* decision, it is also important to note that it was rooted in an Enlightenment worldview that is itself anything but neutral and universal. If the great world religions such as Catholicism and Judaism are "sectarian"—as the Supreme Court's opinions have often referred to them—the worldview in which *Everson* is rooted is surely no less sectarian. As John Courtney Murray wrote two years after the decision, it was rooted in "an irredeemable piece of sectarian dogmatism."[7] He then goes on to explain that "in the effort to prove that 'no establishment of religion' means 'no aid to religion' the Supreme Court proceeds to establish a religion—James Madison's."[8]

I have already noted the extent to which Black's majority opinion and Rutledge's dissenting opinion relied on Madison's views on religious freedom, especially as they related to the struggles for religious freedom in Virginia. Key to Madison's view was the idea that religious beliefs and practices could be divided into those that were common to all religions and important for maintaining public order and peace and those that were peculiar to specific religious groups. The former were public, accessible to all by natural reason and common sense, and sufficient to assure a peaceful, prosperous society; the latter were divisive, troublesome, unnecessary for public order, and best left to the purely private realm. Thus, beliefs and practices peculiar to specific religious groups had no public role to play. This view lay near the heart of the Deist, Enlightenment rationalism popular among the American leadership echelon of the late eighteenth century. And it is this faith that the Supreme Court adopted as its own in 1947. Rutledge's dissenting opinion acknowledged that for Madison "religion was a wholly private matter."[9] Elsewhere Rutledge insisted that religious teaching is a matter "of private right and function," that the religious "function [is] altogether private," that religion "is exclusively a private affair," and that religious training and belief "should be kept inviolately private."[10]

But the fact is that all three of the world's great monotheistic religions originating in the Middle East—Islam, Judaism, and Christianity—insist that religion is not a purely private affair that can be walled off from questions of public virtue and policy without doing violence to the very nature of their beliefs and practices. The concept of religion as a purely private matter was born in the rationalism of the eighteenth-century Enlightenment and has played a role in Western thought ever since. But it is a worldview, a set of faith-based beliefs and assumptions, that is accepted by many and challenged by many. As such, it is a belief that should be free to compete in the marketplace of ideas, not one that is accepted as a starting point for constitutional interpretation and to which all competing religious and secular belief systems must conform.

By rooting its *Everson* decision—with its strict separationism and no-aid-to-religion dogma—in eighteenth-century Enlightenment rationalism, the Court rooted its decision in a perspective every bit as narrow and space- and time-limited as many other religious and secular creeds.

A Decision That Is Not a Principled Basis
for Interpreting the First Amendment

The faults thus far outlined would not be all that serious if *Everson* and the legal doctrines laid down in it had proved to be a principled, predictable basis for future establishment clause decisions that resulted in a broadening of religious freedom for all. There are other landmark decisions of the Court that, while stretching original intent to the breaking point and while rooted in the personal philosophies of the justices, have nevertheless proven to be serviceable foundations for the development and strengthening of constitutional interpretations. This, however, has not proved to be the case with *Everson*. The true nature of the *Everson* disaster can be seen in fifty years of muddled church-state jurisprudence and a constricting of religious freedom.

In *Everson* the Court declared in ringing terms that the wall between church and state must be kept high and impregnable. In a sentence quoted earlier, it clearly drew a line in the sand: "No tax in any amount, large or small, can be levied to support any religious activities or institutions, whatever they may be called, or whatever form they may adopt to teach or practice religion." In light of such rhetoric it is no less than astounding that the Court found no violation of the First Amendment in the public funding of bus transportation to religiously based schools. Justice Robert Jackson complained in his dissent that the Court's decision reminded him "of Julia who, according to Byron's reports, 'whispering "I will ne'er consent,"—consented.'"[11] In this regard *Everson* foreshadowed fifty years of Supreme Court church-state jurisprudence. Strict separationist, no-aid-to-religion language still stands as the official interpretation of the First Amendment, yet countless forms of financial and other types of cooperation between government and religious groups continue. The Supreme Court has approved public expenditures for textbooks for religiously based schools, a paid chaplain in a state legislature, a city-owned crèche as part of a Christmas display, the placement of a cross on a state capitol grounds, and public funding for religiously based colleges and universities, hospitals, and teenage counseling centers.[12] In a recent year, 65 percent of the Catholic Charities' revenues came from government sources, as did 75 percent of the Jewish Board of Family and Children's Services' revenues, and 55 percent of Lutheran Social Ministries' revenues.[13] One study found that a majority of the religiously based child and family service agencies surveyed received over 40 percent of their budgets from government sources.[14] All this occurs in a society whose highest court has declared that its Constitution prohibits "any taxes in any amount, large or small" from going to support "any religious activities or institutions, whatever they may be called." The juxtaposition of soaring rhetoric declaring no aid to religion as a constitutional norm with a host of instances where government aids or supports religion is one of the key legacies of *Everson*.

This anomaly lies at the heart of what is wrong with the *Everson* decision and why it has taken constitutional interpretation down the wrong road. *Everson* approached a complex, difficult area of law and constitutional rights by adopting a simplistic standard: strict separation, no aid to religion, a wall of separation. But this is a standard that cannot be met. In a society composed of many deeply religious persons who are committed to a host of religious faiths, and in a society in which government is actively involved in almost all aspects of society, there is no way there can be an absolute separation of church and state of the nature put forth in *Everson*. Even such widely accepted practices as police and fire protection and water and sewage services for houses of worship, tax exemptions for religious nonprofit service agencies and schools, and the testimony of representatives of religious groups before congressional committees could be seen as violating an absolute church-state separation. To say there must be a high and impregnable wall between church and state that translates into no aid of any sort going to "support any religious activities or institutions" and that religious organizations cannot participate in the affairs of government is to set up a standard that never has been met and never can be met. The fact that the 1947 Court felt the need to find a basis to approve bus transportation to religious schools in the same decision that it created a standard of near absolute church-state separation bears testimony to the impossibility of meeting that standard.

The key problem that has haunted establishment clause jurisprudence ever since is that the *Everson* Court did not articulate any standards or principles by which one can determine what sorts of interactions or cooperative ventures are or are not constitutional. It merely bracketed its absolute-sounding church-state separation rhetoric with calls for government to be evenhanded and neutral in dealing with religion. It declared that "New Jersey cannot hamper its citizens in the free exercise of their own religion. Consequently, it cannot exclude individual Catholics, Lutherans, Mohammedans, Baptists, Jews, Methodists, Non-believers, Presbyterians, or the members of any other faith, *because of their faith, or lack of it,* from receiving the benefits of public welfare legislation."[15] It went on to say that the First Amendment "requires the state to be neutral in its relations with groups of religious believers and non-believers; it does not require the state to be their adversary. State power is no more to be used so as to handicap religions than it is to favor them."[16]

The tough theoretical question never considered by the *Everson* Court was how one squares its calls for an "impregnable" wall between church and state and the proscribing of the use of *any* tax dollars to aid or support religion with its injunctions for the state to be truly neutral in its relationships with all believers and nonbelievers and not to deny the benefits of public welfare programs to believers or nonbelievers because of their beliefs. To provide generally available public services to religious groups necessarily involves breaching the wall; to grant public benefits on a neutral basis to religious and nonreligious groups alike is to grant religious groups in certain circumstances public tax revenues.

The seeds of the subsequent church-state confusions were all present in *Everson.* One can either bar all interactions with, and tax-funded benefits to, religion or have public policies that neutrally make public benefits available to believers and nonbelievers alike; one cannot do both. Or, at least, to do both requires a careful, sophisticated, nuanced approach. In *Everson* the Court majority simply articulated a strict separation standard, then used evenhandedness and neutrality language to adopt a decision that violated its own strict separation standard without ever reconciling—or even attempting to reconcile—the two. Fifty years of confused—some would say chaotic—church-state jurisprudence has been the result.

Subsequent Supreme Court decisions have sought to bring greater clarity to church-state law and to resolve the basic conflict already present in *Everson*— but without success. More specifically, there has been one attempt to pour more meaning into *Everson*'s strict separationist norm and there have been two attempts to circumvent the full implications of its strict separationist norm without violating it. Their very lack of success suggests the conflict present in *Everson* is fundamentally unresolvable.

The *Lemon* test was an attempt to create a standard or test by which courts could determine whether or not the no-aid-to-religion strictures of *Everson* had been violated. This three-pronged test was first articulated by Chief Justice Warren Burger in 1971: "First, the statute must have a secular legislative purpose; second, its principal or primary effect must be one that neither advances nor inhibits religion; finally, the statute must not foster 'an excessive government entanglement with religion.'"[17]

The Court has ruled in most cases involving a challenged practice that there was a valid secular purpose for it. One of the few decisions that turned on this first prong of the *Lemon* test involved an Alabama law that provided at the start of public school class days a moment of silence for prayer or meditation.[18] The Court held that by mentioning prayer as a favored activity, the Alabama legislature was clearly signaling that a religious purpose or goal underlay the challenged provision.

Most practices that have been found unconstitutional based on failing the *Lemon* test have failed the second prong of the test: that they must not have the principal or primary effect of advancing or inhibiting religion. Well-known constitutional law scholar Laurence Tribe has pointed out that, in practice, the

Supreme Court tends not to ask whether the "principal or primary" effect is to aid religion but whether there is any effect at all of aiding religion. "The constitutional requirement of 'primary secular effect' has thus become a misnomer; while retaining the earlier label, the Court has transformed it into *a requirement that any non-secular effect be remote, indirect and incidental.*"[19]

The third prong of the *Lemon* test is that there must be no "excessive government entanglement with religion." The Supreme Court used this test to invalidate a New York City program that supported remedial assistance for children from low-income families in nonpublic schools.[20] It ruled that the system New York had established to make certain that religious elements were not being introduced into the remedial program resulted in an excessive entanglement of church and state.

There are two basic problems with the *Lemon* test. One is that the test has not resulted in settled, principled results. It was designed to reduce the uncertainty created by the *Everson*-articulated norm of strict separation and no aid to religion, but it has failed to do so. If anything, it has added to the confusion and uncertainty in church-state jurisprudence. Today, a majority of the sitting Supreme Court justices have indicated their dissatisfaction with the test,[21] it has given rise to many disputes over its interpretation and application, and there are some decisions reached by the Court where the test has simply been ignored altogether.[22]

The second problem with the *Lemon* test is that instead of bringing greater clarity to *Everson*'s no-aid injunction, the test has, if anything, introduced additional elements of uncertainty and subjectivism. To base decisions on the purpose or intent of the authors of a challenged action (the first prong of the test) places decisions firmly in the midst of subjective judgments of the highest order. Who is to say what the intent or purpose of a legislative body was in enacting a certain measure? Or what if, as Tribe has pointed out, one could demonstrate that a program with a clearly secular effect had a religious motive underlying it? "A legislature might, for example, vote to increase welfare benefits because individual legislators feel religiously compelled to do so."[23] It would be absurd to hold such a program in violation of the First Amendment, yet that is what the first prong of the *Lemon* test could be interpreted to demand.

The third prong—no excessive entanglement—has rarely been used by itself as a basis for finding actions unconstitutional and, as a stand-alone standard, gives little or no guidance. It implies some church-state entanglement is all right but gives no guidance on what constitutes *excessive* entanglement.

That leaves the second prong, namely, that the principal or primary effect of a challenged action must be neither to advance nor to hinder religion. But as seen earlier, this test as applied by the Court has come to mean *no* aid or advancement of religion. When restated in this manner, the test brings one back to the no-aid-to-religion standard articulated by *Everson,* with no further guidance as to what this means or in what circumstances some government cooperation or support of religion is constitutionally permissible and in what circumstances it is not.

One does not have to accept all the rhetorical flourishes that Justice Antonin Scalia has used to deride the *Lemon* test (he once referred to the *Lemon* test as "some ghoul in a late-night horror movie that repeatedly sits up in its grave and shuffles abroad, after being repeatedly killed and buried")[24] to be convinced that the test has not advanced the clarity and fairness of the Court's establishment clause interpretations. It has largely failed as an attempt to give greater clarity and pour more precise content into the sweeping words of *Everson.*

There have also been two means developed by the Supreme Court subsequent to *Everson* that have circumvented the full implications of *Everson*'s strict separation, no-aid-to-religion rhetoric without violating it. In fact, there has been a whole series of decisions approving a host of cooperative efforts between church and state without overturning *Everson*'s no-aid-to-religion language. This seemingly impossible task has been achieved, first, by making a sacred-secular distinction. This approach has been used to find a number of aid programs for religious organizations constitutional. It says that the activities or programs of religious organizations can be divided into secular and sacred, and government may aid, support, or recognize the secular ones without aiding, supporting, or recognizing the sacred ones. The government can thereby grant aid to religiously based organizations without aiding religion, since the aid is only going to the organizations' secular aspects. Thus the bedrock, no-aid-to-religion standard of *Everson* can be upheld while government aid or support can still flow to religious organizations.

Everson itself implicitly made this the basis of its decision to allow bus transportation funds for parents of children attending religious schools. It argued that bus transportation was similar to other public services such as police and fire protection, roads, and sewage disposal, and that such services are "separate and . . . indisputably marked off from the religion function."[25] Thus the New Jersey school district whose transportation reimbursement program was being challenged could reimburse parents for bus transportation without aiding religion. This sacred-secular distinction received fuller development in subsequent decisions. By making a clear-cut distinction between the religious and the secular elements in a college education, for example, and then funding only the secular elements, government financial aid can be given to a religious college without giving aid to religion (at least in legal theory). In one case, the Court observed that the challenged program of aid "was carefully drafted to ensure that the federally subsidized facilities would be devoted to the secular and not the religious function of the recipient institutions."[26]

Another decision noted that "the secular and sectarian activities of the colleges were easily separated."[27]

The problem with this distinction is that it is based on an assumption that in many instances is simply false: that the religious and secular aspects of a single organization or program can be simply and easily separated. In fact, for many deeply religious persons from a wide variety of religious traditions, their faith is inseparable from their daily lives. The basic reason many faiths have been motivated to establish schools, homeless shelters, adoption agencies, food pantries, and more is to live out their religious convictions. To them, all of life is sacred. Religious elements are interwoven into the secular aspects of their activities.

Recognizing that this is sometimes the case, the Supreme Court has held that if a religiously based organization is "pervasively sectarian," it may receive no government funds at all, since the religious and secular elements in such an organization cannot be separated. Thus any public funds would necessarily be aiding religion. In one case dealing with a South Carolina program that assisted in the construction of college and university buildings, Justice Lewis Powell, speaking for a 6-3 majority, wrote: "Aid normally may be thought to have a primary effect of advancing religion when it flows to an institution in which religion is so pervasive that a substantial portion of its functions are subsumed in the religious mission or when it funds a specifically religious activity in an otherwise substantially secular setting." [28] He then went on to make the point that the college whose receipt of government funds was under challenge did not have a pervasively religious character. On this basis, the Court has held that almost all forms of public aid to religious K–12 schools are unconstitutional (because such schools are pervasively sectarian) and public aid to religious colleges and universities and social service agencies is constitutional (because they are not pervasively sectarian).

There are, however, two basic problems with the "pervasively sectarian" distinction. One is that it has never been clearly defined by the Supreme Court. The plurality opinion by Justice Harry Blackmun in *Roemer v. Maryland Public Works Board* is the most complete and carefully crafted of the decisions reached by the Supreme Court in the aid-to-religious-colleges cases. Blackmun includes an extended discussion of the meaning of "pervasively sectarian" and lists six characteristics of the colleges whose receipt of government funds was being challenged that to him indicated they were not "pervasively sectarian." But at the end of this extended discussion Blackmun writes, "To answer the question whether an institution is so 'pervasively sectarian' that it may receive no direct state aid of any kind, it is necessary to paint a general picture of the institution, composed of many elements."[29] It is hard to disagree with the conclusion Justice Blackmun himself reached ten years later when he acknowledged that the "pervasively sectarian" standard is "a vaguely defined work of art."[30]

A second problem with the pervasively sectarian standard is the apparently discriminatory manner in which it has been applied. One's suspicions are immediately aroused by the fact that the Court has found all religiously based K–12 schools to be pervasively sectarian and has found all other religiously based educational or social service organizations whose receipt of public funds has been challenged not to be pervasively sectarian. Yet one study found that many colleges and universities, child and family service agencies, and international aid and relief agencies that receive public funds appear to have many characteristics of pervasively sectarian organizations.[31] But just as there are many colleges and universities, child service agencies, and international aid agencies that appear to be "pervasively sectarian," there also appear to be many K-12 schools that are not "pervasively sectarian." This was the conclusion, for example, reached by the Ninth Circuit Court of Appeals in *Equal Employment Opportunity Commission v. Kamehameha Schools* (1993).[32] This case concerned a private, nonprofit, Protestant school in Hawaii that had a policy of hiring only Protestant teachers. A non-Protestant denied employment brought her case to the EEOC. The school claimed exemption from religious antidiscrimination laws under exemptions the civil rights law provides to religious educational institutions. But the circuit court ruled against the school, holding that it was not religious enough—was not, in effect, pervasively sectarian—and thus the exemption Congress had granted religious educational institutions did not apply to it: "We conclude the general picture of the Schools reflects a primarily secular rather than a primarily religious orientation."[33] Using the "pervasively sectarian" category to hold public funding for religious K-12 schools to be unconstitutional and the funding of all other religious social service and educational organizations to be constitutional appears not to be rooted in the objective, factual situation.

A second basis the Supreme Court has sometimes used to circumvent the full implications of *Everson*'s strict separation, no-aid-to-religion stance is a combination of long tradition, the innocuous nature of certain religious practices, and the secularization of certain religious practices by their ceremonial nature or their accompaniment by secular symbols or practices. In 1984, for example, the Court declared that a crèche owned by the city of Pawtucket, Rhode Island, could be publicly displayed at the Christmas season. "The crèche in the display depicts the historical origins of this traditional event long recognized as a National Holiday. . . . The display is sponsored by the city to celebrate the Holiday and to depict the origins of that Holiday. These are legitimate secular purposes."[34] The Court also went on to note that the inclusion in the display of secular items, such as candy canes and reindeer, helped assure that the crèche would be taken as a secular, not a religious, display.

In embarrassingly clear terms Justice William Brennan, in a dissenting opinion joined by three other justices, declared:

> I would suggest that such practices as the designation of "in God we trust" as our national motto, or the references to God contained in the Pledge of Allegiance to the flag can best be understood . . . as a form of "ceremonial deism," protected from Establishment Clause scrutiny chiefly because they have lost through rote repetition any significant religious content. Moreover, these references are uniquely suited to serve such wholly secular purposes as solemnizing public occasions, or inspiring commitment to meet some national challenge in a manner that simply could not be fully served in our culture if government were limited to purely nonreligious phrases. . . . Their message is dominantly secular.[35]

It has been on bases such as these that a menorah in Pittsburgh's city hall and a chaplain in Nebraska's legislature have received Supreme Court approval.

Thus, *Everson*'s no-aid-to-religion and "impregnable" wall of separation norms can be upheld while still allowing some forms of religion into the public square. It is done by pretending that certain forms and manifestations of religion are in fact no longer religious. But that is, of course, a thinly veiled fiction for many deeply religious persons—and for many militant nonbelievers. To them, prayers at the start of legislative sessions, a recognition of God on coins and in the Pledge of Allegiance, and Nativity scenes are anything but secular. Depending on one's own beliefs, one may find them comforting and reassuring or a source of irritation and discomfort, but innocuous and secular they are not.

In unequivocal terms, *Everson* called for church-state separation and no aid to religion. But if one does not wish to follow this standard to its final conclusion and live with its results, one must find the means by which to have "reasonable" and desired forms of church-state cooperation in spite of the absolute terms laid down by *Everson*. Therefore, the sacred-secular distinction, the pervasively sectarian category, and the secularizing of familiar religious practices were invented for instances when the Court—and American society—wanted some forms of church-state cooperation and support. But the language of *Everson* and the *Lemon* test were always there to be called upon whenever the Court—and American society—wanted to bar a form of church-state cooperation.

There also is a third, more hopeful development in establishment clause jurisprudence, one that builds upon *Everson*'s mention of neutrality and evenhandedness in regard to public benefits. I will consider it in the last section of the chapter. But first it is important to note that *Everson,* the *Lemon* test, and the two means sometimes used to circumvent the full consequences of the strict separationist language of *Everson* have resulted not only in legal confusions but also in a serious constriction of religious freedom.

A Decision Resulting in the Constriction of Religious Freedom

The problems caused by *Everson* are more than simply a few untidy definitions or an underlying uncertainty in constitutional law. I am convinced that he basic reason the *Everson* decision was a disaster is that it has led to a serious constriction of religious freedom in the United States. Because of it, American society is less free and poorer today. This is true for three reasons.

First, when *Everson* is taken literally and its no-aid-to-religion norm strictly followed, it results not in government neutrality on matters of religion but in the disfavoring of religion and a favoring of a secular cultural ethos. Religious neutrality is violated when broadly, but not universally, accepted religious elements are present in government-sponsored activities and programs, as we saw earlier was sometimes the case in 1947; but it is equally true that religious neutrality is violated by their removal from all government programs. When all religious references, acknowledgments, ceremonies, and beliefs have been carefully removed from an activity or institution, one does not end up with an activity or institution that occupies a neutral, middle ground between religion and secularism. Instead, one ends up with an activity or institution that, for most intents and purposes, has been secularized. Political scientist A. James Reichley has expressed it well: "Banishment of religion does not represent neutrality between religion and secularism; conduct of public institutions without any acknowledgment of religion *is* secularism."[36]

What results when religion has been eliminated from the public realm is not a self-conscious, explicit promotion of an antireligious secularism—such would no doubt quickly be found unconstitutional by the courts—but what sociologist James Hunter has termed a secular cultural ethos or a "latent moral ideology" that is supportive of a thoroughly secular view of life and the world.[37] The diffuse, latent nature of the secular outlook that is thereby promoted does not make it any less powerful a force in American society today. Its very diffuse, latent, and therefore subtle nature may make it a more effective force for shaping attitudes and expectations than would one that directly and explicitly attacks religion and religiously based views of life and the world.

The removal of all elements of religion from public programs thereby results in government taking sides in the religious-secular debate taking place in American society today. Legal scholar Michael McConnell has framed the issue well: "In the marketplace of ideas, secular viewpoints and ideologies are in competition with religious viewpoints and ideologies. It is no more neutral to favor the secular over the religious than it is to favor the religious over the secular."[38] When a religious nonprofit organization or school is denied public funds that similarly situated, parallel secular organizations (whether public or private and nonprofit in nature) are receiving, religion is being disadvantaged by deliberate government policy. Or when—in a public school or public social service agency—history, science, and literature are taught or drug dependency, domestic violence, and homeless problems are addressed with no reference to religion or God, by default religion and God are declared unnecessary and irrelevant to history, science, literature, and severe social problems. This is a position to which secularism as a worldview adheres and which religion opposes. Given the size and impact of the modern, comprehensive administrative state—whose expenditures today account for over 30 percent of total domestic output[39]—the consequences for religious freedom are great.

In short, *Everson's* strict separation, no-aid-to-religion norm is anything but neutral. The subtitle historian George Marsden chose for his recent book, *The Soul of the American University: From Protestant Establishment to Established Nonbelief*, is striking.[40] In today's struggle between religious and secular mindsets, government agencies and programs have moved from supporting a generic, consensual Protestant establishment to supporting—implicitly, by default—the establishment of a generic secular cultural ethos. Both constitute governmental establishment of a belief structure; neither meets the norm of genuine governmental religious neutrality.

Some would argue that the loss of religious freedom resulting from *Everson* has been less in practice than in theory, since, as seen earlier, several means have been found to circumvent the strict separation, no-aid-to-religion language of *Everson*. Unfortunately, this is not the case. If anything, the means developed to circumvent the language of *Everson* contain within them even greater dangers of reducing religious freedom. They constitute the second reason why *Everson* has had the effect of constricting religious freedom. The key problem is that the means used to circumvent *Everson* carry with them pressures on religion to tone down its distinctive beliefs and activities, to secularize, to become like the rest of society. One needs to recall that there are two basic means by which religious programs or activities whose governmental recognition or support has been challenged can pass establishment clause scrutiny under *Everson*. One is to segregate one's religious and secular activities and not be too religious (that is, pervasively sectarian). Thus, to obtain the very same benefits that all other similar organizations are receiving, many deeply religious organizations must, in fact or in pretense, play down their religious nature or remove parts of their program from religious influence. Those that refuse to do so run the risk of losing government funding or other help. A study of mine demonstrates that many religious nonprofit organizations receiving public funds under these terms have been able to maintain a significant degree of religious autonomy and freedom.[41] Many of them engage in a variety of religiously motivated practices that seem to run counter to *Everson's* no-aid-to-religion norm and the sacred-secular/pervasively sectarian standard enunciated by subsequent courts. But they do so under an *Everson*-created cloud. I found that many—but not a majority—have experienced overt pressures to remove or tone down their religious practices. Many have been able to withstand such pressures, some have found subterfuges by which to get around them, and still others have toned down or compromised their religious practices. No one should pretend that this is government neutrality on matters of religion.

Similarly, when the Supreme Court says religious symbols can be used and public recognition of religion can take place only when the symbols and the religious tradition being recognized have been secularized by the presence of secular symbols, long tradition, or rote repetition—a second means by which the full implications of *Everson* have sometimes been avoided—religion is being demeaned and degraded. When a menorah is allowed to be displayed at the Hanukkah season only because it is accompanied by a Christmas tree and because the holiday it commemorates allegedly has "a secular status," as the Supreme Court ruled in one case,[42] Judaism and its contributions to American public life are not being honored or acknowledged. It is hard to disagree with Henry Siegman, executive director of the American Jewish Congress, when he reacted to this decision with these words: "We are unhappy that the Court strained to give the menorah a secular meaning. In a sense, this denudes the menorah of its truly religious significance."[43] Whenever religion is forced to pretend it is less than what it really is, religious freedom is being constricted.

A third reason that *Everson* has resulted in the constriction of religious freedom is more indirect and subtle than the first two, but is also probably a more severe limitation on religious freedom. It is that the radical, absolutistic church-state separation language used by the Black majority opinion and its effective invocation of Jefferson's "wall of separation" metaphor have done much to create a mindset or attitude on the part of many Americans that is even more destructive of religious freedom than the actual decision itself. The evidence in support of this conclusion is largely circumstantial, yet persuasive. Most Americans, and especially most Americans in leadership positions in society, accept the proposition that there should be a wall of separation between church and state. One study found 62 percent of the American population agreeing with the statement, "There should be a high wall of separation between church and state," and—even more significantly—95 percent of academics agreed with this statement, as did 81 percent of business leaders, 86 percent of media leaders, and 83 percent of government officials.[44] Clearly, the wall of separation metaphor has become a part of the American mindset.

It is also undeniable that this wall of separation mindset is often used to justify practices that seem clearly to violate persons' basic religious rights. Here, no systematic evidence has been gathered, but anyone who has studied the area of church-state issues will repeatedly come across examples. In one instance a teacher assigned her class to write a research paper. One student wrote on the life of Jesus Christ and was given a zero on the paper because, as the teacher explained, "the law says we are not to deal with religious issues in the classroom" and "we don't deal with personal religion—personal religious beliefs. It's just not an appropriate thing to do in a public school."[45]

In another instance the Department of Commerce rejected an application of Fordham University for federal funding for the construction of a new radio tower for its public radio station.[46] The review process gave the station the highest possible recommendation, yet the Commerce Department rejected the application because the station broadcasts a Catholic mass from the university's chapel for one hour each Sunday morning. The department claimed the broadcast of the mass violated a regulation against the use of funded facilities for religious purposes. The federal district court upheld the decision of the Commerce Department, finding that the restrictions against carrying religious programming "do not inhibit religion." Further, it held, "The challenged regulations are a product of the Secretary's efforts to comply with Supreme Court jurisprudence in this area."[47]

A third example also illustrates the problem. Devils Tower—a monolithic rock rising twelve hundred feet above the surrounding terrain—is a national monument in Wyoming.[48] It is a popular challenge for rock climbers. But it is also held sacred by many Native Americans and, especially in the month of June, is the site of religious rituals. The conflict between recreational climbers and Native Americans seeking spiritual renewal through meditation and religious ceremonies is all too clear. Therefore, in 1995 the National Park Service established a new management plan for Devils Tower National Monument that banned commercial climbing during June and provided, "[I]n respect for the reverence many American Indians hold for Devils Tower as a sacred site, rock climbers will be asked to voluntarily refrain from climbing on Devils Tower during the culturally significant month of June."[49] The plan worked: only 193 persons climbed the tower in June of 1995 compared with 1,293 in June of 1994. But one person, who guides climbers up the monument commercially, brought suit against the National Park Service and, amazingly, won a district court injunction suspending the management plan, since "affirmative action by the NPS [National Park Service] to exclude a legitimate public use of the tower for the sole purpose of aiding or advancing some American Indians' religious practices violates the First Amendment's Establishment Clause."[50] The judge reached that conclusion because the regulation required "climbers to conform their conduct in furtherance of those American Indians' religious necessities. This amounts to impermissible governmental entanglement with religion."[51] The tragic position of the court was that Native Americans' right to the free exercise of their religion was trumped by the necessity of government not to use religion as a basis to interfere with recreational climbers. This is where *Everson* has brought us.

What is most instructive in these three examples is that federal laws or federal court decisions were cited as reasons for the discriminatory action taken against religious persons or groups. If these cases had reached the Supreme Court, it might very well have found in favor of the religious persons or groups, since these decisions seem to go beyond most Supreme Court precedents. But the vast majority of instances that involve some religious slight or disadvantage, of course, never reach the Supreme Court. Thus the language used by the Court—especially when graphic or uncompromising and direct in nature—can have an impact far beyond the formal decision reached.

It is no exaggeration to say that *Everson* and the cases that have flowed from it have seriously compromised religious freedom in the United States and have led to the de facto, informal, subtle establishment of a secular cultural ethos.

A Better Road

There is a better road the Supreme Court could have chosen in 1947, one that is still available. It is the road of religious pluralism that leads to genuine government neutrality on matters of religion. The *Everson* decision articulated some support for the concepts of evenhandedness and neutrality when it comes to the dispensing of public benefits by government, since the Court used these concepts as means to justify its decision to hold government funds for transporting children to religious schools constitutional. If only the Court had developed this concept more fully and held it up as the basic principle to govern the interpretation of the establishment clause, fifty years of church-state confusion and constricted religious freedom rights would have been avoided.

Under the concept of pluralism and neutrality, the key question to be asked is not whether—in isolation from all else that is being done—religion is receiving government aid, recognition, or support. The key question should be one of discrimination or favoritism versus evenhandedness: whether government is favoring any one religion over any other religion in dispensing aid, recognition, or support, and whether government is favoring either religion as a whole or secular worldviews as a whole.[52] In *Everson*, as noted earlier, Justice Black's opinion spoke eloquently of not excluding individual believers or nonbelievers from any public benefits because of their beliefs and called for government to be "neutral in its relations with groups of religious believers and non-believers." What the Court failed to see was that its no-aid-to-religion principle itself violated the call for neutrality found a few pages later. If it had put forward neutrality as the bedrock principle, instead of no aid to religion and strict separation, it would have chosen a road much more in keeping with full religious freedom for all. Then the answer to the remnants of a nineteenth-century de facto Protestant establishment would not have been to bar all religion from the public square, thereby creating an establishment of secularism, but to welcome a plurality of religious and nonreligious beliefs to the public square.

Since the early 1980s a line of reasoning has been developing on the Supreme Court that is moving slowly and hesitantly in the direction of a genuine neutrality or evenhandedness. This line of reasoning was first clearly articulated in the 1981 case of *Widmar v. Vincent,* which ruled against a policy of the University of Missouri at Kansas City that excluded religious student groups from using university facilities for their meetings. That decision argued that excluding religious student groups from the use of university facilities that all other groups could use violated the religious groups' right to free speech and association. Justice Powell went on to argue that allowing the religious groups to use public facilities did not violate the establishment clause. He wrote that "an 'equal access' policy would [not] be incompatible with this Court's Establishment Clause cases."[53] Later he poured more content into this concept of "equal access" when he noted that the university had created an open forum "that is available to a broad class of nonreligious as well as religious speakers" and that "an open forum in a public university does not confer any imprimatur of state approval on religious sects or practices."[54] Both of these concepts—the availability of a public forum or benefit to a wide variety of religious and nonreligious groups and the absence of governmental endorsement or approval of religious groups or beliefs—were to prove crucial in the Court's subsequent development of this line of reasoning. Three cases are especially helpful in seeing this development.

Lamb's Chapel v. Center Moriches School District dealt with a school district's turning down the request of a church to rent a school auditorium to show a series of religiously based films on child rearing. The Supreme Court's unanimous opinion held that since the school district's "property had repeatedly been used by a wide variety of private organizations,"[55] refusing to rent to a religious group violated that group's free speech rights. In addition, the Court held that renting a public school facility to a religious group would not violate the establishment clause, since "as in *Widmar,* there would have been no realistic danger that the community would think that the district was endorsing religion or any particular creed."[56] The concepts of nonendorsement of religion and governmental neutrality in treating religious and nonreligious groups alike were more important to the Court's thinking than a strict no-aid-to-religion standard.

In 1995 the Supreme Court handed down two decisions that significantly strengthened the neutrality line of reasoning. One dealt with the placing of a cross on the grounds of the Ohio state capitol by the Ku Klux Klan. In this case the Court held that there was no establishment clause violation by Ohio's permitting the display of the cross. Justice Scalia, writing for a plurality of the Court, relied on neutrality and equal-treatment reasoning:

> The State did not sponsor respondents' expression, the expression was made on government property that had been opened to the public for speech, and permission was requested . . . on the same terms required of other private groups. . . . We find it peculiar to say that government "promotes" or "favors" a religious display by giving it the same access to a public forum that all other displays enjoy. . . . [I]t is no violation for government to enact neutral policies that happen to benefit religion.[57]

The most important neutrality decision of the Supreme Court is its 1995 decision in *Rosenberger v. Rector.* In this case, the University of Virginia had refused to fund a Christian student publication, even though it had funded fifteen other student opinion publications. In a close 5-4 vote, the Court held that the university's refusal to fund the publication violated the students' free speech rights and that funding it would not violate the establishment clause. In his majority opinion, Justice Kennedy used the language of neutrality to explain the Court's decision:

> A central lesson of our decisions is that a significant factor in upholding governmental programs in the face of Establishment Clause attack is their neutrality towards religion. . . . We have held that the guarantee of neutrality is respected, not offended, when the government, following neutral criteria and evenhanded policies, extends benefits to recipients whose ideologies and viewpoints, including religious ones, are broad and diverse.[58]

A program funding a clearly—some would say pervasively—religious publication was saved from establishment clause violation because religion was not singled out for favored treatment and the funding was extended to "the whole spectrum of speech, whether it manifests a religious view, an antireligious view, or neither."[59]

In summary, there is a recent, developing strain within the Supreme Court's jurisprudence that holds some forms of government accommodation and assistance to religious groups and their activities—even financial assistance—do not violate the establishment clause as long as that assistance is offered equally to all religious groups and to religious and nonreligious groups on the same basis.

The neutrality approach is a clear departure in establishment clause interpretation from *Everson*'s strict separation, no-aid-to-religion principle. When religious groups may not be excluded from participating in public programs or activities in which all other nonreligious groups are participating—even without giving up or segregating the deeply religious aspects of their programs— clearly the no-aid-to-religion principle is being ignored, if not challenged. This can most clearly be seen in the *Rosenberger* case, which involved financial assistance to a Christian student publication by a state university. The four dissenting justices clearly saw that the no-aid-to-religion principle and the sacred-secular distinction under which religious groups have sometimes been permitted to receive public funds were being undermined by that decision. They wrote: "Even when the Court [in the past] has upheld aid to an institution performing both secular and sectarian functions, it has always made a searching enquiry to ensure that the institution kept the secular activities separate from its sectarian ones, with any direct aid flowing only to the former and never the latter."[60] They went on to advocate the continued reliance on "the no-direct-funding principle" over "the principle of evenhandedness" of funding.[61]

This neutrality principle, if it had been adopted by the Supreme Court in 1947 instead of the strict separation, no-aid-to-religion principle, would have effectively scuttled the remnants of an earlier, informal Protestant establishment, as they ought to have been scuttled. But in their place it would not have put a scheme that, masquerading as neutrality, established in a favored position a secular mindset or ethos. Instead, it would have put in place a genuine government neutrality on matters of religion, one that favored no one religious system of belief over any other or either religious or secular belief systems over the other. Under such a system every religious and secular structure of belief would be free, as Justice Douglas once put it, to "flourish according to the zeal of its adherents and the appeal of its dogma."[62]

One can hope that the Supreme Court—however slowly and haltingly—is beginning to revisit the doctrine laid down fifty years ago in *Everson*, and that in the not too distant future it will clearly elevate the principle of government neutrality over that of a sterile no-aid-to-religion standard as an end in itself.

If that happens, the fifty years of constricted religious freedom that the United States has experienced as a result of the *Everson* decision will, in the broad sweep of history, be seen as no more than an unfortunate interlude in a broader movement toward greater religious freedom for all.

Notes

1. Timothy L. Smith, "Religion, Schools, and the Community of Values," in *Christianity and Politics: Catholic and Protestant Perspectives,* ed. Carol Friedley Griffith e (Washington, D.C.: Ethics and Public Policy Center, 1981), 99. On the de facto Protestant establishment of the nineteenth century, see also Stephen V. Monsma, *Positive Neutrality* (Westport, Conn.: Greenwood, 1993), 113–26.

2. *Everson v. Board of Education,* 330 U.S. 16, 18 (1947).

3. *Everson v. Board of Education,* 31–32.

4. *Everson v. Board of Education,* 13.

5. Among the more persuasive are Thomas J. Curry, *The First Freedoms* (New York: Oxford University Press, 1986); Daniel L. Dreisbach, *Real Threat and Mere Shadow: Religious Liberty and the First Amendment* (Westchester, Ill.: Crossway Books, 1987); Michael J. Malbin, *Religion and Politics: The Intentions of the Authors of the First Amendment* (Washington, D.C.: American Enterprise Institute, 1978); A. James Reichley, *Religion in American Public Life* (Washington, D.C.: Brookings Institution, 1985), chap. 3; Chief Justice William Rehnquist's dissent in *Wallace v. Jaffree,* 472 U.S. at 91–114 (1984); and Justice Clarence Thomas's concurring opinion in *Rosenberger v. Rector,* 1995 WL 382046 (U.S.), 17–20.

6. *Everson v. Board of Education,* 31, 33–34.

7. See John Courtney Murray, "Law or Prepossessions?" *Law and Contemporary Problems* 14 (1949): 30.

8. Murray, "Law or Prepossessions?" 31.

9. *Everson v. Board of Education,* 39.

10. *Everson v. Board of Education,* 51, 52, 53, 58.

11. *Everson v. Board of Education,* 19.

12. The relevant cases are *Board of Education v. Allen,* 392 U.S. 236 (1968); *Marsh v. Chambers,* 463 U.S. 783 (1983); *Lynch v. Donnelly,* 465 U.S. 668 (1984); *Capitol Square Review Board v. Pinette,* 1995 WL 38063; *Roemer v. Maryland Public Works Board,* 426 U.S. 736 (1976); *Bradfield v. Roberts,* 175 U.S. 291 (1899); and *Bowen v. Kendrick,* 487 U.S. 589 (1988).

13. On the first two of these organizations, see Sean Mehegan, "The Federal Connection: Nonprofits Are Looking More and More to Washington," *Nonprofit Times* 8 (November 1994): 43. On the third of these organizations, see *1996 Annual Report* (Chicago: Division of Church and Society, Evangelical Lutheran Church in America, 1996).

14. Stephen V. Monsma, *When Sacred and Secular Mix: Religious Nonprofit Organizations and Public Money* (Lanham, Md.: Rowman & Littlefield, 1996).

15. *Everson v. Board of Education,* 16. Emphasis in the original.

16. *Everson v. Board of Education,* 18.

17. *Lemon v. Kurtzman,* 403 U.S. 612–13 (1971). The quoted words are from *Walz v. Tax Commission,* 397 U.S. 674 (1970).

18. *Wallace v. Jaffree,* 472 U.S. 38 (1984).

19. Laurence H. Tribe, *American Constitutional Law,* 2d ed. (Mineola, N.Y.: Foundation Press, 1988), 1215 (Tribe's emphasis).

20. *Aguilar v. Felton,* 473 U.S. 402 (1985).

21. Justices Scalia, Rehnquist, and Thomas have frequently voiced opposition to the *Lemon* test in their written opinions. Justices Kennedy and O'Connor have also indicated their dissatisfaction with the *Lemon* test. See Kennedy's concurring opinion in *Lamb's Chapel v. Center Moriches Union Free School District,* 1993 WL 187864 (U.S.), and his failure to invoke the *Lemon* test in his majority opinion in *Lee v. Weisman,* 60 LW 4723 (1992), an omission that was criticized by Justice Blackmun in a concurring opinion. In a concurring opinion in *Corporation of Presiding Bishop v. Amos,* 483 U.S. at 346 (1986) Justice O'Connor wrote: "I write separately to note that this action once again illustrates certain difficulties inherent in the Court's use of the test articulated in *Lemon v. Kurtzman.*"

22. See *Marsh v. Chambers,* 463 U.S. 783 (1983); and *Lee v. Weisman,* 60 LW 4723 (1992).

23. Tribe, *American Constitutional Law,* 1211.

24. *Lamb's Chapel v. Center Moriches Union Free School District,* 6.

25. *Everson v. Board of Education,* 18.

26. *Tilton v. Richardson,* 403 U.S. 679 (1971).

27. *Roemer v. Maryland Public Works Board,* 426 U.S. 764 (1976).

28. *Hunt v. McNair,* 413 U.S. 743 (1973).

29. *Roemer v. Maryland Public Works Board,* 758.

30. *Bowen v. Kendrick,* 631.

31. See Monsma, *When Sacred and Secular Mix,* 120–27.

32. *Equal Employment Opportunity Commission v. Kamehameha Schools,* 990 F. 2d 458 (1993).

33. *EEOC v. Kamehameha Schools,* 461.

34. *Lynch v. Donnelly,* 680–81.

35. *Lynch v. Donnelly,* 680–81.

36. Reichley, *Religion in American Public Life,* 165 (emphasis in original).

37. James Davison Hunter, "Religious Freedom and the Challenge of Modern Pluralism," in *Articles of Faith, Articles of Peace,* ed. James Davison Hunter and Os Guinness (Washington, D.C.: Brookings Institution, 1990), 66–68.

38. Michael W. McConnell, "Equal Treatment and Religious Discrimination," in *Equal Treatment of Religion in a Pluralistic Society,* ed. Stephen V. Monsma and J. Christopher Soper (Grand Rapids, Mich.: Eerdmans, forthcoming).

39. See Campbell R. McConnell and Stanley L. Brue, *Economics: Principles, Problems, and Policies,* 13th ed. (New York: McGraw-Hill, 1996), 88.

40. George Marsden, *The Soul of the American University: From Protestant Establishment to Established Nonbelief* (New York: Oxford University Press, 1994).

41. See Monsma, *When Sacred and Secular Mix.*

42. *Allegheny County v. American Civil Liberties Union,* 492 U.S. 598 (1989).

43. Quoted in Ari Goldman, "Displeasure with Decision Voiced by Religious Groups," *New York Times,* 4 July 1989, 12.

44. See Ted. G. Jelen and Clyde Wilcox, *Public Attitudes toward Church and State* (Armonk, N.Y.: M. E. Sharpe, 1995), 59, 99. The academic leaders consisted of a sample of 155 respondents from Ph.D.-granting departments of political science, sociology, history, and English; the media leaders were a nationwide sample of members of the Radio and Television News Directors Association and newspaper editors in cities of more than 100,000 population; the business leaders were a sample of 202 respondents from persons listed in *Who's Who in Business and Finance;* and the government leaders were a sample of 106 respondents from the top 3,000 career and political appointees in federal government agencies. See Jelen and Wilcox, *Public Attitudes,* 30.

45. See *Settle v. Dickson County School Board,* 53 F. 3d 152 (6th Cir. 1995); and McConnell, "Equal Treatment and Religious Discrimination."

46. See *Fordham University v. Brown,* 856 F. Supp. 698, 699 (D.D.C. 1994); and McConnell, "Equal Treatment and Religious Discrimination."

47. *Fordham University v. Brown,* 698, 699.

48. For more information on this example, see Mindy Sink, "Religion and Recreation Clash at Park," *New York Times,* 1 July 1996, sec. A, p. 8; and *Bear Lodge Multiple Use Association v. Babbitt,* 96-CV-063-D.

49.. *Bear Lodge Multiple Use Association v. Babbitt,* 2.

50. *Bear Lodge Multiple Use Association v. Babbitt,* 11.

51. *Bear Lodge Multiple Use Association v. Babbitt,* 11.

52. For a more complete discussion of a genuine government neutrality serving as a basic guiding principle for church-state interpretations, see Monsma, *Positive Neutrality.*

53. *Widmar v. Vincent,* 454 U.S. 271 (1981).

54. *Widmar v. Vincent,* 275.

55. *Lamb's Chapel v. Center Moriches School District,* 5.

56.. *Lamb's Chapel v. Center Moriches School District,* 5–6.

57. *Capitol Square Review Board v. Pinette,* 6.

58. *Rosenberger v. Rector,* 10–11.

59. *Rosenberger v. Rector,* 11.

60. *Rosenberger v. Rector,* 24.

61. *Rosenberger v. Rector,* 7.

62. *Zorach v. Clauson,* 343 U.S. 313 (1951).

7

Everson and Moments of Silence in Public Schools: Constitutional and Ethical Considerations

Derek H. Davis

Those who choose to reflect thoughtfully upon the fiftieth anniversary of *Everson v. Board of Education*[1] are likely to divide into two different camps. On the one hand, separationists will celebrate the decision for its enshrinement of Thomas Jefferson's "wall of separation" as the metaphor that best describes the relationship that should exist between church and state in America. Accommodationists, on the other hand, being those who seek a larger role for religion in public life, are more likely to bemoan the decision for the very reason that separationists celebrate it—the "wall" language and the separationist framework it created for addressing church-state issues. But in fact the *Everson* decision was neither a total victory for separationists nor a total loss for accommodationists. While the decision was replete with separationist rhetoric and definitely laid the groundwork for a host of separationist decisions to come, its result—allowing Ewing Township, New Jersey, to reimburse parents for costs incurred to transport their children to and from parochial schools on city buses—was decidedly accommodationist. The Court, in other words, seemed to honor Jefferson by constructing a "high and impregnable wall," but then immediately set out to create at least one wide gate of safe passage.

The current law regarding moments of silence in the nation's public schools is in many ways a microcosm of the kind of separationist "wall"/accommodationist "gate" approach seen in the *Everson* decision. In 1985, in *Wallace v. Jaffree,*[2] the Court struck down Alabama's moment-of-silence legislation but then uncharacteristically assumed the role of counselor by telling legislatures everywhere how to craft a moment-of-silence statute that would pass constitutional muster. Many states subsequently took the message to heart and passed new (in some cases revising old) moment-of-silence statutes. The Court has not seen fit to revisit the issue to put its official stamp of approval on any of these statutes, but it is now widely assumed that moment-of-silence observances are constitutional, provided the Court's unofficial suggestions are followed. So, as in *Everson*, the *Jaffree* Court appeared quite serious about preserving Jefferson's separationist wall but simultaneously willing to cut yet another door for safe passage. While some have argued that the *Jaffree* case was simply another in a long line of church-state cases in which the Court seemed capable only of doublespeak, the Court saw itself as acting with sensitivity to the competing demands of the establishment and free exercise clauses, or, in its own words, of pursuing "benevolent neutrality which will permit religious exercise to exist without sponsorship and without interference."[3]

This chapter will not quibble with the constitutionality of moments of silence. It is conceded that, if drafted carefully, such enactments are probably constitutional. And, of course, moments of silence might in many cases have salutary effects upon participating students. It will be suggested, however, that on balance, for a number of ethical reasons, moments of silence are a bad idea and should not be part of the daily routine in America's public schools. To state it more matter-of-factly, what is legal is not always what is best when it comes to educating America's children.

Moments of Silence and the *Jaffree* Case

When the Supreme Court decided in 1985 to review the *Jaffree* case, twenty-five states already had moment-of-silence statutes.[4] Such statutes generally were responses to public sentiment that some form of prayer should be permitted, even encouraged, in the nation's public schools. More overt forms of prayer had already been held to be unconstitutional in *Engel v. Vitale* and *Abington Township School District v. Schempp*.[5]

In *Engel,* the Court struck down a twenty-two-word nondenominational prayer written by the New York Board of Regents for official use in the public schools of New York.[6] Pupils could remain silent or be excused from the room while the prayer was being recited, but the Court was not persuaded that this made the prayer acceptable. Justice Hugo Black, writing for the majority, wrote that "it is no part of the business of government to compose official prayers for any group of the American people to recite as a part of a religious program carried on by government."[7] He added that "religion is too personal, too sacred, too holy, to permit its 'unhallowed perversion' by a civil magistrate."[8] The Court's decision, needless to say, was one of the most controversial in its history.

Undaunted by the public vilification it received following the *Engel* decision, the Court agreed the next year (1963) to hear two more cases dealing with religion in the public schools. One involved a Pennsylvania statute providing that at least ten Bible verses should be read daily in each classroom in the state; the other challenged a Maryland statute that provided for the daily reading of a chapter from the Bible and/or reciting the Lord's Prayer. Deciding the cases together in *Abington Township School District v. Schempp,* the Court disallowed both practices as violations of the establishment clause.

Neither *Engel* nor *Schempp* dealt specifically with moments of silence. In *Schempp,* however, Justice William Brennan, in making the point that states could not use religious means to achieve secular ends when nonreligious means would suffice, noted by way of example that a state could not be prohibited from permitting "daily recitation of the Pledge of Allegiance, or even the observance of a moment of reverent silence."[9] This seemed to be the opening in the "wall" rationale of *Everson* that many state legislators were looking for. While it was not possible to compose prayers to be recited in classrooms, it did appear that periods of meditation, even periods of silence specifically for prayer, might be constitutional. Thus, not surprisingly, half of the states in the ensuing twenty-year period passed moment-of-silence statutes. The typical statute called for a moment of silence in the classroom for either meditation or voluntary prayer, although some called for meditation only. Lower courts were divided on the constitutionality of these statutes.[10] It was inevitable that the Supreme Court would feel compelled to address the constitutionality of moments of silence. The Court decided to tackle the moment-of-silence issue by reviewing *Wallace v. Jaffree,* a case involving Alabama's attempt to provide a framework for daily silent prayer in its public schools.

Jaffree involved a challenge to three separate Alabama statutes. One provided that teachers could lead "willing students" in a recital of a specified prayer that was set out in the statute. The Supreme Court upheld the lower courts' invalidation of this statute, in essence reaffirming *Engel v. Vitale.* A second statute authorized a one-minute period of silence for "meditation." The district court upheld this statute, and it was not challenged on appeal. It was the opinion of all concerned parties that a period calling for meditation alone did not invoke establishment clause concerns. One might question what possible motivation the Alabama legislature might have had for passing a meditation statute if it were not to provide specifically for a time for prayer, but the statute, all agreed, was facially acceptable. Whether or not such statutes should so readily be deemed constitutionally permissible is discussed below. The third statute provided for "meditation or voluntary prayer." It was this statute that was the focus of the case and that the Supreme Court, in a 6-3 vote, found to violate the establishment clause.

Justice Stevens, who authored the majority opinion, emphasized that the State of Alabama failed to "present evidence of *any* secular purpose"[11] for the statute, as required under the first, or "secular purpose," prong of the three-pronged test articulated in *Lemon v. Kurtzman.*[12] The Court looked primarily to the testimony of the statute's sponsor in the state senate, Donald Holmes, who unabashedly testified that the bill was an "effort to return voluntary prayer to our public schools" and that he had "no other purpose in mind."[13] Stevens noted that "even though a statute that is motivated in part by a religious purpose may satisfy the first [prong of the *Lemon* test], the First Amendment requires that a statute must be invalidated if it is entirely motivated by a purpose to advance religion."[14] Thus, since the statute endorsed prayer as a favored practice, it violated the establishment clause.

It was not Justice Stevens, however, but Justices Lewis Powell Jr. and Sandra Day O'Connor, who, in separate concurring opinions, strongly intimated that a moment of silence untainted by the religious purpose that so obviously characterized the statute in the *Jaffree* case would be permissible. Justice Powell, after concluding that the Alabama statute failed the "secular purpose" prong of the *Lemon* test, commented that a better-worded statute would not necessarily violate the second and third prongs. "I note," he stated, "that the 'effect' of a straightforward moment-of-silence statute is unlikely to 'advance or inhibit religion.' Nor would such a statute 'foster an excessive entanglement with religion.'"[15] According to O'Connor, "the relevant issue is whether an objective observer, acquainted with the text, legislative history, and implementation of the statute, would perceive it as a state endorsement of prayer in public schools. A moment of silence law that is clearly drafted and implemented so as to permit prayer, meditation, and reflection within the prescribed period, without endorsing one alternative over the others, should pass this test."[16] These statements adequately outlined how a constitutional statute might be written. Justice O'Connor even noted that existing laws in many states would likely pass establishment clause scrutiny since they did not "favor the child who chooses to pray during a moment of silence over the child who chooses to meditate or reflect."[17]

Following the *Jaffree* decision, of the twenty-five states that had moment-of-silence statutes, fifteen states, apparently confident that their statutes were in keeping with *Jaffree,* left them intact; seven states revised their statutes to comply with *Jaffree,* although one of these (Arkansas's) was later repealed; and three states invalidated their prior laws altogether. This left twenty-one states with moment-of-silence statutes, but two states enacted new statutes, so that presently twenty-three states have moment-of-silence statutes that would appear to meet the Stevens-Powell-O'Connor guidelines.[18] The typical statute, which leaves the decision for implementation with local school districts, is much like that of Texas: "A school district may provide for a period of silence at the beginning of the first class of each school day during which a student may reflect or meditate."[19] Some, like New Mexico's, require that moments of silent mediation must be implemented only at the request of the students.[20] All of the statutes presuppose that moments of silence are propitious, an assumption that can and should be challenged.

Ethical Arguments against Moments of Silence in View of the *Lemon* Test

Any number of ethical arguments might be advanced either for or against the observance of moments of silence. The latter half of this chapter consists of a presentation of five ethical arguments against moments of silence, some of which have a theological orientation. Most ethical arguments of a theological nature, of course, are not a significant part of the political debate associated with moments of silence because of the Supreme Court's requirement, pursuant to the *Lemon* test, that legislation reflect a secular purpose, that it not have the primary effect of advancing or inhibiting religion, and that it not create an excessive entanglement between religion and government. Since many might object, on the grounds of *Lemon*, to the presentation of theological arguments against moments of silence, it is appropriate to explain briefly why I do not consider these arguments to violate either the letter or spirit of the *Lemon* test.

In terms of political theory, the *Lemon* three-pronged test reflects the Court's understanding that the nation is essentially a liberal rather than a religious state. However, according to most modern accounts of the liberal state, this designation carries requirements that are in addition to the mandates of the *Lemon* test. Most significantly, according to most theorists, participants' dialogue in public discourse within a liberal democracy must be intelligible to other participants. Since religious language is unintelligible to many citizens, it should be translated into nonreligious language accessible to everyone. Religious motivation might lie beneath the veneer of certain legislation, but the arguments for or against the legislation must be essentially nonreligious or secular. By most accounts, this requirement is a logical antecedent to the *Lemon* test, which requires that the final product of public discourse—legislation—carry a secular orientation.

The work of John Rawls, of course, is pivotal for the entire tradition of liberal political thought. In *A Theory of Justice,* he makes these basic points in support of a secular basis for the liberal state.[21] Rawls's work has been highly influential in the United States and has widespread support among political theorists, albeit in varying degrees.[22] In recent years, liberal political theory has been challenged by a host of communitarian thinkers, all complaining basically that Rawlsian liberal theory unnecessarily undermines the viable contributions to the public good that specifically religious viewpoints can make. Among these critics is Stephen Carter, who argues in *The Culture of Disbelief* that religious arguments and even religion-based legislation should be countenanced in a liberal democratic framework.

It is my own view, contrary to Rawls and affirming Carter, that religious *arguments* in public discourse generally should be permitted. Common sense may dictate that on many occasions the one advancing a religious argument should translate that argument into secular language in order that it become more intelligible and convincing to others, but that should be the decision of the one advancing the argument. Nevertheless, it is suggested here, contrary to Carter and affirming Rawls, that when the public debate on a particular issue is completed and legislation is to be enacted—when the relative free-for-all that is American liberal democracy in which every conceivable viewpoint (religious and nonreligious alike) has been entertained—the legislation enacted, consistent with the *Lemon* test, should reflect essentially *secular* aims and effects. The greater weight of evidence is that the Founding Fathers, most demonstrably by omitting the name of God from the Constitution, intended to create what we generally refer to today as a liberal state. The decision to break with traditional political theory that placed human government under divine authority was the result of their belief that the power to frame a new government derived, not immediately from heaven, but from the American people. The Founders created a government that was to be "of the people, by the people, and for the people." This in no way was a denial of their personal religious (mostly Christian) convictions, but the new federal government was to be one in which the people were the responsible parties, not God. The product of public discourse was to be man's law, not holy law. This is the essence of a liberal state.

In the modern lawmaking process, politicians, like the Founding Fathers, may personally hold themselves accountable to God. But whether or not they do, they are in fact accountable to the people. Since the people are of diverse faiths, the product of public debate—legislation—should be religiously neutral (secular) so as to reflect the common good, not merely the good of those who prevailed in the debate. This kind of commitment is what is embodied in the *Lemon* three-pronged test.

In keeping with these principles, then, we turn now to a consideration of various ethical arguments advanced in opposition to moment-of-silence legislation. While many of the arguments presented are distinctly theological in nature, it is submitted that, consistent with the discussion above concerning the legitimacy of religious arguments, they should be considered in the public debate alongside other meritorious religious and nonreligious arguments. Any resulting legislation, however, either allowing or prohibiting moments of silence, should be couched in secular language, reflecting the requirements of *Lemon* and *Jaffree.*

Ethical Arguments against Moments of Silence

The presentation to follow makes five ethical arguments against moments of silence. The presentation is not intended to be exhaustive; certainly other arguments could be advanced against moments of silence. Nor is the presentation intended to be balanced in the sense of weighing the arguments against various arguments that favor moment-of-silence observances in public schools. The presentation, in other words, is decidedly biased against moments of silence. I shall leave to others the task of presenting opposing arguments favorable to the moment-of-silence practice.

To be absolutely clear, I should underscore the fact that the arguments presented are not arguments against the *constitutionality* of moments of silence; rather they are *ethical* arguments that a legislative body might consider in deciding whether or not to enact a moment-of-silence statute. I hope I have adequately demonstrated why consideration of these and related kinds of ethical arguments is not forbidden by our liberal democratic form of government and the *Lemon* test. The constitutionality of a properly worded statute is conceded. Such a statute is constitutional because it constitutes a Court-approved (*Jaffree*) gate in the wall of separation between church and state. Both the "wall" and "gate" were constructs of the *Everson* Court, and *Jaffree* is simply one case in which the Court deemed it appropriate to carve out a gate in the wall. If pressed, I would probably assert that a gate in the wall should not have been created for moments of silence because realistically (as I shall assert further in connection with the first argument to follow) they have the primary effect of advancing religion in violation of the second prong of the *Lemon* test. The Court, of course, did not make such a finding, holding that moments of silence might be promulgated for nonreligious as well as religious reasons. But in all candor, it seems to me that in virtually every case, moments of silence are enacted and observed for fundamentally *religious* reasons. Nevertheless, for purposes of this chapter, I concede their constitutionality and opt merely to advance five ethical arguments against their passage by any particular legislative body.

The Trivialization of Prayer

The first argument is that moments of silence tend to trivialize prayer. They are constitutional because they are supposedly prayer neutral; that is, students may choose to pray during the prescribed time of meditation, or they may use the time in other ways, such as to prepare mentally for the day or just enjoy the silence. Yet no one really disputes that moments of silence are primarily efforts to encourage prayer. As Walter Dellinger has said, "Since a normal school day ordinarily includes any number of occasions during which an individual student acting on her own initiative can engage in a moment of silent prayer or reflection, the formal creation . . . of an organized teacher-supervised moment of silence is an event that has no readily apparent purpose—unless the government is attempting to convey a message."[23] For the same reason, Dean Norman Redlich suggests that "all prescribed moments of silence are highly suspect."[24] Thus, in schools where the moment of silence is observed, school administrators, each day at the appointed time, are actually saying to students, "This might be a good time to pray." And students, being generally smarter than adults give them credit for, are fully aware that the preferred activity during the moment of silence is prayer. Many students, of course, will choose to engage in prayer during the period of silence and be grateful for the opportunity. Nevertheless, it is a sacrilege to expect certain students to pray without necessarily knowing what prayer is, the identity and character of the God to whom they are to pray, what kind of relationship might be possible with the receiver of the prayer, and what the consequences of the prayer might be.

For those within the Christian tradition, this point can be underscored on the strength of what Jesus Christ clearly taught in the New Testament. Luke 11:2–4 (the Lord's Prayer) and Luke 18:9–14 (comparing the prayers of a Pharisee and a tax gatherer) are clear examples of Jesus teaching his disciples *to pray,* but also how *not to pray.* Thus, the faithful Christian would not simply mandate prayer (especially for a child) without instruction as to content and method, that is, without teaching the child how to pray. To do so would be to encourage a child to undertake a spiritual task without the proper tools, which the New Testament suggests is not only unwise but dangerous to the practitioner's spiritual life. Instruction on theological specifics is an important matter about which public schools are prohibited by law from giving instruction. Why not leave prayer where it belongs—in forums outside the school, where there are ample opportunities for full discussion, explanation, training, encouragement, and participation in the religious life?

Some will surely say, in response to this line of thinking, "Well, then, why not explain to the children what prayer is all about?" But who will do the explaining? What will they teach? Do we allow each different religious tradition to give its version, only to confuse the children? Avoiding problems like these is what is behind the American commitment to the separation of church and state.

To expect or hope that some children might pray meaningfully without the advantages of instruction and mentoring is to deny them the benefits of the spiritual life. Moreover, by observing a moment of silence, are school administrators suggesting to students that prayer takes place only one minute per day? One would not generally think so, but young, impressionable children unfamiliar with the spiritual life may indeed receive such an impression. In short, moments of silence trivialize prayer. They may not trivialize prayer for those students whose homes, churches, synagogues, temples, or mosques have trained them to pray, but such students hardly need a moment of silence set aside by their school to pray; they will pray volitionally, perhaps many times during the course of a day. As James David Knight notes, "Prayer which is genuine cannot be prevented by the absence of a daily ritual; on the other hand, a daily ritual can thwart the meaningful purpose of prayer."[25]

The Secular Humanism Issue

Many advocates of religion in the public schools feel that moments of silence, given the Supreme Court's disallowance of more traditional religious exercises, might be the last remaining hope for arresting the trend toward secularism that pervades American public education. They believe that secular humanism is threatening to gain control of the minds of the nation's children, which would virtually assure the eventual demise of America as a godly nation. The absence of any form of prayer in the classroom, they argue, is a capitulation to the forces of secular humanism and a sure sign that God has been removed from the schools. The Reverend Jerry Falwell, for example, accuses public education of being "materialistic, humanistic, atheistic, and socialistic" and claims that many students are now morally bankrupt because "education has moved from centering on God to centering on man."[26]

This kind of reasoning is rejected by those who see the need for the government to remain neutral with regard to religion. John Swomley, for instance, contends that public education in America operates without any humanistic bias against religion. He says that many religious fundamentalists assume that secular humanism rejects a belief in God. They observe that the schools make no effort to teach students to believe in God, so they wrongly conclude that the schools are teaching secular humanism. Swomley then draws an interesting analogy. He points out that Buddhism does not include a belief in a personal god either, but one would not therefore conclude that the schools are teaching Buddhism simply because they are not instructing the students in the Judeo-Christian view of God.[27]

As James David Knight points out, the accusation that secular humanism pervades the public schools is somewhat inconsistent with the claim made by the religious right that 94 percent of Americans believe in God. If such a vast number believe in God, then why are the schools condemned as dens of god-less secular humanism?[28] As James Dunn has so appropriately asked, are all public school teachers being selected from the 6 percent who supposedly do not believe in God? If not, then why should there be such a phobia that the teachers are somehow the purveyors of atheistic humanism?[29]

Finally, related to the view that secular humanism has taken over the public schools is the belief that God has been removed from the schools and that he therefore must be returned to the schools. Donald Shriver considers it irrational for proponents of school prayer to speak of "putting God back into the public schools." He considers such thinking to reflect a feeble understanding of the biblical God. "God," he says, "cannot be brought to earth by our rituals. God does not 'need' our prayers to be in charge of any part of the universe."[30] To speak of putting God back in the schools assumes that someone had the power to remove him in the first place. As Dunn has observed, "It's as if we had the power to dump the Heavenly Father in a wheelbarrow and cart him around."[31] But even if it is granted that God has been "removed" from the public schools and must therefore be readmitted, the real question becomes, Whose version of God will be readmitted? Most schools, in an effort to respect the religious diversity among their students, would inevitably introduce a generic, lowest common denominator version of God. This result, again, would trivialize religion.

Today's Moral Decline

Many advocates of moments of silence claim that some form of religious activity in public schools is needed to stem the tide of rising immorality in America. They frequently point the finger at the Supreme Court for "removing" God from the schools and ushering in a period of moral decline. Christian-nation advocate David Barton, for example, claims that the *Engel* and *Schempp* decisions of the early 1960s have destroyed American society: "Following the judicial rejection of natural law and the embracing of relativism, the United States has become number one in the world in violent crime, divorce, illegal drug use; number one in the western world in teenage pregnancies; and number one in the world in illiteracy. . . . By removing divine law, the Court removed the source of our previous stability."[32]

It should first be noted that neither natural law nor divine law (terms that Barton seems to use interchangeably) has ever been officially enshrined as the basis for American law, nor has either ever been rejected; natural law and divine law exist alongside other modes of thought, philosophies, and world-views that have always served the formulation of law and public policy in the United States. What Barton means, of course, is that the removal of the traditional practices of teacher-led prayer and Bible reading, observed in a nation for many years on the strength of a cultural Christian hegemony, are indications that the nation no longer chooses to be governed by Christian ideals. What he fails to realize is that the federal courts never had the power to favor Christian practices over non-Christian ones, because of establishment clause constraints. And he also fails to recognize that by the time of the *Engel* and *Schempp* decisions, a dozen states had already banned teacher-led prayer and Bible readings, either by statute or by judicial decision. The Supreme Court was merely adopting the view that was already becoming prevalent among the states, a view necessitated not only by the establishment clause but also by the need to protect the growing number of non-Christian public school students against coercive religious discrimination.

That is not the main point to be made here, however. The point is that it is somewhat naive to blame the current moral decline on the Supreme Court decisions of the 1960s. It would be disingenuous to claim that those decisions could not have possibly contributed, however remotely, to the present moral decline, but we live in a complex society, and it should be recognized that many social forces have been at work over the past thirty-five years that might also have played a part. These would include rapid population increase; the post–World War II economic boom that fed materialistic attitudes; increased ethnic and religious pluralism; the rights movements of the 1960s—civil, women's, minority, children's, and criminal rights; the Vietnam War; and the prevalence of sex and violence themes in the media. All of these developments have had searing and lasting effects on our society. All morally minded Americans are vitally concerned about the moral slide that characterizes the times in which we live,[33] but it is inappropriate to blame the Supreme Court for causing it all and to think that government-initiated prayer (and moments of silence do represent government-initiated prayer) is going to solve the problem.

The Perspective of Religious Minorities

It is rare to find Jews, Buddhists, Hindus, Muslims, and members of other minority communities of faith who favor moments of silence. Why is this? First, members of minority religions fear that the decidedly Christian majority that characterizes most schools across America will use the moment-of-silence observance as a stepping stone to more specifically Christian prayer and religious activities. In many sectors of the country, Christians are hostile toward public education and do not mince words about their intention to "reclaim" the nation's schools. While Jerry Falwell could not be said to speak for all Christians, his sentiments are shared by many: "I hope I live to see the day when, as in the early days of our country, we won't have any public schools. The churches will have taken them over again and Christians will be running them. What a happy day that will be."[34] Given such an attitude, it is little wonder that members of non-Christian religions generally support the elimination of school-sponsored religious exercises in the schools. The outlooks of religious minorities, as well as nonbelievers, should be respected. The public schools belong to them, too.

The nation's public schools, from the time of their formation in the first half of the nineteenth century, have been looked upon as a means to unite citizens in educational concerns that are common to all the people, not as a means to divide the people based on their religious differences. The commitment to the separation of church and state, as articulated most forcefully in *Everson,* has for all of the nation's history been good, not bad, for America, because it has protected the sanctity of religion in the private sphere without allowing it to become a divisive force in the public sphere. In the long term, legislation that sanctions government-initiated religious activities such as moments of silence will tend only to divide the American people.

Members of religious minorities also tend to oppose moments of silence for a second important reason. Moments of silence, as opportunities for spiritual reflection or meditation, often carry little meaning for some religious traditions. In the Islamic tradition, for example, there are several forms of prescribed prayer. The *Salat* ritual calls for prayer five times each day, performed while facing Mecca, preferably while kneeling. Each of the five prayers should generally be at least five to ten minutes long, and the prayers typically involve reciting aloud verses from the Quran and invoking one of God's holy names. Obviously, this form of prayer could hardly be executed within the typical moment-of-silence framework.[35] Many school administrators permit Muslim students to be excused to a safe, private area at appropriate times during the day for the offering of such mandatory prayers.[36] Some Muslims also engage in the *Dhikr* form of prayer, which is the glorifying of Allah with certain fixed phrases, repeated in a ritual order, either aloud or in the mind, with special breathings and physical movements. While Dhikr might be observed in a moment of silence, it would not be without some difficulty.[37] *Wird* prayer is also a regular form of Islamic prayer, involving private prayer to Allah at a definite time of day or night. While this form of prayer might be possible during a moment of silence, it would still break with traditional Wird prayers, which involve verbal recitations lasting far longer than one minute.[38]

There are today approximately six million Muslims living in the United States. While many Muslim children attend special Islamic schools, many attend public schools. The worship practices of these children, as well as those of other religious traditions,[39] are often overlooked by school officials who are familiar only with worship, meditation, and prayer practices within the more familiar Judeo-Christian tradition. If legislatures and school officials intend for moments of silence to be an outlet for spiritual reflection by children representing the ever-broadening range of religious practices in the United States, it seems they will have to plan such observances with more information than typically is gathered.

The Need for Religious Expression

Proponents of moments of silence frequently make the argument that a time for silent prayer is needed because the students presently have no opportunities to exercise their faith. If this were true, it would be far more difficult to be opposed to moments of silence. It is not true, however, because students have many opportunities to exercise their faith in the public school setting. The Equal Access Act of 1984 allows for Bible and other kinds of religious clubs to meet before or after the school day in secondary schools. The Equal Access Act has appropriately been upheld by the Supreme Court;[40] it was held that since the act requires religious activity to be student-initiated and student-run, without school officials' oversight and direction, activities consistent with the requirements of the act are protected by the free speech and free exercise clauses and do not violate the establishment clause.

Moreover, students are free to pray privately anytime they choose, before, during, or after school. They are free to read their Bibles, share their faith, pray with other students, distribute religious tracts, or sing religious songs, provided these activities do not disrupt other school activities. All of these activities are protected by the free exercise clause and the Religious Freedom Restoration Act (1993). As President Bill Clinton noted in a speech delivered on July 12, 1995, the public schools are in no way a "religion free zone."[41]

Unfortunately, what often fuels the movement for more religious activity in the public schools is the widespread myth that all religion is banned inside school walls. Admittedly, many teachers and administrators are confused about what schools may and may not do regarding religion and tend, therefore, to err on the side of excluding religion from the classroom. While it is indeed unfortunate that a few teachers are sometimes hostile toward religion and go too far in excluding lawful religious acts of students, the great majority of teachers are respectful toward students of all faith traditions and wish to accommodate those students' religious needs insofar as the law will allow. There are encouraging signs these days that many school districts are taking seriously the need to understand the nuances in the law regarding student religious activity and to familiarize their teachers with what the law allows and disallows. Fortunately, this development comes at a time when the blurred lines between student-initiated religious exercises that are protected by the free exercise clause and government-promulgated religious activities that are prohibited by the establishment clause are coming into sharp focus. Some gray areas, such as prayer at commencement exercises, still exist, but the courts are increasingly providing much-needed clarification on what kinds of religious activities are constitutional.

It is imperative that students learn that religion is an important part of the fabric of life for most people, inseparable from the other dimensions of life. The public schools should never foster the belief that religion is taboo or in some way to be discouraged or suppressed. Public schools have the responsibility to avoid giving students a distorted view of the (highly religious) culture around them, and thus it is important that schools locate the balance between respecting private religious expression without becoming official sponsors of religious activity.

Conclusion

Twenty-three states now permit moments of silence in their public schools. These states assume, probably correctly, that the practice is constitutional pursuant to the guidelines of the *Jaffree* case. In the best tradition of *Everson*, these states take advantage of a wide "gate" in Jefferson's "wall" that permits the moment-of-silence practice. But *Everson* and its progeny do not mandate that every gate be used. It must be remembered that twenty-seven states, in what they deem the best interest of their youth, have chosen to keep the *Jaffree* gate locked. For them, a legal practice is not necessarily a good practice.

Five decades have elapsed since *Everson* was decided. As a separationist, I rejoice that its "wall of separation" framework remains intact. But erecting an absolutely impenetrable wall does not always serve religious liberty, so I also rejoice that *Everson* sanctioned the opening of gates in the wall from time to time. My personal view is that the Court should not have carved a new gate in the wall for moments of silence, because no matter how they are advertised, moment-of-silence observances make the public school the purveyor of religion, the agent of encouraging students, every day, to be religious, something the Supreme Court, in *Everson* and many times since, has said the Constitution does not permit. The inescapable conclusion, nevertheless, is that *Everson* created a flexible framework for protecting religious liberty, and *Jaffree* is proof of that. This makes a remembrance, even a celebration, of *Everson*'s fiftieth anniversary an altogether fitting exercise.

Notes

1. *Everson v. Board of Education,* 330 U.S. 1 (1947).
2. *Wallace v. Jaffree,* 472 U.S. 38 (1985).
3. *Walz v. Tax Commission*, 397 U.S. 664 (1970) at 669.
4. See Ala. Code sec. 16-1-20 (1985); Ariz. Rev. Stat. Ann. sec. 15-522 (1984); Ark. Stat. Ann. sec. 80-1607.1 (1980); Conn. Gen. Stat. sec. 10-16a (1983); Del. Code. Ann., title 14, sec. 4101 (1981); Fla. Stat. sec. 233.062 (1983); Ga. Code Ann. sec. 20-2-1050 (1982); Ill. Rev. Stat., chap. 122, sec. 771 (1983); Ind. Code sec. 20-10.1-7-11 (1982); Kan. Stat. Ann. sec. 72.5308a (1980); La. Rev. Stat. Ann. sec. 17:2115(A) (West 1982); Me. Rev. Stat. Ann., title 20-A, sec. 4805 (1983); Md. Educ. Code Ann. sec. 7-104 (1985); Mass. Gen. Laws Ann., chap. 71 sec. 1A (1982); Mich. Comp. Laws Ann. sec. 380.1565 (West 1984-1985); N.J. Stat. Ann. sec. 18A: 36-4 (West Supp. 1984-1985); N.M. Stat. Ann. sec. 22-5-4.1 (1981); N.Y. Educ. Law sec. 3029-a (McKinney 1981); N.D. Cent. Code sec. 15-47-30.1 (1981); Ohio Rev. Code Ann. sec. 3313.60.1 (1980); Pa. Stat. Ann., title 24, sec. 15-1516.1 (Purdon Supp. 1984-1985); R.I. Gen. Laws sec. 16-12-3.1 (1981); Tenn. Code Ann. sec. 49-6-1004 (1983); Va. Code sec. 22.1-203 (1980); W. Va. Const., art. 3, sec. 15-a. For a useful chart comparing the various statutes, see Note, "Daily Moments of Silence in Public Schools: A Constitutional Analysis," *New York University Law Review* 58 (1983): 364, 407–8. See also Note, "The Unconstitutionality of State Statutes Authorizing Moments of Silence in the Public Schools," *Harvard Law Review* 96 (1983): 1874; and Rodney K. Smith, "Now Is the Time for Reflection: *Wallace v. Jaffree* and Its Legislative Aftermath," *Alabama Law Review* 37 (1986): 345.
5. *Engel v. Vitale,* 4370 U.S. 421 (1962); *Abington Township School District v. Schempp,* 5374 U.S. 203 (1963).
6. The prayer read: "Almighty God, we acknowledge our dependence upon Thee, and we beg Thy blessing upon us, our parents, our teachers, and our country."
7. *Engel v. Vitale,* 425.
8. *Engel v. Vitale,* 432.
9. *Abington Township School District v. Schempp,* 280–81 (Brennan, J., concurring).
10. Compare *Gaines v. Anders*, 421 F. Supp. 337 (D. Mass. 1976) (upholding statute) with *May v. Cooperman*, 572 F. Supp. 1561 (N.D. N.J. 1983) (striking down statute); and *Duffy v. Las Cruces Pub. Schools,* 557 F. Supp. 1013 (D.N.M. 1983) (striking down statute).
11. *Wallace v. Jaffree,* 57.
12. *Lemon v. Kurtzman,* 403 U.S. 602 (1971). The second prong of the test requires that a statute not have the primary effect of either advancing or prohibiting religion, and the third prong requires that a statute cause no excessive entanglement between religion and government.
13. *Wallace v. Jaffree,* 43.
14. *Wallace v. Jaffree,* 56.
15. *Wallace v. Jaffree,* 66.

16. *Wallace v. Jaffree,* 76.

17. *Wallace v. Jaffree,* 76.

18. The fifteen states that retained their statutes were Connecticut, Florida, Illinois, Indiana, Kansas, Maine, Maryland, Michigan, New York, North Dakota, Ohio, Pennsylvania, Rhode Island, Tennessee, and Virginia. Those revising their statutes were Alabama, Arkansas (but repealed in 1993), Delaware, Georgia, Louisiana, Massachusetts, and New Mexico. Those that had their statutes invalidated were Arizona (repealed, Ariz. Rev. Stat. Ann., chap. 268, sec. 26, 1995), New Jersey (declared unconstitutional in *May v. Cooperman,* 780 F. 2d 240 [1985]), and West Virginia (declared unconstitutional in *Walter v. West Virginia Board of Education,* 610 F. Supp. 1169 [SD. W.Va. 1985]). Those passing new statutes were South Carolina (So. Car. Stat. sec. 59-1-443 [West, 1995]) and Texas (Tex. Ann. Stat. sec. 25.082 [West, 1995]).

19. Tex. Ann. Stat. sec. 25.082 (1995).

20. N.M. Stat. Ann. 22-27-3 (1995). "Students in the public schools may voluntarily engage in student-initiated moments of silent meditation."

21. John Rawls, *A Theory of Justice* (Cambridge: Harvard University Press, 1971).

22. See, e.g., Bruel Ackerman, *Social Justice in the Liberal State* (New Haven: Yale University Press, 1980); Thomas Nagel, "Moral Conflict and Political Legitimacy," *Philosophy and Public Affairs* 16 (Summer 1987): 232; and Kent Greenawalt, *Religious Convictions and Political Choice* (New York: Oxford University Press, 1988).

23. Walter Dellinger, "The Sound of Silence: An Epistle on Prayer and the Constitution," *Yale Law Journal* 95 (1986): 1637.

24. Norman Redlich, "Separation of Church and State: The Burger Court's Tortuous Journey," *Notre Dame Law Review* 60 (1985): 1136.

25. James David Knight, "Christian Ethics and Responsible Citizenship in Church-State Affairs: The Debate over Prayer in the Public Schools" (Ph.D. diss., Duke University, 1986), 111.

26. Jerry Falwell, *Listen, America!* (Garden City, N.Y.: Doubleday, 1980), 211, 218.

27. John Swomley Jr., "Secular Humanism—Neutral Ground for Teaching Values," *Report from the Capital* 38 (July/August 1983): 10.

28. Knight, "Christian Ethics," 98.

29. James M. Dunn, "Reflections," *Report from the Capital* 37 (November/December 1982): 15.

30. Donald W. Shriver Jr., "Against School Prayer," *New York Times,* 7 October 1982, sec. A, p. 27; quoted in Knight, "Christian Ethics," 98.

31. Quoted in Knight, "Christian Ethics," 99.

32. David Barton, *The Myth of Separation,* 3d ed. (Aledo, Texas: Wallbuilders Press, 1992), 217. For a similar argument that the removal of God from the classroom has caused moral decay, see D. J. Mattheis, "Religion and Education: A Response," *Educational Leadership* 39 (1981): 209.

33. While a "moral slide" is conceded, one relating primarily to *personal* morality, it could be said that America's *societal* morality, in spite of the end of official prayers in public schools, is on the upswing; witness the new laws banning racial, ethnic, and

religious intolerance; protecting against gender and age discrimination; and assisting the elderly and handicapped.

34. Quoted in Rob Boston, "Public Schools under Siege," *Church and State* 47 (April 1994): 4.

35. Akbar S. Ahmed, *Living Islam: From Samarkand to Stornoway* (New York: Facts on File, 1994), 40.

36. For a good discussion of Muslim religious observance in public schools, see "The Needs of Muslim Children in Public Schools," *Religion and Education* 22 (Fall 1995): 90.

37. *The Encyclopaedia of Islam* (Leiden: E. J. Brill, 1979), s.v. "Dhikr."

38. *Encyclopaedia of Islam,* s.v. "Wirt."

39. For a statement on moments of silence as generally compatible with Buddhism, see José Ignacio Cabezón, "The Case for Silence: A Buddhist Perspective on Prayer in Public Schools," *Religion and Education* 22 (Fall 1995): 72.

40. *Westside v. Mergens*, 496 U.S. 226 (1990).

41. President Clinton's speech is reprinted in *Liberty* 90 (November/December 1995): 20–22.

8

A Skeptical Postmodern Defense of Multiestablishment: The Case for Government Aid to Religious Schools in a Multicultural Age

Robert Booth Fowler

This chapter explores the serious question of what a skeptical postmodern case for government aid to religious schools might look like in an increasingly multicultural society.[1] Skeptical postmodern voices are prominent everywhere in American intellectual life and can hardly be ignored today. Often secular voices, they are always skeptical of any disposition that proclaims the existence of absolute truth, religious or otherwise. This essay challenges the routine assumption that skeptical postmoderns today should—as they overwhelmingly do—line up in opposition to government help for religious-based schools. In making this argument, the highlighted issue is government assistance to elementary and secondary education, the arena of greatest controversy regarding state aid and schools today. Aid to religious colleges, when sought, is far more extensive and, in several forms, has long been held to be constitutional.[2]

A skeptical postmodern perspective does not affirm the truth of any religion, however defined. This is not to say, however, that a postmodern outlook must necessarily be hostile to religion, and in this chapter the postmodern voice is not hostile to religion. Instead, it makes a skeptical postmodern case for state assistance to religious schools. It does so in a spirit that is different from the normal secular or religious (and self-interested) perspectives, but one that is comfortable in the postmodern world in which there are multiple views. The postmodern argument used here is meant to connect with the nation's prospective entry into a new century and with its increasing multiculturalism and the spread of postmodern attitudes. These attitudes properly include the conclusion that skepticism should not somehow be a foundational belief itself countering foundational religious beliefs. Rather, it should constitute an appreciation that sure grounding for all truth claims, including a militant secularism, is beyond our grasp.

There are five arguments that must be made from a skeptical, postmodern stance for the acceptability of state aid to religious schools. First, such aid is a moral response to the increasingly multicultural reality in the United States. Second, government help is a practical response to the widely diverse reality of the contemporary United States. Third, skeptical postmodernism should have a deep self-interest in encouraging free exercise of all religious and non-religious points of view, a commitment that can plausibly justify support for government assistance to religious-based schools. Fourth, in a philosophical mode, a skeptical, postmodern view must be open to multicultural perspectives and modes of life and faith and can offer no foundational reasons to deny them. Finally, a free and dynamic religious environment is the best environment for skeptical postmoderns, despite the ordinary assumption to the contrary. Once this reality, an apparent paradox, is appreciated, ensuring the proper religious/nonreligious environment must be a state priority.

It is one of their strengths that these arguments come from a number of different directions—sociology, philosophy, religion, and political science, a diverse cross section of thought. But all of them lead to the same end. Taken together, they suggest at the least that there is no necessary contradiction between a skeptical, postmodern view of the world and state assistance to religious schools. At best, they suggest that these two go together. The normal view, which assumes otherwise without argument is little more than prejudice masquerading as rationality.

The larger part of this chapter will address standard—and serious—objections to state help for parochial schools. After all, any normative or policy argument is not worth much if it does not engage the inevitable constellation of criticisms and counterarguments. And on state support for religious schools, opposition abounds. This chapter will investigate five objections, often focusing discussion on claims of particular importance to a postmodern skeptic: government assistance is unconstitutional; if government helps parochial schools, religion will be promoted; public schools and thus the larger society will suffer; religious diversity will explode to a dangerous degree in society; and religion will be sadly corrupted.

Before this journey begins, the reader deserves to know the basic situation regarding religious schools in the United States today. Over the past fifty years the ratio of private to public school enrollments has remained steady. Between 10 and 15 percent of students are in private schools, the rest in public schools. While as recently as 1965 the vast majority of private school students were enrolled in Roman Catholic schools, today slightly over half attend non-Catholic institutions. Roman Catholic school enrollment is over two million children, but it has fallen dramatically since 1965. Yet the proportion of private school children who attend religious schools has *not* fallen in recent years and it continues to hover at around 85 percent of total private school enrollment. The substantial expansion in the number of children attending so-called Christian schools has made up for the relative decline in Catholic parochial school enrollment. What is not clear—and this is one of the central problems of the entire issue of government aid to parochial schools—is what these figures might look like were government money to start flowing in a serious fashion to such schools or to the parents of children attending such schools. It is at least possible that these numbers might greatly expand and those from the current situation might turn out to be no more than a footnote to ancient history. No argument for government help for religious schools can ignore this possibility.[3]

The Case for Government Aid

Respect for Persons

In making a case for state assistance to parochial schools from a skeptical, postmodern perspective, I contend the central claim must be that there are significant moral and practical reasons to hold this position. First, there is a powerful moral argument for such aid in the U.S. multicultural society. This argument necessarily involves accepting the legitimacy of multiculturalism, accepting that various groups of people have different but legitimate traditions and ways of life. These naturally include a wide assortment of religious beliefs and practices, often inherited from the past, but frequently created and recreated in the present.

The question is, how can the sympathy for multiculturalism, which does exist among most skeptical postmoderns, be honored unless there is a positive effort to assist multicultural groups, which are often, even usually, defined in part by their religious commitments? Such an effort in turn must mean taking seriously multicultural groups' frequent insistence that they be able to educate their own youth as they wish. In this context, schools, which are undeniably a vital element in transmitting group values, are important. How else can certain values or ways of life be passed on except through the family and the schools? According to this argument based on honoring diversity, government help can make this possible. It takes account of the real-world situation, which is that many persons and some whole groups cannot really afford to select or sustain schools devoted to affirming their culture (including their religion).

To present this argument another way, the issue is one of human respect. In a multicultural society respect must necessarily be accorded to all groups. And if it is to mean anything, it must be evidenced not just by pleasant verbal affirmations such as "celebrate diversity." It must be instantiated in a society's institutions and policies—and these must include government assistance to parochial schools.[4]

Yet the moral issue is also very much about respect for individuals. Respect for individuals involves more than respect for them as members of multiple groups and more than respect for them as a collection of individual atoms, somehow combined with all other atoms to make up the human race. It involves respect for them as individual, living historical beings, in their particular cultures and with their particular values—and religious faiths (or non-faiths). Such respect must also insist that people's actual individual lives and real beliefs—often including religious beliefs—receive serious support within the context of the overall social order. For many individuals, of course, such practical support should and would include state aid to facilitate their children attending religious schools.

This argument about what should be a consequence of respect for persons and for groups connects with the justly famous argument made by Richard Neuhaus in *The Naked Public Square*. Neuhaus argued a decade and more ago that there was increasing pressure in American society to purge religion from public life and purge those in public life who were led by their religious outlook.[5] Stephen L. Carter has made a similar argument more recently in telling detail.[6] Both analysts underline what they judge to be the very real lack of respect, especially in many elite circles, in the United States for seriously religious persons and groups. To be sure, this chapter is not intended to go further and make a case for aid to parochial schools because somehow religious beliefs and/or values are vital for a thriving democracy, as Neuhaus maintains.[7] This fascinating argument must be left aside here.

Of course, most skeptics would see no reason why religion is a necessary condition for a vigorous democracy and might well suggest that secular values and secular bonds can do just as much for democracy as religious ones. Perhaps the pertinent question is whether some needed values and bonding are present, not whether they are religious or otherwise. The larger point, however, remains. For religion to be socially alive, it needs institutions and opportunities for persons and groups who seek to pass on the faith to their children. Aid to parochial schools would be a powerful expression of support for this goal—and for acceptance of those who seek it.

Respect for persons, then, if it is to go beyond bland and meaningless words, may require substantive assistance for religious schools in a multicultural society. This is not to say, of course, that the public currently agrees and thus is ready to endorse such assistance. The concept of broad choice in education—which would be the likely result of such assistance—does have popular support as long as it is presented as an abstract principle. But when the matter arises of paying for other people's children to attend a school affiliated with a religion different from one's own, public sentiment shifts. Then such aid is not popular.[8] Yet the respect-for-persons argument does not, after all, depend on popular agreement as to what this would entail; nor does it depend on popular support for the very idea of respect for persons. Respect for persons, in this case and in too many others, is an ideal that necessarily must pass by particular or temporal popular judgments as to its value and its content.

The Practical Case

A major practical argument must be added to the respect-for-persons view, which has been cast here in a skeptical mode, neither calling on nor necessitating a religious conviction of any sort but still proposing to benefit religious schools. There is nothing fancy about this practical argument. It simply points out the obvious, that multiculturalism is a reality in the United States today—in religious terms as in others—and notes that American society is becoming ever more heterogeneous, not less. While it is true that some groups, such as the American Jewish people, are diminishing (they now constitute less than 2 percent of the population), there is plentiful evidence overall of advancing pluralism—including religious diversity. Indeed, religious pluralism is very much the order of the day. The facts are not in dispute: as the proportion of self-identified Protestants declines to only half the population, the number of "seculars," Buddhists, Mormons, and New Agers, and the combinations of ethnic-religious group adherents steadily expand.[9] It is in light of this situation that the pragmatic case for state help for religious schools is made—even from a skeptical, postmodern outlook.

This might seem surprising because of the presence of those who are ideological secularists, devoted to promoting secularism as a kind of antireligion for everyone. Such individuals or organizations—for example, the aptly named Freedom from Religion Foundation—are as militant in their convictions and as sure of their truth as religious fundamentalists. But for more skeptical secularists, pragmatic adjustment to reality in one's environment in an atmosphere of tolerance is what makes sense. Of course there will be—and there are—religious groups and schools that brazenly undermine this attitude through their actions. They are as intolerant as the most zealously ideological secularist. Helping them is, to say the least, problematic. Yet generally, pragmatism in this situation suggests accepting reality and cooperating with it to a degree. This is the way pluralist politics works in the United States now. It is simply practical to suggest that a live-and-let-live attitude prevail as much as possible. This can mean supporting the schools that multiculturalism creates rather than somehow fighting to bring them down, keeping only the public schools. It also means understanding and expecting that secular schools, public and private, will get aid too, since they also are part of the multicultural reality that makes up U.S. culture.

On the Self-Interest of a Postmodern

A third argument has neither the force of the ethic of respect for persons nor the substantial presence of irreducible practicality behind it. But it has its own appeal, a logic of sheer (or mere) self-interest. It holds that a skeptical perspective in a postmodern mode has a self-interest in government aid to religious educational institutions. The reason is that skeptical postmodernism must necessarily be deeply committed to the free exercise of religion—and nonreligion. In a postmodern world there is no absolute Truth that state or society can or ought to uphold. It follows that all beliefs that do not threaten the very existence of state or society and accord with basic respect for others must be free to be practiced. Free exercise is also needed, for related practical reasons, for those of a skeptical outlook. In such a (relatively) religious society as the United States, those with a skeptical perspective could face serious problems in many places if extensive free exercise were to be hampered. Once again, that means that the society must go from talking about favoring free exercise to allowing and practicing it.

To achieve a situation where free exercise flourishes in practice requires a close examination of the context in which free exercise can be achieved. This necessity brings one again to the fact that many Americans consider that their faith should involve sending their children to religious (or nonreligious) schools of their choice.[10] Yet since they often cannot, an important part of free exercise of religion for them is therefore denied. The reason is the perennial inhibitor, money. Parochial schools' costs, no matter how low, are often quite beyond the financial capacities of many families. This situation, of course, serves to reduce the numbers of such schools (that is, the opportunities for free exercise in this fashion). Few people seem willing even in this postmodern world to grant this argument, but "free exercise" counts only when it enters the very texture of lives; to realize that goal there must be concrete steps to help people to achieve free exercise in practice.

It also, of course, means taking the unconventional step in American experience and recognizing that establishment of religion, in this case the establishment of many types of religious and nonreligious schools through government aid (multiestablishment), is by no means the inevitable enemy of free exercise. On the contrary, greater establishment can at times yield greater free exercise. The Founders saw free exercise and establishment as inevitable enemies. They had plenty of reason to think that way, from the history of humankind, from what they saw in Great Britain and elsewhere, and from what some of them experienced in the American colonies. Yet what was true for them, while it remains normally plausible, is not always applicable today.

In this case what is at issue is what might be called the multiestablishment of religions and nonreligions through state aid to their schools. To increase free exercise today, state help may be necessary for religious and nonreligious private schools. In this instance in our time, what some see as a paradox is actually not a paradox at all: greater establishment, in fact, yields greater free exercise of religion—as long as the focus is on diverse religious and nonreligious schools.[11]

The Open Universe

From quite a different angle, one that is perhaps a bit more philosophical, there is yet another argument that a secular, postmodern perspective should make for state aid to parochial schools. This point of view builds on an agreement with the previous and essential moral and practical arguments. It suggests that in a postmodern universe, where there are no absolute truths, no certain texts, there should be an openness to the issue of truth or interpretation that should welcome, or at least accept, a diverse world of truth claims, perceptions, and understandings. While a skeptical postmodern must necessarily be agnostic about all claims to religious truth, except perhaps those self-constructed, from a broader philosophical perspective the real lesson must be the value of tolerance. More generously, the result of the lesson would be an expansive openness to other viewpoints and especially an environment of other viewpoints. Once again, with this philosophical conclusion as with anything else, to have force, it must take on life. It cannot be just an abstract or passive principle, as are too many principles in philosophical terms and settings.

To take on life here means to create a society genuinely open to all "truths," as much as possible within the wide limits of a functioning society. In this time, place, and context, it is arguable that this should even include support for them, and thus aid for religious schools, among others. A skeptical postmodern argument against such help in this philosophical setting immediately calls into question just how committed (if this is the right word) the skeptical postmodern is. It raises the awkward question of whether beneath such a postmodern argument lies an unacknowledged and undefended foundationalism that denies the central philosophical premise of postmodernism, its skeptical openness.

The Market View

A skeptical postmodern might offer a final argument, on yet another level, for state assistance to parochial schools. This argument derives from the fascinating and controversial recent scholarship on the effects of various market conditions on the flourishing of religion.[12] This scholarship, which often has offended both the pious and nonpious, holds that the vigor of religion in any time and place is closely related to how much religious competition there is. The more actively competitive religions and religious groups are with each other, the more likely religion as a whole will be strong. Similarly, the more government establishes one religion (as in official state churches or religions) and acts to weaken other religions (or nonreligions), the weaker in actual fact all religion will turn out to be.

In short, this is a market-conditions perspective, which holds that free competition benefits religion. One might conclude that this analysis is not exactly congenial to a religious skeptic or a secularist and certainly not to anyone who is willing to accept government aid to religious schools. But this recent research is actually grist for a skeptical postmodern argument. The reason is that a free and dynamic religious environment is also the best setting for a skeptic, indeed better than any other. An open environment allows skepticism to bloom, after all, and definitely restrains government interference or direction in religious and nonreligious matters. Religious freedom is religious freedom, and skeptics are definitely in favor of that. There is no better setting for it than an open society with competing ideas, religions, and places of worship.

A second factor, however, is equally important. If a free religious environment by definition means that there will be a number of competing religious groups and persuasions, any attempt by any one or more of these groups to grasp power over the others could be dangerous. Yet one may predict that the presence of many religious groups, along with nonreligious groups, will block each other. There is no need for an elaborate historical analysis to sustain the claim that religious groups of greatly diverse backgrounds have too often attempted to crush others, sometimes invoking the power of the government, sometimes not. There is no reason to think that there will not be many more such efforts in the future. To be sure, there is no guarantee, none at all, that a freewheeling competitive religious context, where nonreligious groups are very much a part of the mix and the competition, will eliminate such efforts. There are no guarantees in politics. Yet this context should provide greater protection for everybody—of course including religious skeptics or secularists—than any other arrangement. Where is a skeptic likelier to be free? In Spain in the nineteenth century, Iran in the twentieth century, or the United States in the contemporary era?

The few places where secularism is ascendant today, such as Scandinavia, are locales where the state still is much involved in religion and religious institutions, often maintaining aspects of an established state religion. Indeed, according to religious-market scholars, this state involvement explains why religion is so weak in such nations. It has prevented the vigorous religious competition so necessary for religious health and growth. Moreover, even in these relatively secular nations, since the state remains involved in religion, the potential, if not now the reality, of abuse by government also remains ever present. The fact is, dynamic religious pluralism and competition can provide the best protection in societies for the religious skeptics and secularists who often need such protection.[13]

It follows for this argument that state help for religious schools in a competitive religious environment could be a means of ensuring that religious competition continues, a necessary condition for the protection of skepticism. Such aid, however, would need to come in the form of vouchers for parents. It could not come as direct help for assorted religious and nonreligious private schools. Otherwise we would obviously be in a situation that potentially could lead to dangerous government control over religious (and nonreligious) institutions. This is, naturally, just what the skeptic ardently seeks to avoid and the religious-market analyst warns can be fatal to religious competition.

This is an important point to emphasize at the end of this particular argument. Government aid would be acceptable only if it were given to citizens regardless of religious belief or nonbelief and never to institutions themselves. Vouchers would be the best form of such aid and would affirm all the reasons a skeptical postmodern might offer for help for parochial schools. They would respect persons by giving the help to them directly—and thus also acknowledge their diversity. Vouchers would also be the least institutional form of help imaginable and thus the least threatening to skeptics and secularists who might continue to fear any form of government aid.

Five arguments, then, have been explored here that a skeptical postmodern might mount to defend a rare view in such ranks—the legitimacy of government assistance for parochial schools. They are based on reasons of morality, practicality, self-interest, philosophy, and general safety. Others could also be brought forth, but these give a reader a taste of the eclectic possibilities open for a skeptical postmodern willing to consider the case for government aid to religious schools.

These arguments, of course, mostly differ from those propounded in the usual campaigns for government help for parochial schools. Also, they differ from the usual fare for proponents of a school-choice movement intended to include religious schools. Roman Catholics often take the lead in both causes, though the latter cause has attracted a far wider religious and libertarian base of support in recent years.[14] But no one should expect the contentions here to be the same as Roman Catholic or other religious arguments for government help for parochial schools or for broad school choice. The whole point of this chapter, after all, is to take another look at the case for government help to religious schools, one from a distinctly skeptical postmodern outlook.

Responses to Critiques

As with any other policy or normative argument, however, there is much to be said—and a good deal more that has been said—against the case for government aid. These critiques must be taken seriously, and this chapter will do so. Five critiques merit particular attention: constitutional complaints regarding state aid; fears that giving public money directly or indirectly to religious schools will hurt the public schools; concerns that too much religious pluralism will develop; fear that religion may capture government; and, finally, concern that the state will promote religion outright, retard the development of skepticism, and possibly threaten skeptics and secularists.

Constitutional Doubts

First, the constitutional issues demand consideration here, even though they properly receive attention in several other chapters in this book as well. There is hardly a shortage of works that weigh in with firm arguments on the proper constitutional relationship between church and state. The literature on this issue is voluminous. Because the issue is so contested both in terms of fact and preference, there are innumerable arguments.[15] This is the reality of the situation, which should not be lost in the welter of confident factual and normative claims and counterclaims that abound in this arena. There are frequent claims from almost all sides that, at best, the Supreme Court's views on church-state constitutional matters are murky. There are as many claims that the Court's doctrine has often been contradictory and confused. Such common sentiments only reinforce the point that everything is contested in this area.[16] This condition applies equally well to the views of many of those contesting to what extent, if any, the constitution permits government assistance for nonpublic, and especially religious, schools. About all that is clear in this matter is the public's attitude. Abstract public support for separation of church and state and against state aid for religious schools—indeed, any private schools—is widespread.[17]

This reality of division and sometimes confusion over church-state issues among many of those most interested—whatever the general public opinion—is important to understand. It is important in part because the divisions and confusion reflect the actual constitutional situation. They reflect the condition of the constitutional law on church and state and aid to nonpublic schools, a reality that necessarily undermines the claims of those who insist government support of all nonprofit private religious education is self-evidently unconstitutional—or constitutional.

Perhaps the best way to proceed to explore the relevant constitutional law is to look first at the practice regarding state aid to religious institutions in the

United States. This mission requires what rarely happens: an honest engagement with what actually occurs today. What takes place is that the national, state, and local governments grant vast amounts of aid, both direct and indirect, to religious institutions in the United States. The Supreme Court, moreover, has long and repeatedly upheld such aid as constitutional.[18] In this sense, separation of church and state in this country is a myth and should be acknowledged to be so. The government assistance comes in part through aid to all kinds of nonprofit institutions, both religious and otherwise: hospitals, colleges, day care facilities, nursing homes—the list is very long. As long as these institutions are nonprofit, the money flows. State support also comes indirectly though the immense tax relief states and localities grant churches and nonprofit religious facilities from hospitals to schools, while providing them tax-free services such as fire protection, garbage pickup, and the like.[19] This is why multiestablishment—rather than separation of church and state—is a better description of much of the relations between church and state in the United States. No single church or religion is established in any official sense, but almost all receive large or small, direct or indirect, financial benefits from the government. They are financially established, in fact, in ways and to a degree that would surely astound the author of the First Amendment, James Madison.

In the case of the schools, however, the situation is considerably more complex. Because minors are involved and the Court has held that vulnerable minors must be more protected from inappropriate religious influence in public settings, there has been more attention to separation issues. The result has been that the official Supreme Court doctrine is a bit different regarding government assistance. While the usual and significant tax benefits are the same, the Court's official doctrine otherwise employs the famous standard of "neutrality." The reigning case is *Lemon v. Kurtzman* (1971).[20] *Lemon* held that state help to a religious institution is not permissible unless it has a clear secular purpose, secular effect, and avoids excessive entanglement by government in religious affairs.

What this test means and has meant in practice is that the Supreme Court has merrily reserved to itself the right to determine, since it is hardly self-evident. The Court has proceeded to determine its meaning in a piecemeal and disputed fashion over the past twenty-five years. While the Court's decisions in a long (and unending) series of cases have resulted in plenty of confusion, they have also provided some rules regarding government assistance and parochial schools in specific policy areas.

The rules have two dimensions. Employing the *Lemon* test, the first dimension attempts to explain what kinds of aid may or may not be given to religious elementary and secondary schools. It does so with the understanding, of course, that the Supreme Court decisions merely grant states or localities permission to adopt such policies or provisions; there is no assurance that they will do so. With this in mind, the Court has determined that support may be given to parochial schools for secular texts for regular school subjects, for transportation to schools, for diagnostic services, such as those for children with suspected learning disabilities, and for associated kinds of therapeutic help—if they are provided off school grounds. Other forms of potential help are unconstitutional, according to the Court, including payment for teachers' salaries and school supplies other than books.[21]

The logic of why one type of assistance is acceptable under *Lemon* and why another is not is rarely, to put it mildly, self-evident. Thus, each instance is understandably argued both ways in every case. Two recent decisions only underline Jeffrey Rosen's bemused observation: "Bus trips from home to religious schools are constitutional, but bus trips from religious schools to local museums are unconstitutional. . . . Standardized tests are o.k., but teacher-prepared tests are not. Government can provide parochial schools with books but not maps, provoking Senator Daniel Moynihan's quip: 'What about atlases?'"[22]

In *Board of Education v. Grumet* (1994), the Supreme Court held that New York State could not set up a unique public school district treating Hasidic special-needs children and thus relieve taxpayers in an Orthodox Jewish town in suburban New York where the other children attended religious Jewish schools. The Court interpreted this arrangement as too blatant an example of establishment of religion, violating the *Lemon* principle of neutrality. They judged that there was no doubt that the law in question had a religious purpose and a religious effect.[23]

On the other hand, in *Zobrest v. Catalina Foothills School District* (1993), the Supreme Court permitted the government to pay a person who accompanied and helped a deaf student who attended a religious school.[24] In this instance approval was given to government assistance that skated close to providing support for teaching personnel in parochial schools. The Court held in this situation that there was no particular religious purpose or effect, though, of course, there was little doubt that parochial schools were definite beneficiaries of the decision.

While these decisions hardly etch sharp lines of distinction, they do not alter the fact that the Supreme Court has allowed states and localities many avenues for constitutionally providing state aid to parochial schools—and some states have acted on these opportunities. Establishment of sorts, it is fair to conclude, is present even in the arena of the state and religious schools, not just with regard to the state and religious hospitals or churches' freedom from property taxes. As usual, the establishment appears as multiestablishment, as many religious schools of many perspectives are currently drawing assistance from state and local governments.

A second part of Supreme Court standards and government help concentrates on the issue of government assistance to parents and their children who attend religious and other private schools. It is distinguished from direct aid to the schools themselves. While earlier Supreme Court decisions held that various arrangements regarding school tuition, such as voucher plans involving payments to parents for educational costs or tax deductions for such costs, were unconstitutional as establishment of religion, the binding case now is *Mueller v. Allen* (1983).[25] There the Court accepted as constitutional Minnesota's provision of tax deductions up to certain limits for parents sending their children to private (including religious) elementary or high schools. This decision may mean that voucher plans now might also be upheld, a possibility currently being tested in the case of the State of Wisconsin's system of vouchers for poor Milwaukee students who wish to attend private schools, including religious schools.

Even if the federal courts affirm the constitutionality of such arrangements, however, it is not obvious how many such schemes would be enacted. It is apparent that many, perhaps most, state legislatures would not pass such aid bills. Some state constitutions, moreover, have strict and very specific prohibitions against any such action. This situation should be kept in mind by both religious and secular opponents of government help to religious schools. Such assistance is not necessarily likely to become a widely adopted policy.[26]

While it is impossible to predict future directions with any confidence in this turbulent policy arena, contemporary legislative efforts appear to concentrate on vouchers and other forms of government help to parents rather than aid to parochial schools themselves. Ohio has recently enacted a voucher plan, one which is also being tested in the courts. Some other places are poised to do so as well. Everything, however, will turn on the fate of such legislation in the courts, including, eventually, the Supreme Court.

What can now be said confidently is that claims that such policies are flatly unconstitutional should be regarded more as ardent expressions of desire by opponents than anything else. After all, what the Supreme Court decides is what is constitutional, and it would be unwise just now to bet a great deal on what it will say about state aid to religious schools in the form of vouchers. Thus, firm assertions that state aid via vouchers is unconstitutional and that any practical case for this type of assistance to parochial schools is a waste of time are arguments that have no basis at this time.

Effects on the Public Schools

A second argument, heard almost as much as the declaration that such aid is unconstitutional, is based on the fear that support for religious schools will damage the public schools. After all, especially if it included a voucher system, such aid would constitute a dramatic and radical change, well beyond many others debated today.[27] Increase in support for religious schools would be, as is obvious, an important matter of concern for skeptics in this context— and for two reasons. A skeptic would normally want strong public schools— that is likely where his or her children will be going to school, after all, and few of us consciously seek inferior education for our children. Moreover, skeptics, like everyone else in this nation, look for an educated and thoughtful citizenry for the economic, political, and moral health of the sociey. They assume that schools—potentially or actually—are a key to achieving this goal. A strong and effective community needs good public schools, and skeptics and secularists have often joined others in sounding this theme when they opposed state aid to religious schools. This concern is valid and goes quite beyond the legitimate but after all embarrassingly selfish interest of public school teachers' unions, with their relentless search for greater pay, more freedom from systematic evaluation, and more in-service days.

Yet to say there is an important concern here simply does not get us very far toward assessing whether there is a major *problem* here. First, there has to be evidence that the public schools would, in fact, suffer if state aid to religious schools were permitted on a much broader scale than is now the case. This pessimistic scenario somehow assumes that there would be a mass exodus from the public schools of all "good" students from "good" families, leaving only the disadvantaged, special-needs, and problem children. But in an America that is considerably secular, where religious schools would almost certainly still cost more than any state aid received, whatever its form, this contention remains at present just pessimistic speculation. Indeed, quite a different —and equally speculative—scenario is that as the result of state help to religious educational institutions at the primary and secondary levels, there would be a great improvement in public education.

It is hardly necessary to repeat here the plethora of criticisms and doubts about public elementary and secondary education in the United States today. Public uneasiness is often documented in public opinion surveys and derives in part from the serious critical studies of the 1980s, such as *A Nation at Risk* and *A Nation Prepared*.[28] While it is impossible here to evaluate the actual condition of American public schools, it is surely defensible to suggest that their strengthening is a challenge that Americans generally endorse.

From this perspective, the argument is that public schools and teachers who now often exist in a noncompetitive market, or at least one in which competitors are substantially constrained, would face a challenging competitive situation were parochial schools to receive substantial financial help from the government. The public schools would have to show results or encounter disastrous decline. But why should anyone, especially a skeptical postmodern who is committed to the public schools now, be less than optimistic that the public schools could meet the challenge? Why not be optimistic and expect that public education could do so and would emerge improved from its experience in a putative competitive environment?

Part of the benefit may turn out to be that in improving the public schools, public education may learn from—rather than just denounce—successful private school experiences. Indeed, in part because of the already increasingly competitive situation as well as the larger "crisis" in American public education, there is a considerably greater interest now in successful parochial schools, especially Roman Catholic schools. In Chicago, for example, the leaders of the public school system have recently joined their counterparts in the parochial system in monthly consultations, trying to learn from the experience of the Roman Catholic schools in the city. In the process, the idea that parochial school successes can be fully explained by their relatively selective admission policies has been rejected and a spirit of cooperation has replaced the competition between the two huge systems—for the benefit of both.[29]

Studies have established that stressing common values, insisting on student achievement, and maintaining real discipline in the classroom and elsewhere explain much of the higher levels of achievement in Roman Catholic as opposed to public schools, especially in urban areas. Also important is the frequent ability of Roman Catholic schools to establish community: to foster student-teacher closeness in an atmosphere of safe and serious learning and loving, and to involve parents, especially in sometimes chaotic urban settings.[30] The results have sometimes created a mystique concerning these parochial schools, which is why there has been a marked rise of interest in what they may be able to teach public schools. Education schools in institutions of higher education often resist this interest, but they are among the last holdouts. Thus the *New York Times,* hardly known for its pro-Catholic bias, and definitely a bastion of modern skepticism, has of late pursued this topic with unwonted energy and sympathy.[31]

Indeed, it could be argued that the competitive possibilities may really constitute a reason for a skeptical postmodern at least to accept state aid via vouchers to religious schools. If the results of that aid turn out to be even better public schools, would it not be worth it? At this juncture—again, despite confident claims on all sides—there is, however, just scant basis for all the assertions about what the consequences of systematic assistance to parochial schools or parents might be for the public schools. No one knows what the results might be for the health of the public schools and what they may in turn affect—and all contestants should admit it.[32]

This is why one need not maintain that yet another reason for a skeptic to favor government aid is that it will improve the public schools. That is too strong a claim for now, just as the frequent claim that the public schools will be destroyed by government help for parochial schools is a weak argument against such aid at this point. The fact is that in all these realms ideological rhetoric, however sincere, currently substitutes for empirical information— and, indeed, is encouraged to romp freely just because we at present lack solid data. As there are more and more choice arrangements within public school districts, some involving private schools, there will be more data about how to design effective choice arrangements, how to evaluate them, and how best to finance them. Right now about all that is known is that these matters are complicated—and that there is an urgent need for more information to grapple with them.[33]

Religious Diversity and Social Stability

A third objection has its origins in the same general anxiety about the consequences of state aid, though it is rarely mentioned by those who are concerned about the potential effects of vouchers or of increased aid of other sorts to religious schools. This view proceeds from fear that state aid of the kind and degree often proposed is bound to encourage, indeed invite, a never-ending spiral of expanding religious diversity. The reason is simple. Most religious groups will eagerly reach for the state largesse, and it does not take a cynic to suspect that a host of new religious groups will spring up as a result.

The issue is not just that some of these groups will be about as religious or spiritual as sewer covers, though that is likely to be true. It is that the ever more diverse religious environment that is bound to occur will be just another stress on a society and nation already struggling to keep afloat as they are nearly overwhelmed by an endless series of quarreling subgroups. How much such diversity can a nation stand and still survive as a nation? Implicit and hovering not very far in the background, in other words, is the matter of multiculturalism and how much of it can exist in America if the United States is to have a future — just as this issue also hovers, often silently, around those who today anxiously look to preserve the public schools for national unity and shared citizenship.[34]

While concern over the putative consequences of too much multiculturalism rarely focuses on religious diversity as the core of existing or potential problems, religious pluralism is definitely part of the picture. There is hardly any question, as we know, that religious diversity has absolutely exploded in the United States over the past three decades.[35] Proponents of government assistance to religious schools argue for help, as we have seen, partly as a practical means of addressing the multicultural and multireligious reality that exists—and is expanding—in the United States. And critics fear that more aid to religious schools would at the least cement into place the wide-ranging religious pluralism present now and more likely would produce more and more over time.

There is no reason, of course, why a skeptical postmodern should be enthusiastic about encouraging this result. Yet it is unlikely to be threatening to his or her view for the very reason that it would likely lead to an increase in religious pluralism. It is government support for a single religion that poses by far the greatest potential danger for a skeptical perspective, now as always. It is, moreover, decidedly speculative, to say the least, to predict that state aid to religiously based education will contribute to unraveling the United States as a society or nation through an expanding and excessive multiculturalism. This is one more among many "facts" in the case against religious aid that is no fact at all. The reality might be quite different. For example, it might be that government help for religious schools of diverse traditions and cultures would serve to connect them to state and society in all sorts of beneficial ways (for state and society). That might be true in terms of the obvious financial benefits; it might also be true in instilling a respect for a government and a society that honors groups enough to help them as well as protect them. The outcome could be an increase in religious integration as religious groups unite on behalf of their mutual benefits from state and society. Such a consequence would constitute a powerful motive to avoid severing such connections.

Government Corruption of Religion

This last possibility leads one naturally to another significant objection to government assistance to schools under religious auspices. It is the fear that the consequences will corrupt religion terribly, the worry that government, if given a chance, might soon try to direct a religion's basic faith, its organization, its services and programs, indeed its very life. This concern is, of course, hardly a new one in human history—nor is it a phantom one in the tale of human experience. This theme is also important in the history of some parts of Protestantism, and of American Protestantism in particular. Throughout U.S. history, once individual Protestant churches were no longer established by specific states, Protestantism endorsed a separation of church and state, frequently citing the danger of state corruption of religion as a core reason for its stance. This separation was and is a fiction in many ways, and for at least 150 years after the adoption of the First Amendment to the United States Constitution, the Protestant religion was in effect the established religion of the country. Yet this reality does not invalidate the sincerity of the Protestant commitment to separation nor its traditional fear of government corruption.

At this point, however, one must pause and wonder why a skeptical postmodern would care about this matter. From a skeptical perspective it is not self-evident that the issue of government corruption of religious groups is of much concern. Why would it matter to a skeptic whether government gets too involved in the religious business? The answer is that this possibility is exactly what a skeptic fears, whether the arrow of influence goes from religious groups to government, from government to religious groups, or both ways. Concerns about religious freedom and freedom *from* religion are bound to be significant for any religious skeptic. Possible cooptation of religion by the state, or the reverse, is a matter that a skeptic fears.

In more recent years, receipt of considerable state largesse—even sometimes for religious schools—has coexisted in often unselfconscious harmony with strong approval of separation of church and state in almost all sectors of American religion. This separatist sentiment is rarely rigid (very rarely going so far, for instance, as to renounce tax forgiveness for nonprofit religious property), but it regularly includes warnings about the dangers to religion of corruption from too much involvement with government. This theme is sounded most loudly and most consistently by some (but far from all) evangelical and fundamentalist Protestant groups, especially now, as in the past, many in the Baptist tradition. The leading publication from this point of view remains the *Journal of Church and State,* and several political organizations have this agenda as an important part of their work.[36]

While separatism comes in many hues, it is naturally mostly religious analysts whose questions about government assistance to private religious schools have concentrated on potential damage to organized religion. These arguments are familiar versions of older ones, this time applied to the school-aid issue. Their burden is that government help will have several corrupting consequences. Government regulations, they fear, will inevitably follow aid in ways that are subtle as well as blatant. After government regulations will come more open interference—or even outright control—of parochial school systems as the schools come to depend on government help. Even if this pessimistic scenario does not occur, critics fear that as government assistance grows, the sense of conviction and sacrifice within communities sustaining religious schools will inevitably ebb. With it may depart the very life of the religious community that was the reason for establishing the parochial school in the first place.

How real these threats are is impossible to tell at this juncture. They could happen in some cases or in every instance; no one can deny that. The issue will turn around the interests behind government aid and the quality and focus of the state bureaucracy that is involved. There is hardly room for automatic optimism about the effectiveness of government programs and, perhaps especially, government bureaucrats, who are not always known for their flexibility. Yet it is not at all obvious that a voucher plan, for example, would lead to dangerous levels of government control or loss of community élan in a religious group. There are few signs that current state assistance has led in such unfortunate directions in the states that provide it. Endless reporting forms and other "delights" of bureaucracy are something of a necessary nuisance, but they are hardly cosmic threats.

The most realistic danger, perhaps, for religious groups is that a steady and growing diet of government aid might make them just too pliable and weak. But here again, assistance via a voucher plan would create the least danger. It would forge a link to government, but one that would be somewhat indirect. Thus it could encourage the sense among religious communities sponsoring schools that they are decidedly independent and self-sufficient in their faith and life.

Promoting Religion

This brings us to another great reservation from a secularist, postmodern perspective about government help for parochial schools. It is the idea that in the end it will promote religion(s) in the United States. There is just no reason why a skeptical postmodern would want that end, especially when it could endanger his or her own outlook. In practical terms this is obviously a signifi-cant argument, perhaps the most potent, because it is the most obvious of the lot. Yet the concern is also philosophical for a skeptical postmodern: why would a person of integrity want to encourage error?

The fact is that on both practical and philosophical grounds a skeptical postmodernist simply would not want to advance religion or the religious. There is no plausible or even cunning argument that can somehow make it so, certainly not at the philosophical level. Nor is it worth arguing, as some per-versely delight in doing, that religious schools would actually drive students from religion. While this would occasionally occur, there is no evidence that this is what usually happens. In terms of the largest parochial school system, the Catholic schools, what data we have suggests that attendance in Catholic schools tends to encourage loyalty to the religion and the church, despite some well-known literary examples to the contrary.[37]

Frankly, the only basis for accepting state help for religious schools and the good possibility that it might strengthen religion overall in society is to view this putative consequence in straight trade-off terms: that the gains would out-weigh the negatives. The gains would be embodied in the good reasons for government assistance: enhancing the respect for people and their basic reli-gious and nonreligious self-definitions; enabling society to adjust to a multire-ligious and multicultural reality; and nurturing a social order that values the free exercise of religion (and nonreligion).

Naturally, different skeptical postmoderns will draw the balance in different ways; indeed, most have done just that. Yet my argument is not that a post-modernist secularist *must* rally to the cause of state help for parochial schools, but the much more modest claim that there is a plausible case from this perspective for aid in the form of vouchers. In fact, for a skeptical postmodernist today, and for all of us, to be willing to accept—and even support—those we disagree with in our complex multicultural society may be an essential price to pay for our continued collective existence. It may also be an essential test of whether we really do respect persons, in this case our fellow citizens, or whether we just claim that we do—even when they disagree with us about the most fundamental things in life.

Conclusion

From a skeptical postmodern perspective, optimism must be the watchword. Fears can dominate those who worry about religious forces in U.S. culture just as they can dominate those who focus too often on the possible negative results of multiculturalism. But fear, understandable as it is as a human emotion, is not a good basis for making public policy in the postmodern world—or any other. Openness is the appropriate stance of a skeptical postmodern in a world and in a time in which there is no certainty and no text. So is a kind of confidence that people can and will live together in an open, diverse, and multireligious (and nonreligious) society with government as a mediator—and assistant—to all those persons and groups who operate within society's rules. Within this spirit, a skeptical postmodern will be ready to accept state aid to private schools.

Notes

1. As a thought experiment, this chapter should not be assumed to represent the author's personal views.
2. See *Tilton v. Richardson,* 403 U.S. 672 (1971); and *Roemer v. Board of Public Works,* 426 U.S. 736 (1976).
3. John Witte, "Politics, Markets, or Money? The Political-Economy of School Choice" (paper presented at the American Political Science Association meeting, San Francisco, August 1996).
4. For arguments focused not on school-aid issues but on respect for groups, see Iris Marion Young, *Justice and the Politics of Difference* (Princeton: Princeton University Press, 1990); and Lani Guinier, *The Tyranny of the Majority: Fundamental Fairness in Representative Democracy* (New York: Free Press, 1995).

5. Richard Neuhaus, *The Naked Public Square* (Grand Rapids, Mich.: Eerdmans, 1984).

6. Stephen L. Carter, *The Culture of Disbelief* (New York: Basic Books, 1993).

7. Which is the interesting approach of Neuhaus.

8. John F. Witte and Mark E. Rigdon, "Education Choice Reforms: Will They Change American Schools?" *Publius* 23 (Summer 1993): 112.

9. See Robert Booth Fowler and Allen D. Hertzke, *Religion and Politics in America* (Boulder, Colo.: Westview, 1995).

10. Just how many, we cannot know until this experiment actually takes place.

11. Fowler and Hertzke, *Religion and Politics*, 232–34. On the Founders there is no end of literature; a brief sampler of the riches: William L. Miller, *The First Liberty and the American Republic* (New York: Knopf, 1986); Michael Malbin, *Religion and Politics: The Intentions of the Authors of the First Amendment* (Washington, D.C.: American Enterprise Institute, 1978); Robert L. Cord, *Historical Fact and Current Fiction* (New York: Lambeth, 1982); Thomas J. Curry, *The First Freedoms: Church and State in America to the Passage of the First Amendment* (New York: Oxford University Press, 1986); Robert S. Alley, ed., *James Madison on Religious Liberty* (Buffalo, N.Y.: Prometheus Books, 1985); John G. West Jr., *The Politics of Revelation and Reason: Religion and Civic Life in the New Nation* (Lawrence: University Press of Kansas, 1996).

12. For a sampling of market studies: Roger Finke, "The Consequences of Religious Competition: Supply-Side Explanations for Religious Change" (paper presented at the Sundance Workshop, April 1994), 1–32; Roger Finke, "Religious Deregulation: Origins and Consequences," *Journal of Church and State* 32 (Summer 1990): 609–26; Roger Finke and Rodney Stark, *The Churching of America, 1776–1990: Winners and Losers in Our Religious Economy* (New Brunswick, N.J.: Rutgers University Press, 1992).

13. See the *Journal for the Scientific Study of Religion* 35, no. 3 (September 1996) for a lively series of articles on the market-conditions analysis, including a fascinating dispute over its value in explaining the pluralistic but noncompetitive situation in the Netherlands.

14. Witte and Rigdon, "Education Choice Reforms."

15. Some interesting examples: Robert T. Miller and Robert B. Flowers, eds., *Toward Benevolent Neutrality: Church, State, and the Supreme Court* (Waco, Texas: Baylor University Press, 1987); Carter, *Culture of Disbelief*; Leo Pfeffer, *Religion, State, and the Burger Court* (Buffalo, N.Y.: Prometheus Books, 1984); Paul J. Weber, *Equal Separation: Understanding the Religious Clauses and the First Amendment* (Westport, Conn.: Greenwood, 1990); see also Fowler and Hertzke, *Religion and Politics*, chap. 11, for a survey of the current situation.

16. See sources cited in n. 15.

17. René Sanchez, "Who's Vouching for the Vouchers?" *Washington Post National Weekly Edition*, 2–8 September 1996, 34.

18. See, e.g., *Walz v. Tax Commissioner*, 397 U.S. 664 (1970); and *Bradfield v. Roberts*, 175 U.S. 291 (1899).

19. Paul J. Weber and Dennis A. Gilbert, *Private Churches and Public Money: Church-Government Fiscal Relations* (Westport, Conn.: Greenwood, 1981).

20. *Lemon v. Kurtzman,* 411 U.S. 192 (1971).

21. Important cases in crafting this situation are: *Cochran v. Board of Education,* 281 U.S. 370 (1930); *Everson v. Board of Education,* 330 U.S. 1 (1947); *Board of Education v. Allen,* 392 U.S. 236 (1968); *Wolman v. Walter,* 433 U.S. 229 (1977); *Aguilar v. Felton,* 473 U.S. 402 (1985); *Zobrest v. Catalina Foothills School District,* 509 U.S. 1 (1993).

22. Jeffrey Rosen, "Lemon Law," *New Republic,* 29 March 1993), 17.

23. *Board of Education v. Grumet,* 114 S.Ct. 2481 (1994).

24. *Zobrest v. Catalina Foothills Board of Education,* 509 U.S. 1 (1993).

25. *Mueller v. Allen,* 463 U.S. 388 (1983).

26. Witte and Rigdon, "Education Choice Reforms," 111.

27. Mary Anne Raywid, "Choice Orientations, Discussions, and Prospects," *Educational Policy* 6 (June 1992): 105–22; John F. Witte, "Choice in American Education," *Educational Considerations* 19 (Fall 1991): 12–19.

28. U.S. Department of Education, *A Nation at Risk* (Washington, D.C.: U.S. Government Printing Office, 1983); *A Nation Prepared* (New York: Carnegie Corporation, 1986).

29. Dirk Johnson, "Public and Catholic School Chiefs Join Forces," *New York Times,* 16 September 1996, sec. A, p. 8.

30. Lisa W. Foderaro, "In Catholic Schools, Shared Values Include Rigor and Decorum," *New York Times,* 25 September 1996, sec. A, p. 15.

31. Karen W. Arenson, "Parochial School Mystique," *New York Times,* 22 September 1996, sec. E, p. 14; Sol Stern, "The Catholic School Miracle," *New York Times,* 25 September 1996, sec. A, p. 19.

32. Some views here are John Chubb and Terry Moe, *Politics, Markets, and America's Schools* (Washington, D.C.: Brookings Institution, 1990); Peter W. Cookson Jr., *School Choice: The Struggle for American Education* (New Haven: Yale University Press, 1994); Jeffrey R. Henig, *Rethinking School Choice: Limits of the Market Metaphor* (Princeton: Princeton University Press, 1994); Witte and Rigdon, "Education Choice Reforms."

33. John Witte, "Educational Choice in America: The Gap between Theory and Practice" (paper presented at the meeting of the British Educational Research Association, September 1996).

34. Several good sources include David A. Hollinger, *Postethnic America: Beyond Multiculturalism* (New York: Basic Books, 1995); Diane Ravitch and Maris A. Vinovskis, eds., *Learning from the Past: What History Teaches Us about School Reform* (Baltimore: Johns Hopkins Press, 1995); Will Kymlicka, *Multicultural Citizenship* (New York: Oxford University Press, 1996); Lawrence Levine, *The Opening of the American Mind* (Boston: Beacon, 1996); Ronald Takaki, *A Different Mirror: A History of Multicultural America* (Boston: Little, Brown, 1993).

35. For a good account, see Barry A. Kosmin and Seymour P. Lachman, *One Nation under God: Religion in Contemporary Society* (New York: Harmony, 1993).

36. On the Founders, see the excellent discussion in A. James Reichley, *Religion in American Public Life* (Washington, D.C.: Brookings Institution, 1985), chap. 3; on public attitudes and for a discussion of points of disagreement today, see Ted Jelen and Clyde Wilcox, *Public Attitudes toward Church and State* (Armonk, N.Y.: M. E. Sharpe, 1995).

37. On Catholic education, see Jim Castelli and Joseph Gremillion, *The Emerging Parish: The Notre Dame Study of Catholic Life since Vatican II* (San Francisco: Harper & Row, 1987), chap. 9; and George Gallup Jr. and Jim Castelli, *The American Catholic People: Their Beliefs, Practices, and Values* (Garden City, N.Y.: Doubleday, 1987), chap. 10.

9

The Religious Equality Amendment and Voluntary School Prayer

Mary C. Segers

The Supreme Court addressed questions of school prayer for the first time in 1962, holding in *Engel v. Vitale* that a state-sponsored prayer used in public schools in New York State violated the establishment clause of the First Amendment. Thirty years later, in *Lee v. Weisman*, the Court extended the principle of *Engel* to hold that a state may not sponsor prayers at middle- and high-school graduation ceremonies.

But what if such prayers are student initiated rather than state sponsored? Religious right supporters of school prayer argue that student-initiated, voluntary school prayer comports with the free exercise clause of the First Amendment and is therefore constitutionally permissible. Moreover, they contend, many school officials have gone too far in excluding lawful religious acts of students, such as saying a prayer over lunch, praying the rosary on the school bus, or bringing a Bible to school. To remedy this unfortunate stigmatizing of religion in public schools, conservative religious activists introduced a new constitutional amendment in 1995, known as the Religious Equality Amendment (REA). It was designed to protect religious expression in public settings, especially in the nation's public schools. A proposed draft of the religious equality amendment read as follows:

> In order to secure the right of the people to acknowledge and serve God according to the dictates of conscience, neither the United States nor any state shall deny any person equal access to a benefit, or otherwise discriminate against any person, on account of religious belief, expression, or exercise. This amendment does not authorize government to coerce or inhibit religious belief, expression, or exercise.[1]

The nondiscrimination clause in this proposed constitutional amendment was intended to overturn some, if not all, of the cases restricting religious expression in public settings—such as football games and government offices, as well as schools. The "access to benefits" section sought to allow religious institutions to receive public funding under such programs as school vouchers, which allow parents to use public school funds to pay private school tuition, including tuition to religious schools.

This chapter examines the debate about the Religious Equality Amendment. While the Christian Coalition seeks passage of such an amendment to guarantee student-initiated prayer and to enable students to bring in clergy for invocations at graduation ceremonies, opponents of the proposed amendment contend that passage would seriously alter the meaning of the First Amendment's religion clauses and would open wide the gates for an unprecedented merger of religion and government across America. This chapter analyzes the Religious Equality Amendment and explores the political context in which it was introduced. Discussion and evaluation of the arguments for and against the new amendment can shed light on religion and politics generally in the United States and on the vexed issue of prayer in the public schools.

The chapter begins with a review of the historical background and context of the Religious Equality Amendment. In examining the debate about prayer in public schools, it reviews earlier school prayer decisions of the Supreme Court as well as public reaction to those decisions. A lack of compliance by local school officials as well as lack of implementation and enforcement of Court decisions by state and local authorities is also noted. Still another measure of public resistance to Court rulings is the large number of constitutional amendments introduced in Congress to reinstate prayer in public schools. The Religious Equality Amendment is simply the latest example of this general trend.

The second part of this essay describes the Religious Equality Amendment, the problems it addresses, and the arguments for and against it. Finally, it examines alternatives to the REA that will address the concerns of parents for the religious and value education of their children while preserving the free exercise rights of religious minorities.

The Historical Background of the Religious Equality Amendment

In the fifty years since the landmark ruling in the *Everson* case, few Supreme Court decisions have been greeted with such dismay by both the general public and the national media as the school prayer decisions of the 1960s, *Engel v. Vitale* (1962) and *Abington School District v. Schempp* (1963). In *Engel*, a local New York school board requirement that students join in reciting a prayer composed by the state board of regents was deemed a violation of the establishment clause. In *Schempp*, the Court extended this ban on state-mandated prayer to cover a Pennsylvania law requiring the daily reading of Bible verses and a Baltimore, Maryland, practice of Bible reading and recitation of the Lord's Prayer at the beginning of the school day. With these two rulings, the Court seemed to say that officially sponsored religious expression in the public schools was unconstitutional.[2]

The connection between the 1947 *Everson* decision and the Court's school prayer prohibitions in *Engel* and *Schempp* is clear and well acknowledged by scholars of Supreme Court jurisprudence. In order to conclude that devotional exercises such as prayer and Bible reading constituted an impermissible government activity, the Supreme Court relied upon two major interpretive assumptions explicitly stated in *Everson*. The first assumption was that central provisions of the Bill of Rights, including the establishment clause of the First Amendment, applied to state and local governments as well as to the national government. This step was essential, given the fact that throughout American history the public schools have been administered and regulated by local and state governments. The second assumption, also explicitly stated in *Everson*, was that the establishment clause prohibited federal and state governments not merely from favoring one religion over another religion but from aiding or promoting religion over nonreligion. According to *Everson's* doctrine of government neutrality, federal and state governments must be absolutely neutral, not just among all religious groups, but also between religious believers and nonbelievers. "Neither a state nor the Federal Government," Justice Hugo Black wrote in *Everson,* "can pass laws which aid . . . all religions."[3] These two assumptions—application of the First Amendment's establishment clause to state and local as well as to the national government, and the doctrines of government neutrality and strict church-state separation—clearly set the Supreme Court on a course that led, fifteen years later, to the banning, in *Engel* and *Schempp*, of state-sponsored prayer and Bible reading in public schools.

Constitutional law scholar Terry Eastland in his invaluable review of Supreme Court religion cases has noted the generally negative comments on the Court's decision in *Engel* made by liberal newspapers and journals at the time. The *Washington Post* in its editorial comment suggested that a moment of silence might replace prayer at the beginning of each school day "to still the tumult of the playground and start a day of study."[4] The *Christian Century*, a centrist, moderately liberal journal of opinion, stated that nothing in the Court's opinion in *Engel* prevented teachers or pupils in the public schools from engaging in private prayer.[5] The editors of *Christianity and Crisis*, a liberal religious journal founded by Reinhold Niebuhr in 1941, hoped that the Court's ruling did not represent the secularization of the public schools. Such secularization might "amount to the suppression of religion and give the impression that government must be anti-religion. This impression is certainly not consonant with the mood of either the Founding Fathers or our long tradition of separation of church and state, which is based on neutrality and not animosity."[6] The *New Republic*, while agreeing with the Court's opinion in *Engel*, noted that the ruling "has provided the occasion for the most savage controversy concerning the Court since the 1954 desegregation decision" and expressed concern that "the emotional response and sense of alienation from Washington and its institutions apparent throughout the country in the wake of the decision seems to us a factor of authentic importance in the present national political climate."[7] That moderate and liberal publications such as these reacted so strongly in their editorial comments to the Court's ruling in *Engel* suggests the degree of public surprise and shock that greeted the Court's ruling.

Public opinion is another measure of the unfavorable reaction to the Court's rulings on school prayer in the 1960s. A Gallup Poll conducted from July 26 through July 31, 1962, found that 85 percent of those polled approved of religious observances in public schools. Over the years the public has consistently favored reinstating school prayer—by large majorities. In a 1991 *Time/CNN* poll, 78 percent of American adults favored allowing children to say prayers in public schools, and 89 percent favored a moment of silence. According to a *Los Angeles Times* poll in July 1994, 76 percent of those polled favored prayer in public schools.[8] Regarding prayer at school graduations, a 1993 Gallup survey for Phi Delta Kappa, an organization of educators, revealed that 82 percent of Protestants and 72 percent of Roman Catholics wanted *Lee v. Weisman* (the 1992 Supreme Court ruling banning official, state-sponsored prayer at high school graduation ceremonies) overturned. Moreover, more than 70 percent of public high schools surveyed by Phi Delta Kappa in 1993 either permitted student-led prayer at formal graduations or offered seniors a baccalaureate service—that is, a graduation ceremony with prayer.[9]

While mass public opinion has generally favored prayer in public schools, elite opinion has been slightly more divided. Nevertheless, the reaction of leaders and public officials to the Court's rulings in the 1960s was strikingly similar to the negative views of the general public. Commenting on the *Engel* decision, Senator Robert C. Byrd (D-W.Va.) asked: "Can it be that we, too, are ready to embrace the foul concept of atheism? . . . Somebody is tampering with America's soul. I leave it to you who that somebody is."[10] Senator Herman Talmadge (D-Ga.) denounced the decision as "unconscionable . . . an outrageous edict."[11] Representative L. Mendel Rivers (D-S.C.) declared that "the Court has now officially stated its disbelief in God Almighty."[12] Representative George Williams (D-Mich.) insisted that the decision constituted "a deliberately and carefully planned conspiracy to substitute materialism for spiritual values and thus to communize America."[13] For Senator Dale Robertson (D-Va.), father of evangelist Pat Robertson, this was the most extreme ruling the

Supreme Court had ever made in favor of atheists and agnostics. And Representative Frank Becker (R-N.Y.) informed his colleagues that *Engel* was "the most tragic decision in the history of the United States."[14]

Of course, these remarks must be seen in the context of the early 1960s in American society. Southern senators and congressmen, already embittered at the Supreme Court because of its decision outlawing racial segregation in the public schools, were particularly emphatic in their intense reaction to *Engel*. The remark of Representative George W. Andrews (D-Ala.) was typical: "They put the Negroes in the schools, and now they've driven God out."[15]

However, antipathy to the Court's decision was not limited to the South. In 1962, the nationwide Governors' Conference adopted a resolution deploring the decision and calling for a constitutional amendment to overrule it. Former president Herbert Hoover denounced the decision as "a disintegration of one of the most sacred of American heritages" and called for a constitutional amendment that would establish "the right to religious devotion in all government agencies—national, state, or local."[16] Of course many Protestant and Catholic religious leaders were outraged at the Court's ruling, as well. Noted evangelist Dr. Billy Graham said of *Engel*: "This is another step towards the secularization of the United States. . . . The framers of our Constitution meant we were to have freedom of religion, not freedom from religion."[17] Francis Cardinal Spellman, archbishop of New York, declared: "I am shocked and frightened that the Supreme Court has declared unconstitutional a simple and voluntary declaration of belief in God by public school children. The decision strikes at the very heart of the Godly tradition in which America's children have for so long been raised."[18] Episcopal bishop James A. Pike of California, generally regarded as liberal, insisted that the result of the Court's decision in *Engel* was "secularism, whether by intent or by default. I am not implying for a moment that the proponents or supporters of the decision of the Supreme Court intentionally wish an atheistic result. Nevertheless, when it is by default we simply cut off the whole spiritual dimension of life, and without even a reference to it. What we have left is actually a secularist view of life."[19]

Of course, not all religious or political leaders criticized the Court's decision. Dr. Martin Luther King Jr. called it "a sound and good decision reaffirming something that is basic in our Constitution, namely, separation of church and state."[20] Most American Jewish leaders favored the decision. And President John F. Kennedy reacted to the Supreme Court decision in this way:

> The Supreme Court has made its judgment. Some will disagree and others will agree. In the efforts we're making to maintain our Constitutional principles, we will have to abide by what the Supreme Court says. We have a very easy remedy here, and that is to pray ourselves. We can pray a good deal more at home and

attend our churches with fidelity and emphasize the true meaning of prayer in the lives of our children. I hope, as a result of that decision, all Americans will give prayer a greater emphasis.[21]

A year after *Engel*, the Supreme Court handed down its decisions in *Abington v. Schempp* and *Murray v. Curlett*. These rulings prohibited reading Bible passages or saying the Lord's Prayer as religious exercises in public schools throughout the nation. Again, the public reaction was negative, this time perhaps because the Court's ruling had much wider regional and national application than did *Engel*, which, after all, applied only to schools in New York State. Mail to congressmen was heavy, and the message of these letters from constituents was overwhelmingly against the prayer and Bible reading decisions of the Court. Congressional leaders reacted by introducing 146 constitutional amendments to reverse the *Schempp* decision.[22]

Still another indication of citizens' dissatisfaction with the Supreme Court's rulings was lack of compliance and failure to implement the Court's decisions at the state and local levels in various parts of the country. In rural, fairly homogeneous school districts, officials did not always comply with the Court's decisions, and state authorities did not always compel them to comply. In 1967, five years after *Engel*, Leo Pfeffer noted that compliance with the Court ban on state-sponsored and state-mandated prayer in public schools was complete in the Pacific states, virtually complete in the Atlantic coastal states (except south of the Mason-Dixon line), somewhat uneven in the Midwest, and seriously incomplete in Southern states.[23]

In 1966, political scientist Robert Birkby published a study of Tennessee's compliance at the school district level with the Supreme Court's ruling in *Abington v. Schempp*.[24] Tennessee state law had required Bible reading in public schools prior to the Court's decision in *Schempp*. Birkby's survey of 121 school districts reported that by 1966 compliance with the Court's ruling was uneven and in most cases merely procedural: of the 121 districts, 70 still followed the requirements of state law to have Bible reading and devotional exercises in school while the other 51 districts reported some policy changes. Of these 51 changing districts, only one completely eliminated all Bible reading and devotional exercises, while the remaining 50 simply made student participation voluntary and left the decision whether to have devotional exercises to the discretion of the classroom teacher. This strategy of procedural change meant that, in fact, classroom teachers were "voluntarily" conducting Bible reading and devotional exercises just as they did before *Schempp*. Birkby says this general noncompliance was attributable in part to some confusion about the Court's decision: "It was clear enough that required devotional exercises were forbidden but the Court did not commit itself on the status of voluntary programs such as those adopted by the 50 changing districts in Tennessee."[25] However, Birkby's article also indicates that some state officials and citizens questioned the Court's authority to issue its ruling. Obviously, some school board members accepted the decision: one surgeon and school board member stated, "We must conform with Federal law. If we are to teach our children to obey laws we must set an example."[26] But other board members challenged the legitimacy of the Court's decision. One superintendent stated flatly, "Impeach Earl Warren." A college professor and school board member observed that "The Supreme Court decision didn't mean a damn." Another superintendent declared, "I am of the opinion that 99% of the people in the United States feel as I do about the Supreme Court's decision—that it was an outrage and that Congress should have it amended. The remaining 1% do not belong in this free world."[27] The intensity of these negative comments about the Court's ruling in *Schempp* helps to explain why the Court's decision regarding Bible reading and devotional exercises was not self-executing in the Bible Belt state of Tennessee.

Other indications of noncompliance with the Court's school prayer rulings can be seen in the continued efforts by several Southern states to pass legislation permitting a moment of silence in the classroom. In 1978 Alabama passed such a statute; it was later declared unconstitutional by the Supreme Court in *Wallace v. Jaffree* (1985).[28] In 1994, the Georgia General Assembly passed the Moment of Quiet Reflection in Schools Act, which was immediately challenged as a violation of the establishment clause but was upheld by the Federal District Court for the Northern District of Georgia.[29] Also in 1994, the Mississippi legislature passed a school prayer statute permitting "non-proselytizing, student-initiated, voluntary prayer" at various public school events such as, for example, sports events, assemblies, and graduations.[30] Again in 1994 the Virginia legislature directed state school officials to adopt guidelines for prayer in the schools.[31] In Florida in 1996, Governor Lawton Chiles vetoed a bill allowing student-led religious devotions at commencement ceremonies and other school events.[32] These state statutes and the court cases challenging them indicate that, at many levels, a sizable portion of the American public is not satisfied with, and does not accept, the Supreme Court rulings on school prayer.

Finally, the large number of school prayer constitutional amendments introduced in Congress since 1962 is yet another indication of public dissatisfaction with the Supreme Court's rulings. Since *Engel*, more than two hundred proposals in the form of legislation or constitutional amendments have been introduced in Congress to restore religious exercises in public schools. Congress has dealt with school prayer amendments every year since 1962; in 1966, 1971, and 1984, the debate reached serious levels.[33] In each case, however, the two-thirds approval required for passage did not materialize. Despite these setbacks, however, Republican victories in the 1994 congressional midterm elections fueled new hopes among the religious right for passage of a school prayer amendment. In May 1995 the Christian Coalition, founded by Pat Robertson and headed by Executive Director Ralph Reed, issued what it called a "Contract with the American Family," a kind of umbrella document stating the coalition's agenda, part of which was to pursue passage of the so-called Religious Equality Amendment. The coalition sought passage of such a constitutional amendment to guarantee "student-initiated prayer" and to allow students to bring in a clergyman for invocations at graduation ceremonies.

The Religious Equality Amendment

The proposed Religious Equality Amendment was the result of a major effort by religious conservatives in the Republican-controlled 104th Congress to restore school prayer. This effort was centered in the House Judiciary Committee, chaired by Representative Henry Hyde (R-Ill.), and especially in the Judiciary Subcommittee on the Constitution, chaired by Representative Charles Canady (R-Fla.), which held field hearings on the topic "Religious Liberty and the Bill of Rights" in the summer of 1995. However, the REA foundered because of serious divisions within the ranks of the religious right and was never reported out of committee for a floor vote in the House of Representatives. Between November 1995 and September 1996, two versions of the REA competed for congressional support: H.J. Res. 121, proposed by Congressman Hyde, and H.J. Res. 127, proposed by Congressman Ernest Istook (R-Okla.). Hyde was pushing a wide-ranging amendment that would prohibit the government from denying equal access to benefits to anyone because of religious belief or practices. It would also prohibit discrimination on the same basis. By emphasizing the broader freedom of religious expression in public places, Hyde and his supporters believed their amendment would have the effect of permitting school prayer, even though the amendment made no explicit mention of prayer in public schools. The Hyde faction argued that this broad approach was the best way to reverse a legacy of court rulings that overly secularizes public institutions. The original amendment proposed by Congressmen Hyde, Canady, and Goodlatte stated:

> Preamble: Proposing an amendment to the Constitution of the United States in order to secure the unalienable right of the people to acknowledge, worship, and serve their Creator. Text: Neither the United States nor any State shall deny benefits to or otherwise discriminate against any private person or group on account

of religious expression, belief or identity; nor shall the prohibition on laws respecting an establishment of religion be construed to require such discrimination.

Istook saw this as an acceptable start but wanted the amendment to include specific language on what he saw as the main issue: school prayer. Istook's amendment would allow student-sponsored prayer in public schools, forbid religious discrimination, and protect acknowledgment of religious heritage and traditions. The constitutional amendment proposed by Istook and cosponsored by eighty-eight colleagues read as follows:

> Preamble: Proposing a religious liberties amendment to the Constitution of the United States in order to secure the people's right to acknowledge God according to the dictates of conscience. Text: To secure the people's right to acknowledge God according to the dictates of conscience: Nothing in this Constitution shall prohibit acknowledgments of the religious heritage, beliefs, or traditions of the people, or prohibit student-sponsored prayer in public schools. Neither the United States nor any State shall compose any official prayer or compel joining in prayer or discriminate against religious expression or belief.

Hyde objected to the Istook amendment, saying that (1) current law already protects religious acknowledgment by the people of their religious heritage, beliefs, and traditions; (2) Istook's proposal goes much further than Hyde's antidiscrimination remedy, by allowing official government favoritism of the majority faith of a community; (3) the Istook amendment would repeal the establishment clause of the First Amendment and would therefore redefine constitutional law, whereas the Hyde amendment would restore the original meaning of the First Amendment religion clauses.

In the end, Hyde's formulation prevailed (modified to the text that appears on the first page of this chapter). However, it should be noted that the divisions between supporters of these two proposed constitutional amendments were so serious that the Judiciary Subcommittee on the Constitution could not agree on a single proposal. It took approximately five months to hammer out an agreed-upon proposal, and by then it was too late for the 104th Congress to consider the measure adequately.[34] As of this writing, it is unclear whether the new GOP-controlled 105th Congress, elected in November 1996, will make the REA a priority. However, whether or not the REA is voted on by the new Congress, this proposed constitutional amendment merits close analysis because of its remarkably broad, strategic approach to the question of free religious expression in schools and other public places.

The proposed Religious Equality Amendment is aimed at permitting greater religious expression in public places such as public schools, sports arenas, public radio stations, assemblies, and graduation ceremonies. The impetus for this constitutional amendment was provided in part by mounting anecdotal evidence that the rights of students and others were being infringed upon by anxious government and school officials who, through misunderstanding of the law, often went too far in excluding lawful religious acts of students, such as saying grace before meals or praying the rosary on the school bus. In March 1995, for example, when ten-year-old Joshua Burton brought a Bible to his Orange County, Florida, elementary school, his teacher told him he had violated the constitutional provisions on the separation of church and state. The school's principal told the fourth-grader that "he could bring his Bible to school if he read it silently and did not discuss it with anyone." However, two days later, Joshua was expelled after two other students complained that he had been reading his Bible before school.[35]

On June 23, 1995, Joshua and his parents spoke at congressional hearings in Tampa, Florida, before the House Judiciary Subcommittee on the Constitution. Joshua's father, Mark Burton, testified that parents need help raising their children in a socially fraying society that seems increasingly hostile towards religion. As Stephen Carter has noted, this is a problem parents often experience with respect to the public schools—the question of religious values and moral education in a secular society. If the parents are Christians, they worry about moral relativism and about "what it means to school Christians in a liberal society."[36] As Mark Burton stated in his testimony:

> It seems to me that in this age where children are taught by the state school system that they must be tolerant of racial differences, tolerant of homosexuality, tolerant of political differences and tolerant of cultural and language diversity, that this same system should be tolerant when it comes to religious freedom.[37]

In other words, Mr. Burton argued, religion—like race, sexual orientation, and ethnicity—is a fundamental characteristic of individual identity and therefore merits equal respect and consideration in the nation's public schools.

As a proposed constitutional amendment, the REA did not focus narrowly on school prayer but approached the question broadly, as a matter of freedom of religious expression in a variety of different public settings. The root idea behind the REA is to return organized religious expression to public places. Hyde's proposed amendment seeks to prevent discrimination against the expression of religious views, whether in public school commencements or on public radio stations. In fact, Hyde's amendment is silent on the topic of school prayer. As Michael McConnell, a religious conservative and professor of constitutional law at the University of Chicago, testified at hearings before the House Judiciary Subcommittee on the Constitution, the issue is not about school prayer but rather about the fact that the expression of religion has become subordinate to secularism. According to McConnell, "The authentic vision of the First Amendment, and of the Founders, and of the United States until about 40 years ago, was one of pluralistic public space in which all citizens, religious and nonreligious, have equal rights." He noted that the real problem today is "the enforced secularization of public life, not school prayer."[38]

McConnell testified that a constitutional amendment is needed because religion has been incrementally squeezed out of public life as the government's influence has increased over time. That McConnell's conception of the central issue included more than school prayer is indicated by the example he used in his testimony; he cited the Fordham University case where the U.S. Commerce Department denied a grant to the university's radio station because it broadcasts a Catholic mass for one hour each week. Because of this, the Commerce Department concluded the main thrust of the station (WFUV) was sectarian, and therefore the station was not eligible for government funding.[39] McConnell noted that as government becomes increasingly involved with activities in the semiprivate sector, government grant programs are being secularized to the point of denying benefits to any religious entity. Because the current constitutional rule excludes any group that is either pervasively sectarian or engaged in "specifically religious activities," religious discrimination results; and this, McConnell argued, ought to be changed. He suggested a principle of equal access so that whenever secular groups or organizations are given benefits or other government resources for activities that promote the public good, then religious groups and organizations are to be considered on exactly equal terms, notwithstanding their religious nature. Such an approach would show no favoritism or discrimination to any person or group. To achieve this, he concluded, a religious equality constitutional amendment is necessary.[40]

The comments of McConnell, a constitutional law scholar who advised Congressmen Hyde and Canady and helped draft the proposed amendment, indicate the novel, broad, strategic approach conservatives have taken in the matter of free religious expression in the public square. There are several remarkable aspects of this strategy. First, by defining the issue broadly as one of free religious expression rather than the narrow issue of school prayer, conservatives frame their approach as a struggle for religious freedom and religious equality in public schools. By taking on the broader issue of religious discrimination in schools and the workplace, they have expanded the issue from school prayer to cover all aspects of religious liberty under current law and practice in the United States. Moreover, they conceive of this as a matter of equal liberty; that is, they see themselves as involved in a struggle for religious equality defined as nondiscrimination and equal access to benefits.

The second remarkable feature of their approach is the tendency, ingenious and creative, to equate religious expression with free speech and to argue that, as a matter of free speech and religious liberty, believers should not be denied the right to pray in public schools.[41] In adopting this strategy, conservatives are capitalizing on the recent tendency of the Supreme Court to treat free exercise of religion cases as free speech cases under the freedom of speech clause of the First Amendment. This trend in Supreme Court jurisprudence dates from *Widmar v. Vincent* (1981) in which the Court determined that student-initiated religious groups are entitled to meet on the same basis as other student-initiated groups at public colleges and universities.[42] The trend was accelerated by Congress's passage in 1984 of the Equal Access Act, a statute that made it unlawful for any public secondary school receiving federal financing to deny equal access or fair opportunity to students wishing to conduct meetings because of the religious, political, or philosophical content of their speech at such meetings.[43] Continuing the trend toward identifying religious expression and free speech—because speech seems to command greater immunity from restriction—the Court in *Board of Education of Westside Community Schools v. Mergens* (1990) ruled that while a school may not lead or direct a religious club, it may permit student-initiated and student-led religious clubs to meet after school. Granting permission to religious groups for after-school use of facilities in the same manner as other community groups does not, the Court held, convey state approval or endorsement of a particular religion.[44] Then in 1993, in *Lamb's Chapel v. Center Moriches School District*, the Court held unanimously that New York's state education law allowing school districts to rent facilities after school hours for any type of expressive speech except religious speech was unlawful discrimination.[45] Finally, in 1995, the Court in two rulings protected religious speech by appealing to the free speech clause of the First Amendment. In *Rosenberger v. Rector and Visitors of the University of Virginia*, the Court overturned a lower court ruling that the establishment clause required the University of Virginia to exclude Rosenberger's student newspaper from funding because it was a religious publication. Despite funding 118 other student organizations, including 15 student newspapers, the university excluded *Wide Awake*, a Christian newspaper, from receiving money from the student activities fund because of its religious content. The Court ruled that the university had discriminated against *Wide Awake* for its expression of a religious viewpoint. Distinguishing student activity fees from public tax assessments, the Court held that student fees could go to private contractors "for the cost of printing that which is protected under the Speech Clause of the First Amendment."[46] Noteworthy here is the Court's appeal, once again, to freedom of speech rather than to the free exercise of religion clause as the relevant part of the First Amendment at stake in this religion case. Finally, in

Capitol Square Review and Advisory Board v. Pinette (1995), the Court ruled that the establishment clause does not require suppression of private religious speech in a traditional public forum where private secular speech is permitted. In this case, the State of Ohio sought to bar the Ku Klux Klan from displaying an unattended cross in a public park adjacent to the state capitol during the 1993 Christmas holiday. The American Civil Liberties Union argued on behalf of the Ku Klux Klan that the Klan should be allowed to display the cross because a Jewish group had earlier erected a menorah in the area. In its 7-2 ruling, the Court held that in specific cases private groups may display religious symbols on government property, reasoning that, if the sites in question have been used for other types of free-speech activities in the past, religious groups should have access to them also. Again, the Court's tendency to construe or equate the free exercise of religion with free speech activities should be noted.[47]

It is understandable that religious conservatives who favor restoring prayer to public schools would want to emphasize the strong connections between, or even identity of, religious expression and free speech. A liberal, secular society deeply committed to freedom of speech may find it easier to tolerate and protect religious expression defined as free speech rather than as the legitimate exercise of religious liberty protected by the free exercise clause. However, one has to ask whether something is not lost in First Amendment jurisprudence by collapsing religious liberty into freedom of speech and downplaying the religion clauses of the First Amendment. It is no accident that the religion clauses are stated in the very first sentence of the First Amendment and that religious freedom is rightly called "the First Liberty" by many students of American constitutional history.[48] Some historians of political thought go so far as to argue that the civil liberties so dear to American liberals would not even exist were it not for the struggle for freedom of religion that emerged in Europe during the Protestant Reformation and the post-Reformation periods.[49] Thus defenders of religious freedom should be loath to give up reliance upon the First Amendment religion clauses as the first line of defense in the struggle to protect religious expression. In other words, the clever strategy of religious conservatives that lies behind the Religious Equality Amendment may be imprudent and shortsighted. They might succeed in reinstating prayer in public schools as free speech, but they would do so at the cost of emptying the free exercise clause of the First Amendment of all bite and substance.

The third and final aspect of the strategy behind the Religious Equality Amendment has to do with the arguments put forward by its proponents. Congressmen Hyde and Canady insisted that they did not intend to revise the First Amendment, which they fully embrace. However, they questioned the interpretation given to the establishment and free exercise clauses by Supreme

Court decisions in the last thirty years. They argued that the Court, by attempting to prevent government from creating an "establishment of religion," has gone overboard in its interpretation of the Constitution, in effect penalizing religion and subverting "free exercise." They claimed that the Court's interpretation has created a tension between the two clauses that is not historically sound. The Court's current interpretation pits the two clauses against each other, resulting in "no establishment" trumping "free exercise." The result of this improper interpretation of the First Amendment has been the exclusion of religious values from American public life because of court-imposed discrimination against religion. Hyde and Canady said they wanted to recover the true balance between the two religion clauses. To this end, their proposed constitutional amendment calls for equality—for religion to enjoy the same freedom and protection given to secular activities.

Arguments against the Religious Equality Amendment

While the REA's proponents say it is necessary to protect believers against aggressive secularism in the schools and courts, opponents call the amendment unnecessary at best, and a dangerous breach of church-state separation at worst. Congressman Barney Frank (D-Mass.), ranking minority member of the House Judiciary Subcommittee on the Constitution, claimed that any problems of religious equality were resolved with passage of the Equal Access Act in 1984.[50] Citing Court rulings in *Mergens, Rosenberger*, and *Pinette*, J. Brent Walker, general counsel for the Baptist Joint Committee for Public Affairs, called the proposed amendment unnecessary because "the Court has been very generous to religious speech."[51] Moreover, opponents argued that tinkering with the Constitution, particularly something as hallowed as the First Amendment, should not be undertaken simply because someone does not like some court rulings. The Reverend Oliver Thomas, a Baptist minister and special counsel to the National Council of Churches of Christ in the USA, averred: "It's a good thing we're talking about treating religion fairly. But the last thing we need is a new First Amendment."[52]

A fundamental objection to the proposed amendment is that the REA could discourage the expression of minority religions and would be coercive of individual students. According to Jesse Choper, law professor at the University of California at Berkeley, prayer in public schools would have a coercive effect on some students, especially young children who are members of religious minorities. "Sometimes majorities succumb to the passions of the moment," Choper said, but "majorities don't need constitutional rights to protect them. They have the political process to protect them."[53] Yale Law School professor Stephen Carter, who is generally sympathetic to the concerns of parents that public schools should inculcate moral values in young citizens, maintains that the prohibition of public school prayer protects the exercise of religious freedom:

> In each of the Supreme Court's school-prayer cases, the Justices have been trying to avoid, at the minimum, official coercion of children to be religious or endorsement by the state of particular religious practices. If the state writes a prayer, selects a prayer, approves a prayer, or (through a teacher or a principal) leads a prayer, the message that it sends to impressionable children is that it is better if they pray than if they do not. . . . What the Supreme Court has recognized, and school-prayer advocates sometimes miss, is that the ideal of religious freedom means that the state should not express a view on how anyone should pray.[54]

Opponents of the REA also question whether student-led, student-initiated school prayer is really voluntary. Arguing that "voluntary spoken prayer" is neither really prayer nor truly voluntary, they argue that such prayer must be thin liturgical gruel to give no offense to any sect. Moreover, even with such bland, nondenominational prayers, children will feel coercive peer pressure to participate. Spokespersons for the National Council of Churches have repeatedly made this point in the long, thirty-year debate about prayer in public schools.

Opponents of the REA also question the practicality of a school prayer amendment, arguing that in highly diverse school districts such an amendment would only complicate matters in an unduly burdensome way. Jorge Osterling, director of community services for the public schools in Arlington County, Virginia, noted that in his county, students come from over fifty countries and represent nearly twenty religions. "The fact is, we cannot facilitate any public place to pray, because if we do it for one, we have to do it for everybody. We cannot paralyze the school by turning it into a temple."[55] Prudent school administrators note, moreover, the potential for increased litigation and the additional costs schools would face in accommodating each student's demands for religious expression.[56]

REA opponents also argue that this proposed constitutional amendment is a radical solution that is unconstitutional because it threatens to undermine church-state separation. Joseph Conn, a spokesperson for Americans United for Separation of Church and State, claims that the proposed amendment amounts to "a sweeping rewrite of the First Amendment to allow Government support for religious institutions." And J. Brent Walker contends the REA would permit, if not require, government financing of religion.[57] This would amount to a radical departure from the American constitutional tradition of institutional church-state separation—as stated in the *Everson* decision and in

James Madison's "Memorial and Remonstrance." Given the dissenting opinion of Justice Souter in *Rosenberger*, as well as the majority and concurring opinions of Justices Kennedy and O'Connor (which distinguished student fees from public taxpayer financing), it seems unlikely that the Supreme Court as presently constituted would be so radical as to find taxpayer financing of religion constitutional.

Finally, REA opponents seek to counter the impression that overanxious school officials are not allowing students to pray privately in public schools. J. Brent Walker acknowledges that "misunderstandings" about when students can pray have sometimes occurred in public schools. However, he insists that "the answer there is not to amend the Constitution, it's to educate people about what the Constitution allows and disallows."[58] On this view, the best approach to religious liberty would be better public education about existing law.

Alternatives to Prayer in Public Schools

This, interestingly enough, has been the approach of President Clinton and of a wide variety of religious and secular groups. In a major speech on religion in public schools on July 7, 1995, President Clinton affirmed religious liberty in America while stating that such freedom was already guaranteed under present law. Thus there is no need to "reform" or press for a new "Religious Equality" constitutional amendment.[59]

The president argued that "the First Amendment does not convert our schools into religion-free zones." He maintained that in their decisions governing prayer and other religious activities in public schools, the Supreme Court has tried to strike a careful balance, forbidding school-sponsored religious devotions but protecting truly voluntary student free exercise. He insisted that while schools may not advocate a religious viewpoint, students retain broad personal protections. He noted that students may read the Bible or other religious texts during free time, refer to religion in homework assignments, and pray individually, including saying grace before lunch. In many instances, students may form religious clubs, wear religious T-shirts, and distribute religious literature.

The president's speech was timed to coincide with the hearings on religious liberty and the Bill of Rights held by the House Judiciary Subcommittee on the Constitution. Many political analysts regarded Clinton's speech as an effort to defuse the Republican-led Congress's effort to pass the REA. Saying that "the First Amendment as it is presently written permits the American people to do what they need to do," the president directed the federal government to take steps to clarify the role of religion in public schools. To ensure that school officials and parents understand the law on this issue, Clinton instructed the federal Education Department, in consultation with Attorney General Janet Reno, to issue informational materials to all school districts in the country before the beginning of the 1995–96 school year.

One month later, in August 1995, Secretary of Education Richard W. Riley, after conferring with Attorney General Reno, issued an advisory memorandum on religion and public education. The Riley memorandum stated that schools could not discriminate against private religious expression by students but must instead give students the same right to engage in religious activity and discussion that they have to engage in other comparable activity. At the same time, he maintained that schools could not endorse religious activity or doctrine or coerce participation in religious activity. The Riley directive also addressed such issues as teaching about religion and values, the distribution of religious literature on campus, release time for religious instruction, the wearing of religious garb, and the provisions of the Equal Access Act.[60] Copies of the Riley memorandum were sent to all fifteen thousand school districts in the United States in time for the opening of the 1995–96 school year.

Other groups and coalitions have also emphasized the need for better public education about existing law in order to preserve and enhance religious freedom in the nation's public schools. In its January/February 1996 issue, *Liberty* published "A Statement of Principles" that addressed the need for a renewed commitment of American citizens to the principles of the religious liberty clauses in the First Amendment. Sponsors of the statement included a broad spectrum of organizations from both the right and the left: American Association of Teachers, American Center for Law and Justice, Association for Supervision and Curriculum Development, Carnegie Foundation for the Advancement of Teaching, Central Conference of American Rabbis, Christian Coalition, Christian Educators Association International, Christian Legal Society, Citizens for Excellence in Education, the Freedom Forum First Amendment Center at Vanderbilt University, National Association of Churches of Christ in the USA, National Education Association, National School Boards Association, People for the American Way, and Union of American Hebrew Congregations. The statement contained six principles:

1. Religious liberty is an inalienable right of every person.

2. Citizenship in a diverse society means living with our deepest differences and committing ourselves to work for public policies that are in the best interest of all individuals, families, communities, and our nation.

3. Public schools must model the democratic process and constitutional principles in the development of policies and curricula.

4. Public schools may neither inculcate nor inhibit religion. They must be places where religion and religious conviction are treated with fairness and respect.

5. Parents are recognized as having the primary responsibility for bringing up their children, including education.

6. Civil debate, the cornerstone of a true democracy, is vital to the success of any effort to improve or reform America's public schools.[61]

While these principles appear to be general rather than specific, agreement of diverse groups to these shared basic principles can help to resolve disagreements about specific school policies that may develop in the future.

Perhaps the most comprehensive effort to clarify existing law about religious expression in public schools was undertaken by a coalition of thirty-six religious organizations that issued "Religion in the Public Schools: A Joint Statement of Current Law" in April 1995. A drafting committee chaired by the American Jewish Congress included the following groups: American Civil Liberties Union, American Jewish Committee, American Muslim Council, Anti-Defamation League, Baptist Joint Committee, Christian Legal Society, General Conference of Seventh-Day Adventists, National Association of Evangelicals, National Council of Churches, People for the American Way, and Union of American Hebrew Congregations. In addition to these members of the drafting committee, another twenty-four organizations spanning the ideological, religious, and political spectrum endorsed the statement.[62] According to the joint statement, all these religious groups "share a commitment both to the freedom of religious practice and to the separation of church and state such freedom requires." The endorsing organizations issued this statement to dispel the notion that the Supreme Court has declared the public schools "religion-free zones" and to underscore the fact that the Constitution permits much private religious activity in and about the public schools. While these groups might press litigation for different constitutional treatments of some topics, such as graduation prayer and baccalaureate services, they all agreed that the joint statement is an accurate report of what the law currently is. In order to protect religious freedom in public schools, the signatories offered this statement of consensus on current law as an aid to parents, educators, and students.

The document then summarized in practical terms what existing law permits regarding student prayers, graduation prayer and baccalaureates, official participation or encouragement by school teachers and administrators of religious activity, teaching about religion, student assignments, distribution of religious literature, the Equal Access Act, religious holidays, student garb, released time, teaching values, and excusal from religiously objectionable lessons. For example, on student prayers, the statement emphasized that "students have the right to pray individually or in groups and to discuss their religious views with their peers so long as they are not disruptive. Because the establishment clause does not apply to purely private speech, students enjoy the right to read their Bibles or other scriptures, say grace before meals, pray before tests, and discuss religion with other willing student listeners."[63] On graduation prayer, the joint statement maintained that school officials may not mandate prayer at graduation or organize a religious baccalaureate ceremony. However, they may rent out facilities to organizers of privately sponsored religious baccalaureate services if the school generally rents out its facilities to private groups. The document acknowledged that federal courts have reached conflicting conclusions on student-initiated prayer at graduation and that this issue awaits authoritative resolution by the Supreme Court.[64]

Similarly, the statement summarized what is currently legally permissible in teaching about religion. Acknowledging that it would be difficult to teach art, music, literature, and most social studies without considering religious influences, the coalition stated that students may be taught about religion but that public schools may not proselytize or teach religion. Similarly, the document pointed out that public schools may teach about religious holidays and may celebrate the secular aspects of holidays and objectively teach about their religious aspects. However, they may not observe the holidays as religious events.

Finally, the statement asserted that schools may teach values and civic virtues such as honesty, courage, good citizenship, sportsmanship, respect for the rights and freedoms of others, respect for persons and their property, and the dual virtues of moral conviction and tolerance. It said that schools may teach sexual abstinence and contraception; however, they may not be taught as religious tenets. The mere fact that most, if not all, religions also teach these values does not make it unlawful to teach them. In this way, the coalition tried to address the values questions that often lie behind the desire of school prayer advocates to have prayer and devotional exercises reinstated in public schools. The coalition recognized that public schools are not neutral, that they are in the values business. They are involved in, and responsible for, the moral education of their students. Further, the coalition stressed that, with regard to religion, the public schools must treat religion with respect and consideration, thereby conveying an especially important value to their students. Another way of putting this is to say that school officials must certainly avoid giving students the impression that religion is somehow dangerous or unimportant.

By widely disseminating its joint statement, the coalition has sought to educate school administrators, teachers, parents, students, and the general public about what is currently permissible regarding the free exercise of religion in the public schools. It should be obvious that there is actually a fair amount of latitude regarding student rights to pray privately and to learn about the great world religions in American public schools. By broadcasting this view widely, the coalition reaffirms its conviction that the best approach to religious liberty is better public education about existing law. The generous provision of current law about religion in public schools has convinced the coalition that a proposed religious equality constitutional amendment is unnecessary.

The Future of the Religious Equality Amendment

The argument that the REA is unnecessary has much to support it. During the Clinton administration, the executive branch of the federal government has issued educational guidelines to school districts in an effort to clarify the role of religion in public schools. The American Jewish Congress has led a large, ideologically diverse coalition of religious organizations in an effort to educate school officials and the general public about the same issues.

Moreover, the Supreme Court in recent years has upheld the rights of student religious clubs in secondary schools to meet during noninstructional time, to pray, and to read and discuss the Bible or other sacred scriptures. In 1994, the American Center for Law and Justice estimated that 12,000 Bible clubs were operating in American public schools. And a group named Student Venture, a part of the Campus Crusade for Christ International, has helped high school and junior high students organize prayer groups that, in 1994, numbered 177,000 participants. Because these permissible forms of student activity are already there in public schools, especially in the South, a new constitutional amendment seems unnecessary.[65]

Further, the REA is risky and dangerous. It risks violating the rights of individuals and religious minorities. Americans must take care not to coerce impressionable young schoolchildren through government endorsement of religious devotion or through the tyranny of the majority in homogeneous school districts in a nation where 85 percent of the population professes Christianity. The Anti-Defamation League makes this point well: "We oppose organized school prayer—which is usually based on the religion of the local majority—because such prayer sends the message to impressionable schoolchildren that the Government favors a particular religious group."[66] Furthermore, the matter of coercing schoolchildren to pray remains very serious in other ways; for example, how truly "voluntary" is voluntary school prayer? Some argue that "voluntary school prayer" is an oxymoron. Children in public schools are a captive audience; they are required to attend school. They are subject to peer pressure, which can be considerable. They are also subject to subtle pressure from teachers; that is, they may participate in school prayer in order to gain their teacher's approval. Finally, prayer in public schools can be potentially if not actually divisive, pitting students against one another, particularly if prayer at school graduations is decided by majority vote of the student body (as it presently is in a sizable number of school districts around the country). So, for all these reasons, a proposed constitutional amendment such as the REA is, in addition to being unnecessary, a rather risky proposition.

At the same time, it must be acknowledged that the debate about a proposed Religious Equality Amendment to the Constitution has been rather instructive. By citing acts of discrimination and harassment, conservative Evangelicals have succeeded in convincing liberal churches and secular society that problems do exist and that it is very important to prevent any stigmatizing of religion in the public schools. By drawing attention to these problems, they have forced groups such as the National Council of Churches, the American Jewish Congress, and the American Civil Liberties Union to clarify existing law on religion in public schools. Current law, it turns out, is actually quite permissive on a wide range of issues. Children can pray individually and can form groups and religious clubs that meet on school property before or after the official class day, much the way other extracurricular clubs do. The Clinton administration has also weighed in on this issue, supporting through presidential speeches and directives religious freedom in public schools. In this sense, the religious right has done the nation a service—by alerting citizens and officials to the legitimate concerns of parents and teachers about the moral education of future citizens in a democratic republic.

Those who support prayer in public schools argue that the schools are responsible for the moral education of children. Moreover, they claim that morality springs from a religious tradition and that, therefore, there should be school prayer. However, that morality must be religiously based and religiously derived is a debatable proposition. Opponents of school prayer question any logically necessary link between religious devotion and moral education. Stephen Carter, for example, makes the obvious point that little empirical evidence exists to demonstrate the connection between school prayer and a moral citizenry.

> First, no reliable data support the claim that more prayer in public schools would lead to more morally upstanding children. In place of evidence, supporters offer a *post hoc, ergo propter hoc* argument: the rates of teen pregnancy, youth violence, and drug use have increased rapidly in the years since school prayer was banned, and therefore the ban must be the cause. This is reminiscent of the charming but statistically naive point somebody came up with years ago: television viewership and lung cancer were both increasing, so one must cause the other.

Second, throughout much of that often-cited period of American history in which children did pray in the public schools, we as a nation countenanced slavery, Jim Crow, lynchings, child labor, the oppression of women, and much more; that is, there are important ways in which our national morality has improved, not declined, in recent decades. To be sure, intensely religious people were in the forefront of the movements to end these and most other serious abuses and oppressions in our history. But there is no reason to suppose that they were motivated by the classroom prayers of their youth.[67]

A democratic republic, as the Framers foresaw, requires a morally upright, virtuous citizenry, but there is no evidence that religious devotions in public schools will create a moral citizenry. Moreover, the American democratic experiment takes place within the context of liberal constitutionalism. That is, as a liberal democracy, we are especially committed to the religious freedom of individuals and religious minorities. Thus American constitutionalism obligates parents, teachers, and school boards to be especially careful to protect children and teenagers against coercion and peer pressure in the matter of prayer in public schools. As members of a liberal democracy in a pluralistic society, citizens cannot, in the final analysis, constitutionally allow a democratic majority to ride roughshod over the rights of individuals and minorities. Because the proposed REA risks doing exactly that, it is not a constitutional amendment that a liberal democracy should support.

Notes

1. David W. Hendon and James M. Kennedy, Notes on Church-State Affairs, *Journal of Church and State* 38, no. 3 (Autumn 1996): 945.

2. *Engel v. Vitale*, 370 U.S. 421 (1962); and *Abington School District v. Schempp*, 374 U.S. 203 (1963). The following is the nondenominational prayer composed by the New York State Board of Regents in *Engel:* "Almighty God, we acknowledge our dependence upon Thee, and we beg Thy blessings upon us, our parents, our teachers, and our Country." In *Abington v. Schempp*, parents of children in public schools of Abington Township, a suburb of Philadelphia, challenged a Pennsylvania statute requiring the reading without comment of ten verses from the Bible at the opening of school each day. A child could be excused from participation at the parents' written request. In *Murray v. Curlett*, Madalyn Murray, a professed atheist, challenged the daily Bible reading and Lord's Prayer recitation that was a practice in the Baltimore public schools dating to a rule promulgated in 1905 by the city board of school commissioners. The two cases were presented to the Supreme Court together, and a single opinion was handed down in June 1963.

3. *Everson v. Board of Education*, 330 U.S. 1 (1947), in *Religious Liberty in the Supreme Court: The Cases That Define the Debate over Church and State*, ed. Terry Eastland (Washington, D.C.: Ethics and Public Policy Center, 1993), 64.

4. Editorial, *Washington Post*, 28 June 1962, in *Religious Liberty in the Supreme Court*, ed. Terry Eastland, 139.

5. Editorial, "Prayer Still Legal in Public Schools," *Christian Century*, 4 July 1962, in *Religious Liberty in the Supreme Court*, ed. Eastland, 140.

6. Editorial, "The Regents' Prayer Decision," *Christianity & Crisis*, 23 July 1962, in *Religious Liberty in the Supreme Court*, ed. Eastland, 141.

7. Editorial, "Engel v. Vitale," *New Republic*, 9 July 1962, in *Religious Liberty in the Supreme Court*, ed. Eastland, 143, 145.

8. For the 1962 Gallup poll, see Jacquelene R. McKee, "Crafting a Republican Strategy for Religious Freedom: Congressman Henry Hyde and the 104th Congress" (M.A. thesis, Regent University, 1996. table 2, p. 67). For the 1991 *Time/CNN* poll, see Nancy Gibb, "America's Holy War," *Time*, 9 December 1991, 64. The 1994 *Los Angeles Times* poll is reported in McKee, "Crafting a Republican Strategy," table 2, p. 67.

9. Stephen L. Carter, "Let Us Pray," *New Yorker*, 5 December 1994, 61. See also Kirk W. Elifson and C. Kirk Hadaway, "Prayer in Public Schools: When Church and State Collide," *Public Opinion Quarterly* 49, no. 3 (Fall 1985): 317–29.

10. "Church and State: The Court Rules," *New York Times*, 1 July 1962, sec. 4, p. E9; see also Leo Pfeffer, *Church, State, and Freedom* (Boston: Beacon Press, 1967), 466.

11. 108 *Congressional Record* 11675 (1962), as cited by William M. Beaney and Edward N. Beiser, "Prayer in Politics: The Impact of *Engel* and *Schempp* on the Political Process," in *The Impact of Supreme Court Decisions*, ed. Theodore Becker and Malcolm Feeley (New York: Oxford University Press, 1973), 22–36.

12. *Washington Post*, 7 July 1962, cited in Anson Phelps Stokes and Leo Pfeffer, *Church and State in the United States* (New York: Harper & Row, 1964), 378. This is a revised one-volume version of the original three-volume work by Anson Phelps Stokes.

13. For Congressman Williams's comment, see 108 *Congressional Record* 11734 (1962), as cited in Beaney and Beiser, "Prayer in Politics," 23.

14. For Senator Robertson's comment, see 108 *Congressional Record* 11708 (1962); for Congressman Becker's comment, see 108 *Congressional Record* 11719 (1962), both cited in Beaney and Beiser, "Prayer in Politics," 23–24. It is interesting to note the reaction, thirty years later, of Senator Robertson's son, evangelist Pat Robertson, to the Supreme Court decision on prayer at middle- and high-school graduations in *Lee v. Weisman* (1992). In response to this ruling, Pat Robertson and the American Center for Law and Justice (which he founded) actively campaigned to encourage high school students to vote for voluntary school prayer at their commencement ceremonies. See "Robertson Trying Again to Put Prayer in Schools," *New York Times*, 16 April 1993, p. A12.

15. *New York Times*, 1 July 1962, sec. 4, p. E9.

16. Beaney and Beiser, "Prayer in Politics," 27.

17. "Opinion of the Week: Prayer in School," *New York Times*, 1 July 1962, sec. 4, p. E9.

19. Senate Committee on the Judiciary, *Hearings on Prayer in Public Schools and Other Matters before the Senate Committee on the Judiciary,* 87th Cong., 2d sess., 56,

quoted in Beaney and Beiser, "Prayer in Politics," 26.

20. Pfeffer, *Church, State, and Freedom,* 468–69.

21. Beaney and Beiser, "Prayer in Politics," 27.

22. Beaney and Beiser, "Prayer in Politics," 28.

23. Pfeffer, *Church, State, and Freedom,* 478. See also the discussion of the impact of the Supreme Court prayer decisions in Kenneth Dolbeare and Phillip E. Hammond, *The School Prayer Decisions: From Court Policy to Local Practices* (Chicago: University of Chicago Press, 1977), 32.

24. Robert H. Birkby, "The Supreme Court and the Bible Belt: Tennessee Reaction to the Schempp Decision," in *Impact of Supreme Court Decisions*, ed. Becker and Feeley, 110–18.

25. Birkby, "The Supreme Court and the Bible Belt," 115–16.

26. Birkby, "The Supreme Court and the Bible Belt," 116.

27. Birkby, "The Supreme Court and the Bible Belt," 116–17.

28. *Wallace v. Jaffree*, 472 U.S. 38 (1985). In this decision, the Supreme Court ruled unconstitutional an Alabama statute authorizing a moment of silence in public schools for "meditation or voluntary prayer" for the sole express purpose of returning voluntary prayer to the schools.

29. David W. Hendon and James M. Kennedy, Notes on Church-State Affairs, *Journal of Church and State* 38, no 2 (Spring 1996): 459. See also Ronald Smothers, "School Prayer Gaining Ground in the South," *New York Times,* 22 February 1994, p. A12. The challenge to the Georgia statute is *Bown v. Gwinnett County School District* (ND Ga 1995).

30. Linda Greenhouse, "Supreme Court Roundup," *New York Times*, 5 November 1996, p. A16. See also Peter Applebome, "Prayer in Public Schools? It's Nothing New for Many," *New York Times*, 22 November 1994, p. A21.

31. "Taunts Follow Family as Mom Fights Use of Prayer in Mississippi Schools," *Star-Ledger* (Newark, N.J.), 2 January 1995, 11. See also Ronald Smothers, "School Prayer Gaining Ground."

32. "Florida Governor Vetoes Prayer Bill, despite Religious Right Barrage of Attacks," *Church & State* 49, no. 7 (July/August 1996): 15.

33. In 1984, Congress came closest to passing a constitutional amendment to reverse the Supreme Court decisions on school prayer. The Senate debated the following proposal: "Nothing in this Constitution shall be construed to prohibit individual or group prayer in public schools or other public institutions. No person shall be required by the United States or by any State to participate in prayer. Neither the United States nor any State shall compose the words of any prayer to be said in public schools." The Senate vote in favor of school prayer was 56-54, far short of the two-thirds majority necessary for congressional submission of a proposed amendment to the states. See George McKenna and Stanley Feingold. eds., *Taking Sides: Clashing Views on Controversial Political Issues* (Guilford, Conn.: Dushkin Publishing Group, 1997), 279.

34. The split between Hyde supporters and Istook supporters was so serious that it merits additional study. See McKee, "Crafting a Republican Strategy." I am grateful to Professor Hubert Morken for making this fine thesis available to me. See also "School

Prayer Delayed by GOP Squabbles," *CQ Weekly Report* 54, no. 36 (7 September 1996): 2529.

35. "Prayer Amendment Unlikely despite Push from Right," *CQ Weekly Report* 53, no. 27 (8 July 1995): 1998.

36. See Stanley Hauerwas and John Westerhoff, eds., *Schooling Christians: "Holy Experiments" in American Education* (Grand Rapids, Mich.: Eerdmans, 1992), vii. By the "schooling of Christians," the editors understand "the manifold ways, in schools and out, in which Christians are made." For Stephen Carter's views, see *The Culture of Disbelief* (New York: Basic Books, 1993) and also his "Let Us Pray," *New Yorker*, 5 December 1994, 60–74.

37. "Prayer Amendment Unlikely," 2000. Joshua Burton and his family did not wait for Congress to pass a constitutional amendment. With the help of an Orlando law firm specializing in religious liberty cases, the family sued the school in federal district court.

38. David W. Hendon and James M. Kennedy, Notes on Church-State Affairs, *Journal of Church and State* 38, no. 2 (Spring 1996): 461.

39. *Fordham v. Brown*, 856 F. Supp. 1268 (D.D.C. 1994). This case is summarized in McKee, "Crafting a Republican Strategy," 26–27. See also "Prayer Amendment Unlikely," 103.

40. U.S. Congress, House, Subcommittee on the Constitution, Committee on the Judiciary. Religious Liberty and the Bill of Rights, 104th Cong., 1st Sess., 8 June 1995, 79–85. Summarized in McKee, "Crafting a Republican Strategy," 26–27.

41. It is important to note that the religious right has consciously taken the approach that the issue of school prayer is one of students' rights to free speech, rather than a question of religious rights. As one high school principal in Tennessee put it, prayer is "a student free-speech issue, just as the wearing of black arm bands by students in school to protest the Vietnam war in the 60's was a free-speech issue." Smothers, "School Prayer Gaining Ground."

42. *Widmar v. Vincent*, 454 U.S. 263 (1981).

43. Public Law 98-377, Title 8 (11 August 1984); 98 Stat. 1302-04; 20 U.S.C. 4071 et seq. There are several conditions attached to this access, including requirements that the meeting be student initiated, not sponsored by the school or government, and employees or agents of the school may be present only in a nonparticipatory capacity. Basically, the Equal Access Act extended to the secondary education level the right granted colleges under *Widmar.* See McKee, "Crafting a Republican Strategy," 87.

44. *Board of Education of Westside Community Schools v. Mergens*, 496 U.S. 226 (1990).

45. *Lamb's Chapel v. Center Moriches School District*, 113 S.Ct. 2141 (1993).

46. *Rosenberger v. Rector and Visitors of the University of Virginia*, 63 USLW 4702 (1995). See also Rob Boston, "A Crack in the Wall," *Church & State* 48, no. 8 (September 1995): 4.

47. *Capitol Square Review and Advisory Board v. Pinette*, 63 USLW 4702 (1995).

48. See, e.g., William Lee Miller, *The First Liberty: Religion and the American Republic* (New York: Alfred A. Knopf, 1986).

49. See, e.g., George Sabine, *A History of Political Theory*, 3d ed. (New York: Holt, Rinehart & Winston, 1961).

50. McKee, "Crafting a Republican Strategy," 24. See also Derek H. Davis, "A Commentary on the Proposed 'Religious Equality/Liberties' Amendment," *Journal of Church and State* 38, no. 1 (Winter 1996): 5–23.

51. Gustav Niebuhr, "Victory on Religion Rulings Was Limited, Groups Say," *New York Times*, 1 July 1995, 7.

52. "School Prayer Delayed," 2530.

53. "Prayer Amendment Unlikely," 2000.

54. Carter, "Let Us Pray," 62.

55. "Prayer Amendment Unlikely," 2000.

56. "School Prayer Delayed," 2530.

57. David W. Hendon and James M. Kennedy, Notes on Church-State Affairs, *Journal of Church and State* 38, no. 2 (Spring 1996): 461.

58. Niebuhr, "Victory on Religion Rulings Limited," 7.

59. Todd S. Purdum, "President Defends a Place for Religion in the Schools," *New York Times*, 13 July 1995, p. A1. See also Joseph L. Conn, "Public Schools Aren't 'Religion-Free Zones,'" *Church & State* 48, no. 8 (September 1995): 9–10.

60. David W. Hendon and James M. Kennedy, Notes on Church-State Affairs, *Journal of Church and State* 38, no. 2 (Spring 1996): 457–58.

61. David W. Hendon and James M. Kennedy, Notes on Church-State Affairs, *Journal of Church and State* 38, no. 2 (Spring 1996): 459–60.

62. Endorsing organizations included American Ethical Union, American Humanist Association, Americans for Religious Liberty, Americans United for Separation of Church and State, B'nai B'rith International, Christian Science Church, Church of the Brethren, Washington Office; Church of Scientology International; Evangelical Lutheran Church in America, Lutheran Office of Governmental Affairs; Federation of Reconstructionist Congregations and Havurot; Friends Committee on National Legislation; Guru Gobind Singh Foundation; Hadassah, the Women's Zionist Organization of America; Interfaith Alliance; Interfaith Impact for Justice and Peace; National Council of Jewish Women; National Jewish Community Relations Advisory Council; National Ministries, American Baptist Churches, USA; National Sikh Center; North American Council for Muslim Women; Presbyterian Church (USA); Reorganized Church of Jesus Christ of Latter Day Saints; Unitarian Universalist Association of Congregations; United Church of Christ, Office for Church in Society.

63. "Religion in the Public Schools: A Joint Statement of Current Law," April 1995, 2.

64. The issue of student-initiated prayer at graduation ceremonies will eventually have to be settled by the U.S. Supreme Court. In the wake of the Court's ruling in *Lee v. Weisman* (1992), which forbade state-sponsored prayer at graduations, many school districts have decided to permit students to vote on whether to have graduation invocations and benedictions. At the present time, there are at least three conflicting rulings by U.S. circuit courts of appeal on this issue. In *Jones v. Clear Creek Independent School District* (1992), the United States Court of Appeals for the Fifth Circuit ruled

that student-initiated prayer at graduation ceremonies was legal when it was spontaneous, initiated and led by students, was nonsectarian, and did not proselytize. The Fifth Circuit's ruling permitted students at a suburban Houston high school to incorporate prayer into their high school graduation. The Supreme Court subsequently refused to review that ruling, leaving it standing in the Fifth Circuit, which includes Texas, Louisiana, and Mississippi. See Smothers, "School Prayer Gaining Ground."

In *Joint School District No. 241 v. Harris* (1995), the Ninth Circuit Court of Appeals ruled student-initiated graduation prayer unconstitutional. However, on June 26, 1995, the U.S. Supreme Court dismissed the case, declaring the issue in this Idaho prayer controversy moot because the student who filed the challenge had graduated. Rob Boston, "Supreme Court Ducks Idaho Graduation Prayer Case," *Church & State* 48, no. 8 (September 1995): 8.

Finally, in *ACLU v. Blackhorse Pike Regional Board of Education* (1996), the U.S. Third Circuit Court of Appeals ruled that decisions about prayer at high-school graduations may not be left to majority rule by students. In this 9-4 decision on May 24, 1996, the full federal appellate panel overturned a New Jersey school board policy allowing graduating seniors to vote on whether to have prayers at the commencement ceremony. The Blackhorse Pike Regional District had adopted the policy in 1993 in response to the Supreme Court's ban on clergy-led devotions at graduation ceremonies in *Lee v. Weisman* (1992). Noting that the rulings of the Third and Ninth Circuit Courts differ from that of the Fifth Circuit, the majority opinion in *Blackhorse* all but invited the Supreme Court to take up the issue of student-conducted worship at graduation ceremonies. See "No Majority Rule on Graduation Prayer, Rules Appeals Court," in *Church & State* 49, no. 7 (July/August 1996): 16.

65. Applebome, "Prayer in Public Schools?"

66. Abraham H. Foxman and David H. Strassler, letter to editor, *New York Times*, 27 November 1994, sec. E, p. 10. Foxman is national director and Strassler is national chairman of the Anti-Defamation League.

67. Carter, "Let Us Pray," 64.

10

Litigating *Everson* after *Everson*

William Bentley Ball

This book is devoted to "the" *Everson* case, but in fact there are several purported *Everson* cases. One is the *Everson* that upholds the absolute separation of church and state. Another is the *Everson* that justifies unlimited governmental aid to churches. A third *Everson*, in conflict with the first two *Everson*'s, is the *Everson* that holds that states may provide free busing, but no greater benefits, for children attending religious schools. A fourth *Everson* holds that government may fully subsidize religious schools; a fifth, that it may reimburse parents for the cost of sending their children to such schools. I shall not attempt here to delve into those many themes and variations on the music from *Everson*. All such claims should inevitably drive one back to the black print of the opinion of the Supreme Court and to that of the dissents in the 5-4 *Everson* decision. Over the course of the past thirty years I have repeatedly done that very thing. Once again I tackle that black print—this time simply reflecting on the role it has played in the rather momentous court events I've witnessed these past four decades. As I risk burdening the reader with what she or he already knows, I am conscious, in view of the "several purported *Everson* cases," of the discipline Justice Brandeis imposed upon himself of personally drafting his statement of the facts of each case coming before him as "his private assurance that he would not be seduced by the fascination of legal analysis until he had grounded himself in the realities of the case."[1] Here is my grounding in *Everson*:

In 1941 New Jersey enacted a statute authorizing local public school districts to provide for the transportation of children attending public schools and of those attending nonpublic schools. Provision for the latter depended upon provision being made for the former and, for all, was limited to established public school routes. Excluded were children attending schools operated for profit. Not excluded were children attending nonpublic schools that were religious. A local school district (Ewing Township Board of Education) "acting

219

pursuant to the statute" (as the U.S. Supreme Court would later describe the district's proceeding) chose, not the actual furnishing of transportation to any children, but making cash payments to both public and nonpublic school parents to reimburse them for fares they paid to the public transportation system to carry their children. Ewing Township Board of Education made such payments to parents of children attending Catholic schools. A district taxpayer sued in state court challenging both the statute and the making of those payments as violating the New Jersey and federal constitutions. Losing in the New Jersey courts, he appealed to the Supreme Court on the ground that the statute and payments violated the due process clause of the Fourteenth Amendment and the establishment clause of the First Amendment. The Supreme Court, in an opinion by Justice Black, supported by Chief Justice Vinson and Justices Douglas, Murphy, and Reed, held them to violate neither. Here, said the Court, was no taking of a taxpayer's money to serve a private purpose, hence no violation of the Fourteenth Amendment. Instead, a purely public purpose was served—the provision for public transportation of children to schools where they would receive education.

Black's opinion in *Everson* then dwelled upon two provisions of the First Amendment—its establishment clause and its free exercise clause. He provided eloquent dictum on the first and a ruling triggered by the second. His discourse on establishment, characterized by Justice Jackson in dissent as "the undertones of the opinion," described the establishment clause as providing a high and impregnable wall of separation, not simply between church and state, but apparently between religion and state. His ruling on the issue presented by the case—reimbursement of money to parents that they had expended for transportation of their children to religious schools—was based on the free exercise clause, even though neither the school board nor any of the parents had raised a free exercise issue. After his long exposition of the establishment clause, Black turned to the "command" of the free exercise clause that government may not exclude individual believers, because of their faith, from receiving the benefits of public welfare legislation.

The *Everson* holding, then, comes to this: furnishing the public welfare benefit of busing to children to transport them to religious schools and to secular schools, in either of which they meet state compulsory attendance requirements, does not, insofar as the former are concerned, violate the establishment clause, because to hold that it does (and thus deny the transportation to children attending religious schools) would violate the free exercise clause. While the Court, in *Everson*, was careful to infer that not all government programs for the public welfare must be extended to individuals who would seek to enjoy them through religious agencies, it held that if a general welfare program were extended to benefit persons through secular private agencies, it could not exclude those who seek them through religious private agencies.

Everson, therefore, may be regarded as a *free exercise* decision. The Court upheld the providing of the service not only on the ground that that fulfilled a public purpose (that would not save it from establishment clause attack) but because the establishment clause attack that was made was nullified by free exercise principles.

The establishment clause dictum in *Everson* became the centerpiece of the Court's decision next term in *McCollum v. Board of Education*.[2] Here the Court (in an opinion, again, of Justice Black and with but one dissent) nullified an interfaith community program whereby, at no public cost, religious teachers of Protestant, Catholic, and Jewish faiths were permitted to offer religious instruction to children of those faiths on public school premises. The Court held the program to violate the establishment clause, stating that "it falls squarely under the ban of the First Amendment . . . as we interpreted it in *Everson v. Board of Education*."[3] Thus was dictum made into governing law.

In the early 1960s, a public question factually similar to that reviewed in *Everson* exploded in Pennsylvania—a proposed amendment to the public school code[4] to provide free bus transportation to children attending nonprofit, nonpublic (including religious) schools. The explosion was occasioned by the facts that the measure had been promoted by the Pennsylvania Catholic Conference (the public affairs representative of the Catholic dioceses of Pennsylvania) and that its principal beneficiaries would be parents of children enrolled in Catholic schools. So suit was instituted to enjoin operation of the act— based in part on *Everson* (the Black "no aid" dictum). Representing parents in defense of the act, I relied mainly on *Everson*'s actual holding. The Pennsylvania Supreme Court upheld the act, it, too, resting its decision on *Everson*.[5] The challengers sought U.S. Supreme Court reversal by appeal. The Supreme Court dismissed the appeal without oral argument.[6] A successor Pennsylvania nonpublic school busing statute, now extending the benefit of transportation beyond school district boundary lines, was similarly found constitutional against establishment clause attack in 1979 in *Springfield School District v. Department of Education*.[7]

Everson, prior to these two bus cases, had already found its way into Pennsylvania law in *Schade v. Allegheny County Institute District*.[8] There it was cited to defend the federal and state constitutionality of counties' paying of public funds to sectarian agencies to purchase care for dependent and neglected children placed there by orders of juvenile courts. The Pennsylvania Supreme Court held such purchases of services to be simply the fulfillment of a public purpose. It found no violation of church-state separation principles, citing *Everson*.[9]

As the first of the Pennsylvania busing cases was making its way through the courts, I was called upon to aid parents in the state of New York in a case then before the Supreme Court of the United States. New York had enacted a statute empowering public boards of education to lend to children attending public or private schools in their districts textbooks designated for use in the public schools. Two school boards sued to enjoin the loan of books under the act to children attending religious schools. Parents of children residing in the East Greenbush School District and attending Catholic parochial schools under the compulsory attendance law had been granted status as intervenors, and it was they I now came to represent. The school boards, in the courts below and now before the Supreme Court, relied heavily on the *Everson* dictum, especially as that had been given status as controlling precedent in *McCollum*, calling *Everson* "the seminal case on the impact of the establishment clause on a state's power to tax."[10] In this, the boards were supported by an impressive array of amici.[11]

While it was obvious that the parents' case should rely largely on *Everson*, by 1967, when the Supreme Court docketed the textbook loan case (as *Board of Education v. Allen*), it had also provided us with a decision that seemed to me complementary to *Everson* and highly useful in defense of the East Greenbush parents' interests. This was the case involving Bible reading and prayers in public schools, *School District of Abington Township v. Schempp.*[12] The Court, in *Schempp*, had moved to a new statement on the establishment clause. To withstand the strictures of the clause, said the Court, governmental action must have "a secular legislative purpose and a primary effect that neither advances or inhibits religion."[13] The Court cited *Everson* at the conclusion of the quoted language.

A second decision complementary to *Everson* had also been handed down by the Court in 1963. This was *Sherbert v. Verner,*[14] where the Court held that South Carolina had violated an individual's right to free exercise by denying her application for unemployment compensation after her discharge from employment for refusal to work on Sunday, the Sabbath day of her faith. The Court declared that its holding was based on *Everson*.[15]

With *Everson* and its two juridical descendants (*Schempp* and *Sherbert*) in hand, I felt that our parents should prevail as we now approached the Supreme Court. Arguing that the benefit of a secular textbook to a child in a religious school is constitutionally indistinguishable from the benefit of transportation of that child to that school, we considered no establishment clause problem to exist. We went on, however, to tell the Court that the school boards' complaint triggered vital free exercise concerns:

> Where the state compels attendance at some schools, and conscience . . . compels the selection of a particular school (where the requirements of law may be

fulfilled), serious free exercise problems would arise if those particular children were to be cut off from the benefits of a general public welfare statute applicable to all children in the State.[16]

This *Everson*-based argument we could now combine with the *Schempp* "purpose and effect" teaching. Surely, the furnishing of secular textbooks to children was in fulfillment of a secular purpose and had no primary effect of advancing religion.

The Supreme Court, by a vote of 6-3, upheld the textbook loan act, with its inclusion of children in religious schools. Justice White, writing for the majority, noted "the citation of *Everson* by the *Schempp* court to support its general standard" and wrote that "[t]he statute upheld in *Everson* would be considered a law having 'a secular legislative purpose and a primary effect that neither advances nor inhibits religion.'"[17]

Thus, in *Allen*, the "holding" side of *Everson* governed, while in *McCollum* the "dictum" side would be invoked to invalidate a series of legislative enactments aimed at including children in religious schools as beneficiaries of general welfare programs.

The most memorable of these (memorable because of its effects for a quarter century and down to the hour) is *Lemon v. Kurtzman*.[18] In 1968 Pennsylvania enacted a statute that seemed to its general assembly and its governor to follow logically from *Allen* (hence from *Everson* as developed in *Schade* and *Schempp*). Under the statute, Act 109 of 1968, the commonwealth would purchase secular educational services from nonpublic schools, both secular and religious. These services were confined to instruction in mathematics, modern foreign languages, physical science, and physical education. Governmental purchase of secular services from religious institutions was a technical device familiar in health care and, as was seen in *Schade*, child care. Why not, Pennsylvania reasoned, apply it in the field of child education? Act 109 was immediately challenged on establishment clause grounds in a federal three-judge district court and found constitutional by that court. The plaintiffs appealed to the U.S. Supreme Court. Again representing before the Court parent and child beneficiaries of Act 109, I pressed the holding in *Everson*, with its factual congruence with our case: (a) the public purpose in the service to individual children, (b) the secularity of that service, (c) the fact that the legislative program was of *general* benefit, not limited to children in religious schools but for all children in nonpublic schools and, further, simply extending to such schools public support of four required areas of secular instruction in public schools. I relied also, of course, on *Allen*, with its adoption of *Schempp*'s "purpose and effect" test. The Supreme Court in its decision made but brief reference to *Everson*, purporting to distinguish it on the sole basis that Act 109, unlike the

Everson and *Allen* programs, provided a "direct money subsidy" to church-related schools.[19] Thus ignored by the Court was the whole *Everson* "child benefit" rationale. Surprisingly, the Court also bypassed the *Schempp-Allen* "purpose and effect" test except to the extent of according "appropriate deference" to Act 109's declaration of the public purpose. Not finding that the act had a primary effect advancing religion, the Court struck down the act on a ground it had never before employed as a basis for decision, namely, that the act created "excessive entanglements" between government and religion. I will not here comment on what I deem the baselessness of the "excessive entanglements" notion.

Lemon simply left *Everson's* holding by the juridical wayside, while *Everson's* "no establishment" dictum for much of the next quarter century would constitute the core of decisions of the Court in cases involving statutes supportive of parental choice of religious schooling for their children. In 1973, again representing parents, I argued the case of *Sloan v. Lemon*[20] before the Supreme Court. This involved a simple statutory plan to reimburse parents for tuition expenses incurred in sending their children to nonpublic (including religious) schools. While I again sought to focus the Court on the implications of *Everson*, the Court used *Everson* to suggest a political conspiracy by which the Catholic Church was continually seeking to aggrandize itself at public expense through legislation in aid of its schools. As Justice Powell, writing for the Court, now said:

> Yet such aid [buses and textbooks] approached the "verge" of the constitutionally impermissible. Everson v. Board of Education, 330 U.S. 1, 116, . . . In Lemon, we declined to allow Everson to be used as the "platform for yet further steps" in granting assistance to "institutions whose legitimate needs are growing and whose interests have substantial political support."[21]

Argued the same day was the *Nyquist* case involving, inter alia, four programs again calling for the use of public funds for tuition reimbursement and, in addition, state income tax relief for parents of children attending nonpublic schools. Relying extensively on the *Everson* dictum, the Court voided the programs. Notable, if not prophetic, were now three strongly stated dissenting opinions on the issues of tuition reimbursement and tax relief. These opinions, by Chief Justice Burger, Justice White, and Justice Rehnquist, were rendered commonly for both the *Sloan* and *Nyquist* cases. A joint opinion penned by the chief justice went directly to *Everson* in attacking the Court's decision:

> I believe the Court's decision on those statutory provisions ignores the teachings of Everson v. Board of Education . . . and Board of Education v. Allen. . . .

While there is no straight line running through our decisions interpreting the Establishment and free exercise clauses of the First Amendment, our cases do, it seems to me, lay down one solid, basic principle: that the establishment clause does not forbid governments, state or federal, from enacting a program of general welfare, under which benefits are distributed to private individuals even though many of those individuals may elect to use those benefits in ways that "aid" religious instruction or worship.[22]

The opinion then goes on to stress *Everson* and, in particular, the free exercise aspect of its holdings.

[T]he balance between the policies of free exercise and establishment of religion tips in favor of the former when the legislation moves away from direct aid to religious instruction and takes on the character of general aid to individual families.[23]

The three dissenters also joined in separate opinions by Justices White and Rehnquist, both additional opinions basing themselves on the *Everson* holding.

I raised *Everson* two years later in yet another case arising in Pennsylvania, *Meek v. Pittenger*.[24] There a statute provided that all children enrolled in nonpublic schools would receive, at state expense, "auxiliary services" (counseling, testing, psychological testing, speech and hearing services, etc.) and that their schools would receive loans of instructional materials and equipment. Striking down these provisions as violating the establishment clause, the Court was forced to grapple with the implications of its *Everson* holding. The Court stated that, according to the holding, "as part of general legislation made available to all students, a State may include church-related schools in programs providing bus transportation, school lunches, and public health facilities—secular and nonideological services unrelated to the primary, religious-oriented educational function of the sectarian school."[25] But these, said the court, were "indirect and incidental" benefits, while the "massive aid" of instructional materials and equipment, under the new Pennsylvania program, was "neither direct nor incidental."[26]

Two observations are in point. First, the Court here departs from the stress given in *Everson* (and reported in the *Sloan-Nyquist* dissents) upon the liberality that the Constitution allows when the governmental aid is to individuals. It treats *Everson* as upholding *institutional* aid, and it seems to find institutional aid unconstitutional only where it is on a large scale. Second, neither the *Meek* Court nor the dissenters in *Sloan-Lemon* focused on a problem inherent in aid that is technically directed to institutions but that has no other public purpose than to aid the individuals in them. In *Meek* we therefore argued that, while public purposes may be achieved through government aid to individuals, *Everson* should not be read as meaning that government does not, and may not, aid individuals by directing the aid to the institutions where they, of right, choose to be.

Yet the *Everson* dictum rode on. In 1985, the Court struck down two state programs calling for use of public school employees to provide secular education courses on the premises of religious schools. In both cases, *Grand Rapids School District v. Ball* and *Aguilar v. Felton*,[27] the Court expressly relied upon the dictum (as well as the dictum's accumulations in *Lemon, Nyquist,* and *Meek*). The decisions in both *Grand Rapids* and *Aguilar* were accompanied by dissenting opinions from Justices Rehnquist, O'Connor, and White and Chief Justice Burger. These now repudiated the course of establishment clause development that, since 1971, had driven the *Everson* dictum to more and more extreme interpretations. Chief Justice Burger suggested that the majority in the two cases was driven by paranoia,[28] while Justice O'Connor deplored as "tragic" the terminating, after nineteen years, of the services of public teachers to help impoverished children in religious schools.[29]

While, in those decisions, the *Everson* dictum had prevailed over the *Everson* holding, the holding had been given expression in 1983, over the dissents of four justices. The case was *Mueller v. Allen,* wherein the Court upheld, over establishment clause objection, a Minnesota statute providing tax deductions for individuals for public and private school expenses they had incurred.[30] The Court found here the elements of "programs such as those in *Allen* and *Everson*" (a public welfare benefit, to a broad class of individual citizens).

Justices Marshall, Brennan, Blackmun, and Stevens, dissenting, found the decision of the Court as contradicting all the decisions—*Lemon, Nyquist, Meek*—that had been built upon the *Everson* dictum, concluding, indeed, by quoting the dictum's language that "no tax in any amount . . . be levied to support any religious activities or institutions."

In 1986 the Court had before it the case of one Larry Witters, a blind young man who had sought payments of government money for his education at a Bible school, under a vocational rehabilitation program of the state of Washington.[31] The Supreme Court of Washington held the payments to violate the establishment clause. The U.S. Supreme Court reversed. Critical to the Court's reasoning was the fact that the payment was to an individual, a student who would then transmit it to the educational institution of his choice. Hence any aid to that institution would come to it only as the result of that independent choice. Further, the aid was available without regard to the sectarian or nonsectarian nature of the institution and gave no greater benefits to recipients who would choose religious schools than to those who would not. The *Witters* decision, therefore, fit precisely the doctrine of the *Everson* holding. *Everson*'s true descendants—*Allen, Mueller,* and *Witters*—would now be of great service to a profoundly deaf boy and his parents whom, in 1988, I came to represent.

Jim Zobrest was a student at a Catholic high school in Tucson, Arizona. His parents asked the local school district to provide him a sign-language interpreter under the provisions of the federal-state programs of aid to education of the disabled.[32] The school district declined on establishment clause grounds. I brought suit in the U.S. district court at Tucson to require the service to be provided to Jim. That court granted summary judgment to the school district, the Ninth Circuit affirmed, and our case was accepted for review by the Supreme Court. Just as the Court, in *Grand Rapids* and *Aguilar*, had based itself on decisions that were the progeny of the Everson dictum, so now the Court, in reversing, would cite *Mueller* and *Witters*—direct and legitimate descendants of the real *Everson*.[33]

After some decades of handling litigations in cases in which *Everson* has logically been involved, I have now reached this conclusion as to its meaning, post *Zobrest*: Government may afford material aid to individuals exercising a choice to be served by religious educational institutions where the individual and not the institution is the beneficiary of that aid. The programs must provide benefits to a broad class of citizens and be religiously "neutral" (i.e., not be primarily religious in character, create no greater or broader benefits to recipients who apply their aid to religious education, and not limit the benefits in part or in whole to students at religious institutions).

Thus, after half a century does the *Everson* music continue to play. As I concluded this chapter, there came to me an odd little thought that often tiptoes into my mind as I think of famous cases: Whatever has become of those whose names the cases made notorious? Where now are Vashti McCollum, Edward and Sidney Schempp, Adell Sherbert, Alton Lemon, Dr. David Kurtzman, and all the others whose names we keep repeating, though they have mostly passed into the shadows of history? Maybe they are still around. Some may have been used as dummies, simply for signatures on complaints generated by ambitious partisans; for others the case may have been a cause. Archie Everson's action, years ago, has had all the extraordinary effects this book describes and has, in fact, generated the book. In the distant future, after this book has been reprinted for the last time, the themes of this case—the public interest, church-state relationships, religious liberty, parental rights—will be with us, and *Everson* will continue to be cited, interpreted, transmogrified, and doubtless put to even more uses than those I mentioned at the start of this chapter. But that is as far as I dare prophesy.

Notes

1. Paul Freund, *On Understanding the Supreme Court* (1949), 50.
2. *McCollum v. Board of Education,* 33 U.S. 203 (1948).
3. *McCollum v. Board of Education,* 210.
4. The amendment was adopted as Act 91 of 1965, 24 P.S. sec. 13-1361.
5. *Rhoades v. School District of Abington Township,* 228 A. 2d (Pa. 1967), appeal dismissed 389 U.S. 11 (1967).
6. Where appeal is the route for review of a state court decision, dismissal of the appeal is the equivalent of affirmance on the merits. See *Eaton v. Price,* 360 U.S. 246, 247 (1959). In 1972 the busing statute was amended to provide that children attending nonpublic schools may be bused beyond school district lines. The new act was challenged in court on both state and federal constitutional grounds. Agan it was upheld by the Supreme Court of the United States. *School District of Pittsburgh v. Pennsylvania Department of Education,* 443 U.S. 901 (1979).
7. *Springfield School District v. Department of Education,* 397 A. 2d 1154 (Pa. 1979), appeal dismissed 443 U.S. 401 (1979).
8. *Schade v. Allegheny County Institute District,* 386 Pa. 507 (1956).
9. *Schade v. Allegheny County Institute District,* 513.
10. Brief for Appellants, 9.
11. American Jewish Committee and eight allied Jewish organizations. Protestants and Other Americans United for Separation of Church and State. Amici urging sustaining of the act were the United States (through the solicitor general) and, through their attorneys general, the States of Rhode Island, Pennsylvania, Vermont, Louisiana, and New Mexico. The amici, on both sides, all insisted on *Everson* as the commanding precedent.
12. *School District of Abington Township v. Schempp,* 374 U.S. 203 (1963).
13. *School District of Abington Township v. Schempp,* 203.
14. *Sherbert v. Verner,* 374 U.S. 398 (1962).
15. *Sherbert v. Verner,* 410.
16. Brief for Intervenor-Appelless, 61.
17. *Board of Education v. Allen,* 392 U.S. 236, 241–42.
18. *Lemon v. Kurtzman,* 403 U.S. 602 (1971).
19. *Lemon v. Kurtzman,* 621.
20. *Sloan v. Lemon,* 413 U.S. 825 (1973).
21. *Sloan v. Lemon,* 832–33.
22. *Sloan v. Lemon,* 788–89.
23. *Sloan v. Lemon,* 802.
24. *Meek v. Pittenger,* 421 U.S. 329.
25. *Meek v. Pittenger,* 329, 364–65.
26. *Meek v. Pittenger,* 329, 365.
27. *Grand Rapids School District v. Ball,* 473 U.S. 373 (1985); *Aguilar v. Felton,* 473 U.S. 402 (1985).
28. *Aguilar v. Felton,* 419.

29. *Aguilar v. Felton,* 431.

30. *Mueller v. Allen,* 463 U.S. 38 (1983).

31. See *Witters v. Washington Department of Services for Blind,* 474 U.S. 481 (1986).

32. *Individuals with Disabilities Education Act,* 20 USC secs. 1400 et seq.; Ariz. Rev. Stat. Ann. secs 15-761 et seq.

33. *Zobrest v. Catalina Foothills Board of Education,* 509 U.S. 1, 113 S.Ct. 2462 (1993).

General Index

Case Index

237